Digital Healing

Digital Healing
People, Information, Healthcare

Marc Ringel

LONDON AND NEW YORK

Routledge
Taylor & Francis Group
711 Third Avenue, New York, NY 10017

© 2018 by Marc Ringel

Productivity Press is an imprint of Taylor & Francis Group, an Informa business

No claim to original U.S. Government works

Printed on acid-free paper

International Standard Book Number-13: 978-1-138-06936-7 (Hardback)
International Standard Book Number-13: 978-1-351-11575-7 (eBook)

Library of Congress Cataloging-in-Publication Data

Names: Ringel, Marc, author.
Title: Digital healing : people, information, healthcare / Marc Ringel.
Description: Boca Raton : Taylor & Francis, 2018. | "A Routledge title, part of the Taylor & Francis imprint, a member of the Taylor & Francis Group, the academic division of T&F Informa plc." | Includes bibliographical references and index. |
Identifiers: LCCN 2018002609 (print) | LCCN 2018013530 (ebook) | ISBN 9781315115757 (eBook) | ISBN 9781138069367 (hardback : alk. paper) | ISBN 9781351115757 (eBook)
Subjects: LCSH: Telecommunication in medicine. | Internet in medicine.
Classification: LCC R119.9 (ebook) | LCC R119.9 .R56 2018 (print) | DDC 610.285—dc23
LC record available at https://lccn.loc.gov/2018002609

Visit the Taylor & Francis Web site at
http://www.taylorandfrancis.com

and the Productivity Press site at
http://www.ProductivityPress.com

Contents

Acknowledgments

I am indebted to many people who provided me with invaluable help and encouragement in the course of writing this book. Among them are: 2 consultants, 5 editors, 11 friends, 2 informaticists, 3 librarians, 1 musician, 4 physicians, 2 policy analysts, 3 publishers, 1 research scientist, 5 teachers and 5 writers. (Obviously most of them fall into multiple categories.) In producing this work, I've demonstrated to myself once again the truth of the book's main theme, that it's the people who count. So, thank you, all of you. You have counted big for me: Dana Abbey, Jeff Bauer, Charlie H. Bennett, Deb Bennett-Woods, David Bloom, Jim Fittz, Stephen Greenberg, Alexandria Gryder, Brittany Heer, Evon Holladay, Michael Kahn, Don Katz, Peggy Wagner Kimble, Alan Lembitz, Veronique Mead, Kristine Mednansky, Nancy Meyer, Bryan Nation, Don Nease, Kevin Nelson, Alex North, Mike Oberman, Donato Perl and Dennis Troutman.

About the Author

Marc Ringel grew up in Chicago. He earned a bachelor's degree with honors from Tulane University, majoring in philosophy.

After a summer driving buses for the Chicago Transit Authority, Ringel enrolled in the University of Illinois Abraham Lincoln School of Medicine in Chicago. He stayed on at Cook County Hospital for his postgraduate medical training, concentrating in pediatrics. Though he was a dyed-in-the-wool Chicagoan, several years later he found himself working as a general practitioner in Yuma, Colorado, a prairie town of 2000, as a National Health Service Corps doc. There he became enamored of family medicine, country people and rural ways. So he completed board certification as a family physician and founded a private practice in Ripon, Wisconsin, where he worked for five years.

After Ripon, Marc returned to the prairie to spend nine years teaching family medicine at North Colorado Family Medicine Residency Training Program in Greeley. He then practiced part-time for 15 years in Brush, Colorado, devoting the rest of his work life to consulting, writing and speaking on rural healthcare, telehealth and continuing medical education. Ringel's most recent job in patient care was three years as a hospice medical director.

Marc has appeared as a regular columnist in a number of newspapers and magazines, as well as delivered a bi-weekly radio commentary for over 16 years on KUNC, a Colorado public radio station. He has authored many articles and several books for professionals and for lay audiences.

Over the years, the day-to-day business of caring for patients provided Marc with endless concrete experience wrestling with a question that has fascinated him since he was an undergraduate philosophy major. What sorts of problems is science good at addressing and what sorts is it not? This book, with one foot in science and technology and one in the intimate knowledge that comes from having been doctor to thousands of patients, is a continuation of Ringel's life work.

Marc has lived in Greeley since 1985. He has three grown children and two grandchildren. In his spare time, which he has more of lately, he bicycles, gardens, hikes, reads and writes and tries to capture the beauty of the prairie in photographs. Now that this book is written, he is considering filling some of that freed-up time with writing a novel and/or learning Latin drumming and, of course, spending more time with his grandkids. He still does some consulting and speaking.

Introduction

Both words that make up this book's title, "digital" and "healing," can be found in any dictionary. There are multiple meanings for each, which is a good part of the challenge of making sense of this unusual word paring. By "digital" am I referring to fingers and toes or to calculating with discrete units? Is "healing" used here as a noun, an adjective, a transitive or an intransitive verb?

What if you were to input this two-word title into a computer driven by a traditional rule-based program and ask its language-processing program to make sense of it? The machine would probably start by looking up the definitions of both words. Because remembering, sorting and delivering data at the speed of light is what calculating machines do, I expect the computer would produce many more definitions than I mentioned above, making many more pairings that generate many more possible meanings than you'd ever get out of me, un-coached. Next the electronic device would parse these dyads and throw out the ones that didn't make any sense at all, for example, "digital" referring to a type of audio recording paired with "healing" meaning to cleanse of sin. (For what it's worth, my human brain can make this connection via a tortuous route that runs through the great Marvin Gaye song, "Sexual Healing.")

I don't mind that there is some ambiguity and squishiness to the title of my work. Language, thought and life have plenty of ambiguity and squishiness to them. My goal in writing this book is to explore the ever-fascinating blurry boundary that lies between biology, human consciousness and machines. (Actually, I think that boundary is not so blurry as it is fractal: complicated and endlessly interesting, no matter whether you view it through a telescope or microscope.)

Over the course of this work I will present some telescopic views and some microscopic ones, with the goal of engaging you in a discussion about a subject that is absolutely critical to our wellbeing. How can we human beings use electronic information and communication technologies, that become more powerfully clever by the day, in ways that enable us to be more human and become healthier in the process?

This is a large question, way bigger than medicine and healthcare. Our whole civilization needs to pose hard questions about the role of information technology in work, education, politics and virtually every other aspect of our lives. Having devoted most of my life to practicing, teaching and thinking about medicine and healthcare, I'll limit myself in this work to discussing what I know best.

In recent years, the word "healing" has come to connote more complementary and alternative medicine than the sorts of things my colleagues and I learned about in medical school. The stage was set 1971 when James Reston, an American journalist, became ill in the course of accompanying President Richard Nixon on the historic trip that opened relations between the U.S. and China. The press breathlessly reported how Reston's post-operative appendectomy pain had been controlled by acupuncture. Afterwards, the floodgates opened to legitimate consideration of diagnostic and therapeutic modalities that were way outside the sorts of things sanctioned by the American Medical Association.

Rather than confine the meaning of "healing" to describing what those other guys do, I mean to use the word in its broadest sense: as an intransitive verb that means to get better; as a transitive verb meaning to help someone get better; and as an adjective that identifies a desirable quality for everything we do in healthcare.

Everybody who cares for patients, in any way, participates, or ought to participate, in healing. That includes the receptionist who greets patients at the medical office, the phlebotomist who draws their blood and the housekeeper who empties the trash can in their hospital room. (See Chapter 5, "Data versus Story," for an anecdote about a healing person who delivered my food tray when I was a hospital patient.)

* * * * * *

In a typical family medicine practice it has been estimated that only about 30% of patient visits result in a firm, physiologically-based diagnosis. Doctors make educated guesses way more than we like to admit and than the public likes to believe. Practitioners frequently write "try this" prescriptions when we are not sure what the diagnosis is or what drug might work best. Nevertheless, I quickly learned, with every prescription I issue, to deliver it with words like, "This is just the right drug for what you've got." When I convey this message I am consciously and overtly making use of my physician persona to enhance the healing power of the medication, even should it turn out not to be the right one. Innumerable studies have shown that, for so many of the tried and true drugs that address real disease mechanisms, 50% or more of their power is still attributable to the placebo effect that derives from the patient's faith in the remedy. Medical science plus human connection is a very potent combination.

Most of the time that I provided hard copies of care instructions to patients in my family practice, in the days before prescribing and patient instruction writing were relegated to computers, I chose to whittle them down to what would fit on a single sheet from my prescription pad. First of all, brief is better. Second of all, that piece of paper, inscribed with a caduceus, was taken from the most potent implement in my healing arsenal, my prescription pad. (Actually, I consider it my second most potent implement. The first is, by far, the relationship with the patient.)

* * * * * *

In the medical field, electronic technologies born of the scientific revolution, have heretofore been used mostly to further the scientific aspects of healthcare, as well as the business. Actually, business came before science. Medical enterprises had electronic billing, accounting and inventory systems decades before they had electronic medical records. (For a fuller conversation of money, medicine and information technology, see Chapter 6, "Economics.")

Only now are electronic medical records (EMR) becoming nearly universal in the United States. Ask a number of professionals who use EMRs today how much the systems help them provide better patient care and you'll get very mixed reviews. The current struggle to incorporate the electronic medical record into medical practice is one of the main impetuses for writing this book at this time.

We clinicians stagger along, extolling the virtues of: putting well-organized scientific and personal information at the fingertips of everybody who participates in taking care of a patient; assuring that all of these folks are in touch with each other; not having to remember so many things like drug interactions and when immunizations are due; communicating more closely and consistently with the patient; being able to do important medical research cheaply by mining enormous patient databases; and on and on. Way too often we find instead that these systems, if they exist, don't talk to each other and that they present barriers to really connecting to our patients.

We need to take a bigger view of what we are doing in healthcare today. Healing needs to be re-emphasized, especially when we consider how we employ technology. As with every other tool humans have used since we started out hammering things with rocks and poking things with sticks, the important thing is not the tool itself, but how we use it.

Engaging my readers is as important to me as an author as engaging my patients is to me as a physician. That's why this is a book with: ample room for exposition and discussion; illustrative examples; points of view that range from telescopic to microscopic; a glossary and a suggested reading list. I want to engage you. I encourage your comments and dialog. You can reach me at marc@marcringelmd.com.

Chapter 1

Logical Conclusions:
How Modern Medicine
Fits into Western Culture

Science is the tool of the Western mind and with it more doors can be opened than with bare hands. It is part and parcel of our knowledge and obscures our insight only when it holds that the understanding given by it is the only kind there is.

—Karl Jung[1]

The discoverer of an art is not the best judge of the good or harm which will accrue to those who practice it.

—Plato (Phaedrus)[2]

I chose philosophy as my college major because I was interested in most everything: science, math, literature and philosophy. A little later I added music and art. My natural inclination is to come at any topic, especially this one, from the widest perspective possible, which is what I will endeavor to do in this work.

By any measure—health indicators, number of uninsured, total cost, per capita cost, consumer bankruptcies, political inertia—the United States is at a crisis point in healthcare. Rather than just continue tinkering with valves and relays to keep this obsolete engine limping along, it behooves us to step back from the machine for a bit and seek the wider perspective we need in order to make some smart decisions and to take some smart actions that could really fix things.

Sometimes I think it would be best if we could just blow up this damn jury-rigged healthcare non-system and build a new one that gets people what they really need, and does it efficiently. That may or may not happen in my lifetime.

When I was a medical student in the early '70's, my comrades and I did expect the economic and political system to collapse, possibly led by what we perceived, even back then, to be a remarkably inefficient and unjust healthcare system. I actually had a friend who had switched careers from social work to nursing in order to acquire the skills she imagined would be needed to care for the wounded on the Revolution's barricades. At that time, the healthcare sector accounted for 6% of the GNP. Today it stands at 18% and is likely to be more by the time you read this.

Sooner or later our unsustainable healthcare non-system must reach an inflection point, where things really do collapse and reorganize in a radically different way. The cost curve cannot go up forever, nor can citizens' discontent with the healthcare they're getting (and not getting); nor health professionals' unhappiness with the meaning and quality of their all-important work. Over the course of my career, I've predicted four of the last zero healthcare system collapses. Which leaves me with the question, what should be done in the meantime?

I hope, with this book, to contribute to a deeper understanding of how healthcare works, the first step toward making smart strategic decisions about which subsystems of this oh-so-complicated machine most merit our attention and energy. I will make the case that one subsystem that touches all the others, and consequently has huge potential leverage to shift the direction of healthcare at least a few degrees shy of straight over the brink, is information technology.

An Ultra-Wide Angle View

Let's start our journey of understanding with views from an ultra-wide-angle (hopefully not fisheye) lens. I'll begin with a little philosophy.

The ancient Greeks started Western philosophy and culture down the path toward understanding the world by observation and mathematization at least six centuries before the birth of Christ. These two approaches were melded during the Renaissance to become the scientific method. Francis Bacon, English scientist, philosopher, statesman and jurist (the world used to be full of generalists) first codified the principles of this way of understanding the world. His method for discovering what is true boils down to a cycle of observing, modeling, predicting and observing. (I beg forgiveness of my philosophy professors for compressing more than two millennia of intellectual history into a single paragraph.)

Lord Kelvin, the 19th Century Scot best known for his formulation of the first and second laws of thermodynamics, said, "When you can measure what you are speaking about, and express it in numbers, you know something about it, *[sic.]* when you cannot express it in numbers, your knowledge is of a meager and unsatisfactory kind; it may be the beginning of knowledge, but you have scarcely, in your thoughts advanced to the stage of science." A century or so later Peter Drucker, the renowned American business guru, intoned his version, "If you can't measure it you can't improve it." The people who run American healthcare today appear to have taken both Kelvin and Drucker at their word.

The modern intellectual revolution was initially led by sixteenth century astronomers like Galileo, Brahe and Kepler. But it didn't take long for the scientific method to be applied to understanding biology and medicine. *De Motu Cordis*, published in 1628 by English physician William Harvey, was world-changing, as much for its methods as for its conclusions. Harvey proved via unassailable experimental evidence that blood circulates in the body.

Medical scientists, aided by an ever-longer list of measuring devices, including microscope, thermometer, barometer, and most importantly, by close observation, rapidly expanded the scope of understanding of how the human body works in health and in disease.

Once the Dutch spectacle makers, Zacharias and Hans Janssen, opened an unseen world to the human eye and mind with their invention of the compound lens microscope in the 1590s, the world would never be the same.* Three centuries later, Robert Koch, a German microbiologist, building on the work of his predecessor, Louis Pasteur, the Frenchman who founded microbiology, published his four postulates. Fulfilling these four conditions, Koch reasoned, was proof that a specific organism caused a particular disease.

1. The microorganism must be found in abundance in all organisms suffering from the disease, but should not be found in healthy organisms.
2. The microorganism must be isolated from a diseased organism and grown in pure culture.
3. The cultured microorganism should cause disease when introduced into a healthy organism.
4. The microorganism must be re-isolated from the inoculated, diseased experimental host and identified as being identical to the original specific causative agent.[3]

Research guided by Koch's Postulates brought understanding of pathogenic bacteria, parasites and later, of viruses, leading to antibiotics and huge improvement in individual and population health.†

---

* The Janssens may have had a hand in making the first refracting telescope a decade later, extending human vision into the Universe in the other direction too.

† Water supplies, sewage treatment, adequate housing and other public health measures are still credited with the lion's share of the reduction of deaths from the likes of dysentery and tuberculosis. For example, in 1854, thirty years before Robert Koch definitively identified the bacterium, *Vibrio cholerae*, as the responsible pathogen, John Snow published his study of the Broad Street cholera epidemic in London, which led to separation of drinking water and sewage streams throughout the developed world, sending the rate of cholera mortality on a precipitous decline.

Thanks to the successes of the last century-and-a-half in addressing infectious diseases, the ghost of Koch's Postulates still holds sway over the medical mind, even though we doctors know better than to expect to find a single infectious agent at the root of most of chronic afflictions, like coronary artery disease, cancer and stroke.*

It would be lovely if there were a cure or prevention for every disease that worked as reliably as antibiotics do for *H. pylori*; vaccine does for HPV; and penicillin still does for strep throat 75 years after it was added to the medical armamentarium by Alexander Fleming.

We don't even bother to vaccinate for smallpox any more. Thanks to the small-pox vaccine, introduced by Edward Jenner over 200 years ago, the disease and the virus that causes it have been wiped from the face of the earth (except in a few repositories, in case the pathogen is "needed" as a biological weapon).

We are not going to find a single infectious culprit for most of what afflicts us today. Koch's Postulates don't apply to these complicated maladies caused by multiple factors. As they stand, the Postulates are just too simple to capture even large parts of the reality of infectious disease.

Consider the host. Every human being is biologically unique. This even holds for identical twins who start out with the same genes that come to be expressed more or less differently as a result of each individual's life experience. In the course of learning its job of distinguishing every person from everything else in the world and every good cell in the body from every bad one, the immune system "constructs" a unique biological identity for every human host, defending it against infection and malignancy.

Over a lifetime, the nervous system, conscious and unconscious, also participates in the process of identity-building. Medical science is constantly uncovering ways in which the nervous system and the immune system are intertwined.†

It should be obvious that the concept of an average host who mounts an average response to a single infectious agent is useful only up to a point. We have learned a ton of physiology, pathology, immunology and biochemistry since the time of Herr Professor Koch. Researchers know to cast a much wider net than for a single organism and a unitary host response when investigating most maladies.

Multiply the uniqueness of individuals with the complications of aggregating them into families, cohabiting groups, workplaces, cities and societies. Smallpox was eradicated not just because of the vaccine that primed individual immune systems to recognize and fight off the culprit virus, but because, for two centuries, public health workers, who depended for their success on understanding each

---

* A couple of notable exceptions are the discoveries in the last few decades that the bacterium, *Helicobacter pylori*, causes the bulk of stomach and duodenal ulcers and that *human papilloma-virus (HPV)* is responsible for almost all cervical and penile cancer. *H. pylori* is curable with a combination of common antibiotics. Most *papillomavirus* infections, and hence genital cancer, are preventable with a vaccine administered to preteen girls and boys.

† There is one other major organism-wide integrator, the endocrine system. Its hormones hook up to receptors on cells throughout the body to effect changes in function. The endocrine system is thoroughly enmeshed with the nervous and immune systems.

society and culture in which the disease appeared, kept after disease occurrences and unvaccinated populations.

As a metaphor, these wonderfully simple four Postulates still exert a great deal of influence on medical reasoning. By comparison, Euclid's Geometry, that most elegant deductive reasoning system that we cut our wisdom teeth on in high school, starts with five postulates.

Searching for simple answers to complex problems is a fundamental impetus of medical science, and of science in general. Reductionism lies at the heart of the scientific method. Control as many variables as you can, while you manipulate just one variable at a time, and observe the outcome. This is a way to learn what each factor does. Then combine the factors into a model that makes predictions and test it experimentally.

Experimental testing may be done in a laboratory, employing test tubes, culture dishes, or live animals. Clinical experiments often occur in healthcare settings. For example, a group of clinic patients is administered a drug while a comparable group gets a placebo. Treatment or placebo is assigned randomly and neither patients nor researchers know who's gotten which. This sort of double-blind randomized experiment is considered the gold standard for sussing out all sorts of facts, including what effect a drug really has, in spite of what the patient or researcher may have expected.

An experiment may be observational, based in clinic or community, following a set of parameters in a population over time and calculating correlations. Or it may be done solely by mining medical and public health databases for clues to how things work. (See Chapter 12, "Research.")

Science is a unique universe of knowledge. It depends on being able to test and retest every observation and every theory. Only those facts that stand up to the most intense public scrutiny are considered reliable building blocks upon which to construct the next advance in knowledge. "Public," in this sense, does not mean the general citizenry. It is restricted to fellow experts.

Of course, the elite public of scientists is wrong sometimes. New theories must often swim against the stream of "established" expertise. For starters, consider the travails of Darwin, Einstein and Galileo in defending their earthshaking theories.

Facts and theories that are considered bedrock scientific truth one day may be overturned the next. That a brick can be removed from the scientific edifice because it has been falsified is as critical to the power and credibility of science as it is that new bricks of knowledge and understanding can be added.

The ever-advancing scientific frontier leaves in its wake a body of knowledge that grows exponentially, as well as a rubble heap of discredited facts and theories. For example, after I had spent three decades of my career nagging every woman over twenty to do a breast self-exam, I abruptly stopped. New studies had shown no improvement in disease course or survival of women who had discovered their malignancies as a result of self-exam. Rather, these patients had more procedures, worry, discomfort and expense than women whose tumors had been discovered by their health care provider, by mammogram, or noticed incidentally by themselves.

This may seem counter-intuitive, based on the belief that it's always better to catch tumors earlier; which illustrates why we cannot depend on common sense alone for making medical decisions. We always need good research. (Of course, anybody who does find a breast lump should still see a health professional about it right away. Ignoring a lump is never a good strategy.)

Couple science with technology and you have the synergy to transform every aspect of human life, including healthcare. If I were to try to name all the technology—from stethoscope to functional MRI; from petri dish to DNA sequencer; from punch card to supercomputer; from horse-and-buggy to remote activity monitor—that physicians have counted on to care for patients since the beginning of the modern age, I might never get to the end because things are being introduced today faster than I could list them.

The result has been world-changing. Our power to prevent, diagnose, treat, ameliorate and cure disease is many orders of magnitude more than it was in Sir William Harvey's day. At least in the developed world, medical science has changed everything about life: how we are born, live and die; families; expectations; and our relationship to disease and suffering.

Reductionism

I would like to go back a few paragraphs and pick up the concept of reductionism. Breaking the world into smaller pieces (concepts), seeing how each piece works, then putting them back together in a model that makes testable predictions, is what science does. As time passes, we seem intent on examining smaller and smaller pieces that later we try to reassemble into a working whole. Modern physics—theorizing on scales that range from the quantum, Planck length 1.616199×10^{-35} meters, to the cosmological, diameter of the visible universe 4.4×10^{22} meters—strives to unite it all under a Theory of Everything (ToE).

A ToE has eluded the best minds, including Einstein's and Hawking's, for over a century. It is supposed to combine relativity with quantum physics, that is, gravity with the other three forces of nature (electromagnetism, strong nuclear force and weak nuclear force).

Even without a ToE, it was hoped that quantum physics could eventually explain everything about chemistry, which would inform biochemistry, which would tell us all we need to know about biology. Continuing on up the building block scale, biology was supposed to explain psychology.

In the grip of Western culture's love affair with science, French philosopher Auguste Comte founded positivism in the early 19th century. Positivism set out to discover the principles of human life on an anthropological, social, political, even on a historical level, applying the same observational and theory-building techniques as had been so grandly successful in physics, chemistry, biology and medicine. By exploiting what they learned, positivists expected to make huge strides in reducing human misery, empowered by their knowledge, to strike at the causes of suffering, illuminated at its very core by science. Positivists gave sociology, the science of society, a revered place among the newly scientific disciplines.

And so it goes, on up the hierarchy of sciences, from physics and chemistry, the hardest of the hard scientists, through biology and on to psychology, sociology, anthropology political science, economics and history, the softest of the soft. Where does medical science stand on this ladder?

Medical science doesn't really fit into this hierarchy because it is a hybrid of all of these things, including politics and economics. Though American medicine often seems to be blind to it, the role of social, political and economic factors as determinants of health and disease is undeniable. (Discussion of reasons for this blindness is beyond the scope of this book.)

Physicists may one day manage to meld relativity and quantum theory into a single Theory of Everything. Still, it is unimaginable that starting with these few principles, no matter how elegant and complete, scientists will be able to understand and explain everything else. The world is way too complex. Each level of organization—physical, chemical, biochemical, biological, psychological, sociological, historical—has its own organizing principles and emergent properties.

Emergent properties are behaviors that depend on the function of the system as a whole, behaviors that could not be predicted, no matter how thoroughly the system's pieces are understood individually. There is way more to a cell and how it works than a complete enumeration of its genome and proteins could foretell; way more to a body than the sum of its cells; way more to an animal's behavior than its biology; way more to a society than you could predict by knowing all about each individual.

There are ideas at the cutting edge of science itself—like self-assembling systems, fractal forms of organization, emergent properties and complexity theory—that go beyond the deterministic, reductionist views of old science, best exemplified by Pierre-Simon Laplace's demon, "an intellect which at a certain moment would know all forces that set nature in motion, and all positions of all items of which nature is composed, if this intellect were also vast enough to submit these data to analysis, it would embrace in a single formula the movements of the greatest bodies of the universe and those of the tiniest atom [for all eternity]."[4]

It is especially true that medical science, depending as it does (or ought to) on all these various ways of looking at the world, will never have its own simple set of first principles, which, when correctly applied, would give the correct diagnosis and prescribe the right treatment for every person with every malady for all eternity.

This is one of the reasons I love practicing medicine. I get to immerse myself in the rich stew of human life with its endless textures and layers of flavor and try to make sense of it all. One of the most useful traits for a doctor, especially for a generalist doctor as I am, is the ability to live with uncertainty.

The closest the science of clinical medicine has come to having a broad-enough take on its role in addressing the human condition is the biopsychosocial model proposed in a paper published in the journal *Science* in 1977 and taken up shortly thereafter by US family medicine training programs.[5] The author, psychiatrist George Engel, placed the person, the default focus of clinical practice, in the middle of a set of concentric circles that proceed along the usual reductionist focus inward through organ systems organs, tissues, organelles (subcellular structures), molecules, atoms and subatomic particles. The individual is also situated within concentric circles that move outward through two-person, family, community, culture-subculture, society-nation and biosphere. Engel argued that the outwardly-directed realms were just as much within the scope of medical research and practice as the inward ones.

There has been plenty of lip service paid to the biopsychosocial model in the intervening years. But the standard biomedical model (sans the psychosocial part) that we have learned and labored under still holds sway in day-to-day practice.[6]

Under the *Zeitgeist* of the modern age, ruled as it has been by science and technology, a large share of sociologists, anthropologists, political scientists and economists, and even some historians, strive to make their disciplines more scientific. They collect data, analyze them statistically, build models and test them. This obsession with measurement and mathematization is part and parcel of our times.

Healthcare managers are equally taken with quantification. They labor under the "if you can't measure it you can't improve it" banner, endlessly prodding people on the front lines to collect data that will quantify their performance, writing reports on what they've found and passing them up the chain of command. The whole process has contributed greatly to the discontent of clinicians, who feel inundated by meaningless metrics, resentful of the time they have to spend collecting and responding to a slew of numbers. (See Chapter 5, "Data Versus Story.")

Some cultural critics say we now live in the Postmodern Age and that we have been since two unimaginably destructive world wars disillusioned us with the proposal of Comte and his positivitist colleagues that science would make life endlessly better. A host of modern movements, from existentialism to deconstructionism, position themselves in contradistinction to the modern idea that science is the one and only way to understand anything reliably.

Still, science holds sway. Its achievements are everywhere.

In medicine, we remain in the position of having to insinuate the "soft" (not based on hard science) stuff into medical curricula and discussions. American medicine definitely has not arrived at the Postmodern Age.*

---

* My classmates and I used to caricature the seemingly endless lectures that we sat through for the first couple of years of medical school as going like this, "Of course, when caring for a patient with this illness you should take into account the whole person. First slide please. You'll note that in the smooth endoplasmic reticulum…" (The smooth endoplasmic reticulum is a microscopic sub-cellular organelle whose function is mostly to synthesize carbohydrates and lipids [fats].)

Psychology

My introductory college psychology course was taught by a behaviorist of some renown, whose reasoning moved effortlessly from pigeons to rats to people. The things he measured, like attention and reaction time, helped him to understand how animals, including human beings, learn. He applied these lessons quite successfully to helping the military build better aircraft instrument panels and train their pilots. The professor and his behaviorist colleagues took as a given that, for the purpose of scientific study, if they couldn't observe and measure something, it was not worth their consideration as serious scientists. This meant that an animal's interior life, including a human's, was *terra incognita*. A "black box," they called it.

Though their systems of thought yield some tangible good outcomes, like well-trained pilots and resolved phobias, in recent decades behaviorists have come under a good deal of well-deserved criticism for overzealous reductionism. Their two-dimensional caricature of human beings has led behaviorists too often to study bathwater instead of babies.*

There are plenty of other schools of psychology not nearly so enamored of the observable and measurable at the expense of the larger reality of the organism. Researchers and practitioners from these camps are subject to criticisms opposite to those leveled at their behaviorist colleagues. Instead of reductionist, they are called unscientific.

Look at what has happened to the reputation of Sigmund Freud since he formulated the theory and practice of psychoanalysis in the late 19th and early 20th centuries. Freud's rich observations of the internal lives of his patients—informed by his deep and wide understanding of neurology, hypnosis, anthropology and history—contributed hugely to understanding the human psyche. But his work is anecdotal, wholly lacking the sorts of replicable data and outcome measures that make for respectable science.

A large share of the edifice that Freud constructed has rightfully been torn down. Neurochemistry has shed insight into and provided targeted treatments for a host of psychological maladies for which psychoanalysis might, at worst, lead away from a graspable handle on a patient's mental illness.

As I said above, there are plenty of other forms of psychotherapy. Cognitive behavioral therapy (CBT), for example, has a good deal of data-driven validation. Though the cognitive part of CBT is located inside the head, where it's not directly observable, there are many professionals today who are willing to call CBT scientific. (That the "B" stands for "behavioral," doesn't hurt CBT's claims of scientific validity.)

---

* A classic joke among psychologists goes, What does a behaviorist say to another behaviorist after having sex? I can see it was good for you, but was it good for me?

Sigmund Freud always insisted he was doing science. He began his medical career as a researcher in cerebral anatomy at Vienna General Hospital. In many ways, he did do science throughout his career. And, in many ways, he didn't. That is one reason why his work remains so interesting today. Freud crossed a number of intellectual boundaries. He addressed, with remarkable insight, a large share of the complicated *gemish* that makes up human life, including infant experience, parenting styles, dreams, language, culture and societal pressures. Science was but one of his avenues of understanding.

Which is the real point of this chapter. Science is but one avenue of understanding. To be sure, in medicine, it is one of the most important. Many would say it's *the* most important. But still, just one among many. Since science and technology are hand-in-glove, it follows easily that technology is part and parcel of advancing and applying scientific knowledge. Information technology is especially crucial to today's scientific endeavor, particularly in medicine.

It also follows that the parts of human life and healthcare that are not to be understood scientifically are less amenable to technological fixes and more addressable by real human beings.*

I believe that, by using technology in smart ways, we can extend not just our power to understand and address those things that science is best at doing, but also enhance those "softer" emotional, interpersonal, connectional, intuitive capacities that have too often gotten short shrift in this age of scientific medicine.

---

* At least not yet to be understood scientifically. An ongoing battle rages today in philosophy circles, especially in the field of consciousness studies, as to whether there are things that cannot be understood by scientific means, and what those things might be. There is an interesting parallel here to vitalism, the theory that held that every living organism of necessity contained some non-physical element, a vital spark that distinguished it from non-living things. Though they by no means comprehensively understand even the simplest of living cells, biologists of today are fully convinced that they can describe and study life without resorting to a special energy or a soul. Many non-Western and alternative medical traditions, including acupuncture, chiropractic, osteopathy and therapeutic touch, depend on unscientific energy-like concepts for their understanding and treatment of disease. So does the Freudian model of the psyche.

Chapter 2

What Computers Do Better Than Humans

The information age is to medicine as the Protestant Reformation was to the Catholic Church.

—Michael Millenson[1]

Knowledge is of two kinds. We know a subject ourselves, or we know where we can find information upon it.

—Samuel Johnson

Human beings are great at some things. And remembering ain't one of them.

—Larry Weed, inventor of the problem-oriented medical record

I dare you to name an aspect of your life that has not been affected by electronic technology: your mother's famous coffee cake, emailed recipe to a friend; your daughter's baseball swing, videoed and reviewed; the carburetor on your muscle car, rebuilding technique viewed in an online tutorial; your gas bill, meter read remotely, bill paid online; new diabetes medications, side effects and drug interactions checked out by your provider's electronic prescribing system.

It's everywhere. The majority of us carry computers in our pockets that far surpass the number-crunching power of the giant university computing centers of the 1960s and that make the computer astronauts carried with them on their way to the moon look like a Playskool Activity Center.* Today's gizmos are so powerful and are (sometimes frustratingly slowly) becoming so easy to use that in 2013 there were 6.8 billion active cellphone contracts to serve a population of 7 billion earthlings.[2]

And that's just cell phones. There are laptops, desktops and tablets everywhere; mainframes, supercomputers and server farms; hardwiring and wireless networks to connect it all; not to mention silicon chips embedded in everything from alarm clocks to refrigerators to autos.

I could go on and on, of course, about how information and communication technologies are changing our world. Let's look instead at how information technology changes our language and changes us.

The Written and Printed Word

Socrates, via his self-appointed mouthpiece, Plato, railed against the written word. The acknowledged father of Greek philosophy, hence of Western philosophy, foresaw what would be lost with the eclipse of the spoken word. A big chunk of the engagement and personalization that are the essence of oral, face-to-face communication would be cast off. Poetry, spoken or sung, laden with rhythms and rhymes and gestures that, by addressing multiple human faculties, enhance a work's emotional impact and recall-ability, was eclipsed by the linearity of prose.

Written poetry does preserve some of the emotional aspects of literature. Music, drama and poetry slams add group experience to the written word. Sung and chanted words, from opera to church to rap, keep us connected to our hearts and to each other in ways that reading Plato or our car manual never can.

The bard Homer's long epic poems, *The Iliad* and *The Odyssey*, composed to be performed from memory, were crystallized when they were written down up to four centuries after the poet's death, to be read by millions of people in the ensuing millennia. Innumerable high school and college students have slogged through these works, in Greek or translated into dozens of different languages.

Illiterate Homer and anti-literate Socrates might be pleased to learn that, in the course (so far) of about 2700 years, their cultural influence has been immeasurably enhanced because someone took the trouble to write down their words. They would also be the first to point out what was lost when their thoughts were concretized

---

* Early computers that seem laughably primitive to us now (just as the devices we're using today will make our grandchildren giggle) are still not to be taken lightly. In the eleven years that one of the first general electronic computers, a room-sized device based on vacuum tubes, the Electronic Numerical Integrator and Computer (ENIAC), designed by the US Army primarily to calculate artillery shell trajectories, performed more calculations than the entire human race had done in all of history up to 1946. It could do in 30 seconds what it took a human calculator 30 hours to do. (Peskowitz, David. Modern Art. *Wired*. 11/99.)

into written words, printed, translated, and recently, digitized and made searchable for use by innumerable students who write term papers and scholars who produce erudite commentaries on their works. Nobody today can recite this literature, which started as Homer's poems and Socrates' conversations, by heart.

Denizens of today's digital world are waking up to what's being lost in our rush to digitize, which explains the recent resurgence in sales of vinyl records (200,000 a week in the United States in 2017), print books (sales up for three years in a row), independent bookstores, board games and theater tickets. Even at Google, web designers are required to do their first brainstorming with paper and pen because it leads to freer exchange of ideas than does capturing them on a digital screen.[3] (See Chapter 4, "What Humans Do Better Than Computers," for a lengthier conversation on the advantages of analog versus digital.) After all, humans are analog devices.

When we can look up written stuff, our brains are no longer geared to remember things so well. I really do cherish still being able to recite the few Shakespeare speeches I was required to learn in high school. As poetry, I find them easier to remember than the phone number that my brother has had since 1996. His number used to be written down in a contact file card that I kept in a recipe box. Now the contact information resides in a database on my phone. Needless to say, things I had to memorize in medical school, like ramifications of the axillary plexus (nerves in the armpit) and metabolic pathways of amino acid metabolism, are long-long gone. When I need these factoids, I look them up, more easily than ever before, on a website or a downloaded database.

With Johannes Gutenberg's invention of the moveable type printing press in the fifteenth century, the power of the written word was multiplied a million-fold. Now it was possible to get those words into the hands of an enormous audience, no longer limited to the few learned priests, aristocracy and royalty with the prerequisite leisure, motivation and instructors to master reading, as well as the means to afford documents that had been handwritten on parchment.

The world and the human mind have not been the same since. In the West, the Renaissance, the Reformation, the scientific revolution, industrialization and subsequent popular political revolutions owed their existence in large part to this revolutionary technology. Benedictine monks were right when they protested Gutenberg's invention saying, "They shamelessly print, at negligible cost, material which may, alas, inflame impressionable youths."[4,5]

Rather than launch into a long and tedious recounting of some of the gazillions of ways our world is being changed thanks to electronic information technology, perhaps even more and certainly faster than Gutenberg's invention shook things up almost 700 years ago, I'll reminisce instead about the good old days, almost 50 years ago, when the only things I owned that had a transistor in them were the 6-function calculator that had replaced my slide rule and the dashboard radio in my car. My television and home stereo amplifier functioned with vacuum tubes.

(I know I'm dispensing here a pretty big dose of an old fart tale, not unlike the ones my parents used to tell about the Great Depression or my grandparents about the Cossacks. I will continue to refer now and then to the "old days" with the goal, not of indulging my nostalgic side, but of demonstrating just how much things have changed, and continue to change at an ever-accelerating pace, in the course of one man's career. Feel free to join my children in rolling your eyes.)

Here's how, as a medical student and intern in the early seventies, I'd look for an answer to a medical question that a fellow-trainee, attending physician, or textbook couldn't supply. I'd head over to the library at the medical school or hospital, haul down the index volume of the *Cumulated Index Medicus*, which was published by the National Library of Medicine (NLM), and copy down a list of promising citations. If I wasn't sure of what search term to use (you could only use one term at a time), I'd stop first at the outline of indexing categories at the beginning of the work.*

I'd start with the quarterly unbound editions, beginning with the latest and working my way backwards. Then I'd proceed to the annual volumes. Each tome, weighing about ten pounds, consisted of the year's quarterly editions, bound together. I'd continue my search, from newest to older, until I felt I'd found enough pertinent citations to suit my (or my attending's or my resident's) needs.

I trained at a large medical school and hospital where I had access to substantial medical libraries, which meant they had extensive stacks of journals that they subscribed to, bound, stored and displayed at high cost. Holdings of more important journals sometimes went back decades, taking up more than a whole rack of shelves.

I'd schlep armloads of bound journals to a library table, spread out before at least a couple of seats and take notes on the chosen articles, one at a time. At least I was spared the chore of replacing the volumes in the stacks, as librarians preferred to minimize the risk of misfiling by doing it themselves. If I got really stuck, I'd ask the medical librarian to help me. She (they were all women at that time) actually had a computer link to the National Library of Medicine.

I did find one lament for the loss of the old leafing through old volumes way of doing literature searching. It was in an article published in the journal, *Science,* in 2008. The author observed that, as scientific articles had become available online, organized in electronic indexes and accessed via hyperlinks, the number of citations per paper and the length of time that citations stretched into the past had diminished. He wondered if the scientific literature was losing a certain depth, richness and historicity as a result.[6] The author was right, at least in observing that technological change does bring cultural change.

In both of the states where I first practiced, one of my first steps on arrival was to make contact with the library at the state medical school to arrange for

---

* In 1961, the National Library of Medicine published its Medical Subject Headings (MeSH) nomenclature. This really marked the start of the modern era in medical informatics.

bibliographic help. I'd call with an occasional query. A (dot matrix) printed bibliography would arrive in about a week. I'd circle citations to the articles I was interested in, mail the document back and receive a small stack of photocopied articles by mail within a couple more weeks.

Computerized Medical Information

When it comes to access to the medical literature, thanks to computers and electronic communication, things have just gotten better and better. While writing this chapter, I Googled "history *Index Medicus*" so I could supply some of the details about the olden days that no longer reside in my memory. When I couldn't find the information I needed, I sent an email message to the NLM and got a response from the chief librarian for the history of medicine in two days.[7]

If I want a more technical and in-depth look at a subject, I sometimes consult Google Scholar, which uses different strategies than plain vanilla Google to catalog websites and produce links that go beyond the information needs of the average layperson. In some fields, entries may be listed in order of how many times the articles have been cited, a down and dirty measure of impact or academic weight.

Computers store and retrieve information very effectively, at least information that is well indexed. The National Library of Medicine and others continue producing and promulgating standard nomenclatures of medical terminology and knowledge, such as the NLM's Systematized Nomenclature of Medicine (SNOMED), the World Health Organization's International Statistical Classification of Diseases and Related Health Problems, 10th revision, (ICD-10), the American Medical Association's Current Procedural Terminology (CPT) and the American Psychiatric Association's Diagnostic and Statistical Manual for Mental Disorders, 5th edition, (DSM-V). With excruciating detail, these documents provide the framework that assures that the information you're recording or looking for means what everybody thinks it means.

Professional wikis, patterned after Wikipedia, the grandparent of all cooperatively-generated online information resources, are a bottom-up way to hang medical information on official nomenclature armatures. In November 2017, Wikipedia listed nine active medical wikis and three defunct ones. Who is allowed to contribute and how information is vetted and edited are issues with any wiki.

I carry my smartphone with me everywhere. The device is especially important to me when I practice my trade. It provides access to a few well-chosen databases of medical and drug information. With these organized and vetted facts at my fingertips, I can answer most questions that come up in the course of seeing patients.

Compare this to an unsettling article published in the *Annals of Internal Medicine* in 1985. The authors followed 47 internists around during a typical half-day of office practice, debriefing them after each patient encounter. Of the 269 questions the doctors raised about patient management, *only 30% were answered* before the patient left the office, usually by asking a colleague. If you assume the average doctor saw about 10 patients per half-day, that works out to 1.7 questions per patient per encounter, of which 1.2 were unanswered.[8]

Would you want a doctor caring for you who leaves on the average one stone unturned every time you see her? Could you have trusted that she had the right textbook or journal article in her office to find the answer after you left and adjusted your course of treatment based on that? What if she had to resort to the *Cumulative Index Medicus* or ask a librarian for help? How long before she'd get the answer she needed to take care of you?

A study published in 2008 found that clinicians were able to answer 83% of 883 questions that came up in the course of caring for patients by accessing *UpToDate*, the same comprehensive medical database that I carry on my smartphone. Obtaining an answer usually took under five minutes for the 30 practicing internists and 40 internists-in-training involved in the study.[9]

An article published in 2017 about augmented reality glasses gives us a peek at the sort of information that will soon be at our finger- (or eyeball-) tips in the near future. The paper's authors found that pediatric residents performed even better on simulated patient resuscitations if they wore Google Glasses loaded with the clinical protocols than if they referred to resuscitation protocols that they carried in the pockets of their lab coats.[10]

The legal system, which holds professionals being sued for malpractice to a "generally accepted standard of care," has not yet arrived at making access to online medical information a standard of care, as predicted in commentary that ran in the *Journal of the American Medical Association* in 1983.[11] But case law is inching in that direction.[12] At least in Colorado, as of 2013, having an electronic health record did not appear to affect one way or another the likelihood of being sued.[13]

Anna Konopka, a New Hampshire physician, did lose her license in 2017 for not using a computer and therefore not being able to meet that state's requirements for accessing its online prescription drug monitoring program for controlled substances.[14]

As a family practice residency faculty member, I used to recommend to soon-to-graduate residents that they check out the personal medical libraries in the offices of possible future partners. If the only books there had been purchased in medical school or gifted by pharmaceutical salespeople, I'd suggest steering clear of that practice. Now that I haven't purchased a medical text for over a decade myself, my advice has changed. A routine piece of the assessment I do of practicing physicians in the course of my work in remedial continuing medical education is to ask what electronic medical references they use inside and outside the exam room. The education plans I write routinely call for establishing access to and using good internet-based medical information resources.

Providing quick, easy and ubiquitous access to medical literature is one thing that computers do way better than humans and the paper- (or parchment- or clay tablet-) based information systems that came before the electronic revolution. Nicholas Negroponte, the visionary co-creator of MIT's media lab, famously chanted, "Move bits, not atoms," meaning that when it comes to doing stuff with information, it is infinitely more efficient to accomplish by electronic means than in the solid world of things (referred to by geeks as "meatspace," as opposed to cyberspace). It's the difference between the 1.1 gigabyte (that's 1.1 *billion* bytes or 8.8 *billion* binary digits) of the *UpToDate* medical database that reside in my 4-ounce iPhone and update continuously, versus the hundreds of pounds of *Cumulative Index Medicus* citations that can be found today only in medical museums alongside tons and tons of bound medical journals.

A key concept in informatics is summed up by this simple equation:

$$\text{information usefulness} = \frac{\text{relevance} \times \text{validity}}{\text{work to acquire}}$$

Most of the time "work to acquire" trumps the other two terms on the right side of the equation.[15]

Needless to say, my iPhone loaded with *UpToDate* beats the hell out of the *Index Medicus* in the "work to acquire term," and in "relevance." *UpToDate* wins in validity, too, because trusted experts in each medical field have done the work of selecting and updating reliable information for the database, whereas the *Index Medicus* just listed what was out there.

Electronic "brains" do way better than human ones when it comes to accessing information. The crucial step is to get the right handles on the information when it is put in so it can be grabbed when needed, while avoiding too many less-than-right handles that return too much less-than-relevant information. This depends on indexing, a process that started way before the electronic revolution and continues apace.

Computerized Patient Information

Organizing and retrieving patient information is a good deal harder than organizing and retrieving medical literature. Especially when it comes to humans, nature is way, way more varied, subtle and complex, even than the sum total of everything that's been written since 3200 B.C., when some merchants in Mesopotamia made marks in wet clay with a wooden stylus to help them keep track of their goods and accounts. Just assuring that a set of records in one system pertains to the same patient in another system is a challenge, due to misspellings and the like.[16]

Three of the ECRI Institute Patient Safety Organization's annual list of Top Ten Patient Safety Concerns for 2017, including concerns number one and three, have a direct connection with information technology.*

Reducing medication errors is a shining example of how information technology can improve the quality of medical care. In a single year, a basic e-prescription system installed in 15 primary care adult practices in the Hudson Valley, New York, reduced errors from 42.5 per 100 prescriptions to 6.6. Admittedly, a number of the errors prevented, such as use of inappropriate abbreviations, were in themselves, of little consequence. But others, such as dose errors, were potentially quite harmful.[17]

By requiring physicians to enter drug orders via a computerized order entry (CPOE) system, Brigham and Women's Hospital in Boston reduced its rate of serious medication errors by 88% within a few years.[18] Still, in 2015, the Leapfrog Group (an influential organization composed mostly of large businesses that purchase healthcare) found that hospital CPOE systems failed to flag 39% of potentially harmful drug orders.[19]

Huge efforts and resources have gone into designing electronic medical records that capture the richness and complexity of the patient and her illness, while providing the indexing that gives immediate access to what one needs to know about that patient, or about a group of patients in the course of caring for them.

Based on well-tested indexes, like the ICD-10 disease classification, which is attached to every patient encounter for billing purposes, it is easy to sort through an entire practice or covered population and find everybody who's been seen for diabetes, for example. Other information, easy to obtain and naturally classifiable—like age, sex, zip code, weight, height, etc.—is also eminently searchable. Add in lab test results, recorded as numbers that are the natural language of computers; drug prescriptions, which refer to a finite number of products; and medical procedures, all duly coded for billing, and you've got a whole lot of information on most everybody who comes in contact with the health care system. Everybody (including too many people who shouldn't have it [see Chapter 7, "Security and Privacy"]) is happy to have access to these vital data.

---

* ECRI Institute Patient Safety Organization 2017 list of Top Ten Patient Safety Concerns:
  1. Information Management in EHRs
  2. Unrecognized Patient Deterioration
  3. Implementation and Use of Clinical Decision Support
  4. Test Result Reporting and Follow-Up
  5. Antimicrobial Stewardship
  6. Patient Identification
  7. Opioid Administration and Monitoring in Acute Care
  8. Behavioral Health Issues in Non-Behavioral Health Settings
  9. Management of New Oral Anticoagulants
  10. Inadequate Organization Systems or Processes to Improve Safety and Quality [https://www.ecri.org/press/Pages/Top-10-Patient-Safety-Concerns-for-2017. aspx]

Sadly (I'd say "tragically" if I were more dramatically inclined), though basic patient data are easily encoded by standard indexing systems, the information itself remains locked up in databases that mostly don't "talk" to each other. If I want to know all about what happened to my patient when she visited an out-of-system emergency room or specialist, it's quite likely that a member of my staff or I will have to call the hospital or the doctor to get either a faxed or mailed paper copy of a report or a voluminous electronic file that is 95% extraneous garbage. For lack of standardization, medical information is stored in a hodgepodge of silos that stand within sight of one another, only able to communicate with the equivalent of smoke signals. (See Chapter 6, "Economics," and Chapter 8, "Electronic Medical Record," for discussions of the barriers to information sharing.)

Let's go back to the patient information that I do have in electronic format. It is relatively simple to use these data to remind me of all sorts of things that my fallible human brain, or even a paper-based reminder system, does a whole lot less competently. Well-placed and timed alerts can improve the quality of the care I deliver, often without even involving me. The record can keep track of when children are due for immunizations, for example. In a well-organized office, a medical assistant can arrange to get the vaccines into the kids. The same goes for reminders to patients for pap smears, mammograms, colon cancer screening, glycohemoglobin tests to measure control of diabetes, and a host of other life-preserving measures, all of which can be accomplished without taking up a moment of the doctor's expensive time.

If prescriptions are written electronically, the system can provide an immediate warning if the provider has selected a medication that appears on the patient's allergy list. A sub-routine that checks among drugs for adverse interactions can run in the background whenever a new prescription is written and alert the prescriber immediately if, for example, the antibiotic prescribed for a urinary infection risks making the patient's birth control pills temporarily less effective or the new anti-inflammatory prescribed for arthritis will increase the risk of gastric bleeding for the patient taking a blood thinner.

The developers of most every electronic medical record system are making a continuous effort to turn the data that their products store and sort and display into actionable information, at least within each system. (See Chapter 8, "Electronic Medical Record," for examples.) Moving information across systems remains a colossal impediment to realizing the potential that having patient information in electronic form could provide.

When it comes to information systems, the healthcare industry usually places near last in effective use of information technology. (See Chapter 6, "Economics.."). Taking cues from other sectors, healthcare organizations are slowly learning more effective ways to display data. Dashboards are an outgrowth and refinement of executive information systems, first developed in the 1980s. These systems are designed to display critical data clearly and simply to support organized decision-making. They depend heavily on graphics and charts, coded for easy interpretation.

In healthcare, a dashboard may present what one needs to know about a single patient with heart failure: weight, blood pressure, symptoms, functional level, other diagnoses, etc., or what the hospital needs to know about patients treated there in the last year for heart failure: length-of-stay, procedures, status on discharge, readmission rate, cost per admission, deaths, etc. Graphics can compare individuals or groups to target values, professional standards, norms, last year's performance, or whatever else may be useful.

Here are some very basic principles for graphical presentation of data, which means making the most effective link between information and the human nervous system:

- Simple, communicates easily
- Minimizes distractions that could cause confusion
- Supports organized business with meaning and useful data
- Applies principles of human visual perception to visual presentation of information

A team of academicians analyzed how German hospitals reported their mortality rate for coronary angiography and came up with these simple recommendations for making hospital report cards intelligible to the general public:

- Avoid tables without symbols.
- Include bar charts with symbols.
- State explicitly whether high or low values indicate good performance and provide a good quality range.
- Avoid reporting incomplete data.[20]

In a way, we're getting back to pre-literate communication by appealing to a wider range of perception than pure well-chosen words can. At its best, electronic technology allows us to engage audiences on more levels than we can with written data and words. With the enrichment of pictorial, auditory, visual, video and even virtual reality technologies that add kinesthetic and tactile channels to communications, we are gradually finding our way back to the multi-sensory engagement that Homer counted on and Socrates so lamented the loss of.

Chapter 3

Technology

The influence of this invention [the telegraph] over the political, commercial and social relations of the people of this widely-extended country…will…of itself amount to a revolution unsurpassed in moral grandeur by any discovery that has been made in the arts and sciences.…Space will be, to all practical purposes of information, completely annihilated between the States of the Union, as also between the individual citizens thereof.

—F.O.J. Smith, US Congressman, circa 1850

Were we to examine the armamentaria of the general practitioners of medicine, we would find that where they had electrical apparatus, it would, as a rule, be the farthest from up-to-date of any appliances they might have.

—Caleb Brown, The Use of Electricity by the General Practitioner, *Journal of the American Medical Association*, 1898

We have to be very careful that we don't automate the current chaos.

—Larry Weed

We are stuck with technology when what we really want is just stuff that works.

—Douglas Adams, *The Salmon of Doubt*

This chapter is the hardest one to justify devoting expensive atoms to, rather than cheap electrons. In plain English, these days printing a hard copy of a treatise on information technology, rather than just putting it out in effortlessly updatable electronic format, doesn't seem to make much sense. Things change so rapidly that, by the time it's written about and the words are edited, printed and distributed, technology has moved on to the next big thing.

Here is a partial list of next big things that have held us followers of health-care informatics in thrall over the last few years: big data, business intelligence, analytics, cloud versus closet, artificial intelligence, accountable care organization, population health management, learning health system, precision medicine, interoperability, patient engagement, internet of things, meaningful use, mobile health, electronic medical record, electronic health record, personal health record, telemedicine, telehealth, health information exchange, health information management, patient portal, natural language processing, change fatigue, disruptive innovation, gamification, service recovery mode, patient centered medical home, wearables, tokenization, pay for performance…and on and on. One would find few terms that are on the list of what's hot now in a catalog of buzz words from a decade ago.

A number of items mentioned above are covered in this book, or at least included in the glossary. But I could not justify expending all of this paper on saying a little bit about each of the things that happens to be on the front burner today. Tomorrow, many of these ideas won't even be on the stovetop.

Let me reiterate the pledge I made in the Introduction to write something less ephemeral, from a perspective that penetrates below the surface geography of healthcare. In this chapter and others, I hope to offer insight into the larger structures and forces that drive technology so you can have a better idea where it is galloping off to and how to harness it so that it takes patients, providers and organizations where we really need to go.

Once most everybody has the same technology, how it is employed determines who actually gets a boost from using it. And that depends on people and on relationships. Ultimately, people are what make or break any system, not technology.

So, here's a chapter on technology that starts out stating it's the people who are most important. You'll hear me say that multiple times over the course of this book. If you get only that message, I'll have considered my labor a success.

Bandwidth

Bandwidth is simply the rate at which a channel can carry a signal. That channel may be made of copper wire, fiber-optic cable, or devices that "talk" to each other over the airwaves, through the atmosphere or a vacuum.

In the olden days (late 1980s), I purchased the first home computer, an Epson Equity desktop model with 5.25" floppy disk drive and a 10 Mb hard drive. I added a 1024 baud modem so my device could communicate with other computers. "Baud" is an old-fashioned term meaning bits-per-second. Messages were sent over telephone lines, wonderfully nicknamed "twisted pairs," referring to the standard pair of copper wires that used to connect the vast majority of individual phones to the national network.

When I worked in my first wired office, the Ethernet-based intranet system, constructed of coaxial cables that made it faster than a twisted pair, competed with the Nikenet, which was comprised of people who put on their sneakers, uploaded their data onto floppy disks and walked them down to the hall to the recipient.*

On an average day, I work on my laptop from the dining room table, the sunniest place in my house, connected to the internet at a rate of 15 to 20 Mbps. That's at least 12,000 times faster than the 1200 baud I started out with in the Stone Age. The signal is carried into the house from a utility pole in the alley via a coaxial cable. My modem/router receives the signals and transmits them wirelessly throughout my home. Access to my home WiFi is protected by a password.

When the United Nations declared internet access to be a basic human right in 2011, they did not specify a minimum bandwidth, just that people should have unhampered access to the information they need to live a rich, productive, connected life. A significant rural/urban gap in broadband internet access at home persists in the United States. In 2017, the FCC reported that 60% of rural Americans, versus 5% of urban dwellers, live in what the FCC calls "double burden" counties, which have low rates of internet connectivity as well as high rates of chronic disease, like diabetes. Preventable hospitalizations are 50% higher in the 214 least connected counties, 175 of which are rural.[1]

According to the Pew Trust, in 2016, 73% of American households had broadband internet service. For internet access from almost anywhere, 77% of the population (including 92% of young adults) owned smartphones.[2]

Wireless is often the best solution to the "last mile problem." To bring enough bandwidth to carry television programs into homes, cable companies need franchises from local governments before they can make use of existing power and telephone poles. Then, they must string a coaxial cable to reach each home. This is expensive. Now many of us have little dish antennas on our roof that pick up signals from a distant satellite. Though it costs a bundle to build and launch a communication satellite, a single spacecraft can broadcast to thousands of square miles and millions of customers at a low cost per user.

Many folks have dropped their landline telephone service. In 1990, the Census Bureau found that 97.6% of American homes had telephones, all of which received their service via a twisted pair attached the national phone network. In 2015, only 60% of homes had landline phones.[3]

---

* Today's equivalent of the Nikenet, is Amazon's Snowmobile Service, the ultimate in bandwidth. At the heart of Snowmobile is a 45 foot-long water-resistant, climatecontrolled semi-truck trailer that parks at a data center where it can download up to 100 petabytes (100 million gigabytes), which is the equivalent of five comprehensive copies of the entire internet, going back forever. The truck then drives to an Amazon cloud data center, where the data are uploaded. Were you to upload 100 petabytes via an ultrafast standard connection, such as the 1 gigabyte/second Google Fiber, it would take over 28 years. (Finley, K. Amazon's snowmobile is actually a truck hauling a huge hard drive. *Wired*. December 2, 2016).

The US did not even make the top ten in the 2015 ranking of average internet speed.[4] (South Korea came out at the top of this heap.) We lag because of the peculiar mix of free-market economic principles we claim to uphold. (See "Alignment of Incentives" in Chapter 6, "Economics.") Still, even for us here in the lower bandwidth USA, connectivity is rapidly growing in speed and in availability and will continue to do so for the foreseeable future.

Iridium, the first attempt at worldwide wireless coverage via satellites, was dubbed in 2009 by *Time Magazine* to be "One of the Ten Biggest Tech Failures in the Last Decade."[5] The company, which spent $5 billion to build and launch its system of 66 school bus-sized satellites, managed to sign up just 10,000 customers. Iridium ended up defaulting on $1.5 billion of debt.

Today the deep-pocketed likes of SpaceX, Boeing and OneWeb are planning to launch, via reusable rockets, constellations of thousands of cheap, standardized, miniature communication satellites to provide broadband service literally everywhere on the globe.

In the early 1990s, the High Plains Rural Health Network (HPRHN), a group of hospitals in the northeast corner of Colorado where I worked, got a big federal grant to fund the state's first telehealth system. HPRHN purchased a lot of hardware, including cameras, codecs (the video equivalent of modems) and their own servers. The central videoconferencing codec cost $110,000. And they spent a lot of money to rent high bandwidth lines from the phone company. Each station, installed in a hospital, on a clumsy cart that could be wheeled from emergency room to conference room to consulting room, cost $55,000. The three-year grant was for $400,000

The system never got much use, clinical or otherwise. In my mind, one of the most important reasons for failure was that the urban hospitals that were to provide the consulting services for these country hospitals constantly fought each other for control of the system. The city guys figured that, by getting first dibs on all this pricey equipment and bandwidth, they could outcompete their rivals. While the big guys bickered over turf, nobody was out there doing the marketing groundwork to assess customer (patient, hospital, professional) needs and find ways to meet them via telemedicine or otherwise. The HPRHN system died a slow death.

Today, you can purchase a basic telemedicine base station for a few hundred dollars. Add in bells and whistles, like electronic stethoscope and dermatoscope (for viewing skin lesions), and it could cost some thousands. Transmission can be done via standard secure internet protocols, using the bandwidth that is available to almost everybody almost everywhere.

In other words, just about anyone has or can have the technology at reasonable cost. It has become a commodity, making it impossible to corner the telehealth market on the sole basis of having the right machines and bandwidth. How you use this commodity to serve patients while improving work life of staff is now and always has been the way you win in the marketplace.

Miniaturization, Embeddedness and Portability

There is a repair shop in the town I live in where they'll fix most anything, including bicycles, chainsaws and lawnmowers. The current proprietors are grandsons of the gunsmith who built the machine shop. The workspace has changed little since it was constructed in 1925. Stepping into it is like stepping back in time. A pulley on the shaft of a ten-horsepower electric motor on the floor is connected by a belt to a pulley on an overhead shaft. Each machine—drill press, lathe, table saw, band saw, grinder, milling machine—is powered by its own drive belt that can be cinched to deliver power from a pulley on the drive shaft to a pulley on the power tool.

In order to run and maintain this system, one has to know how to align each of the pulleys and shafts, tension each of the belts, and lubricate the whole shebang. I'm sure a whole lot of power is lost to friction. But back in the day when electric motors were heavy and expensive, it was smart to purchase just one motor to run multiple tools. This machine shop's system doesn't make much sense in today's world, where every tool has its own relatively lightweight, inexpensive and efficient motor to power it. I am so glad that, for the sake of tradition, these two brothers have maintained the old equipment and have kept, into their middle age, the skills to run it.

Nowadays, on a typical day, you use myriad electric motors without ever thinking about them: the fans in your furnace and blow dryer; the compressors in your refrigerator and air conditioning; the windshield wipers, washer fluid pump and electric windows in your car; the motive force in your hybrid or electric vehicle. If you spend time in your shop after work, the power tools, from Dremel to table saw, all have small, efficient, quiet motors to power them. In the kitchen, there's the blender, disposal and dishwasher. You don't have to know anything about operating any of these motors except where the on-switch is. The motors that serve you have retreated into the background.

By a similar only much more dramatic process, electronic devices are getting smaller and fading into the background. Your phone, car, thermostat, television, sound system, security system, copier, even your refrigerator, all rely on computer chips to run them. Since the 1970s, computer memory chips, the cornerstones of electronic computing, have obeyed Moore's Law, which means that they have about doubled in processing power every two years. As a geometric progression, the number of transistors and calculating power of such a chip grows very big very fast. Today the most powerful memories have 20 billion transistors on a single chip.

As the size of individual processors shrinks and they get squeezed closer and closer together, chip designers bump up against fundamental constraints of physics, like the speed of light, the spread-out nature of electrons, and the heat generated by jamming so many circuits into such a small space. Moore's Law has been declared dead more times than Francisco Franco was on the old "Saturday Night Live" television show.

Clever engineers have continued to find new ways to squeeze ever more circuits into and to wring ever more performance out of the computer chips they design.

Of course, nothing (not even healthcare spending) can grow exponentially forever. Sooner or later Moore's Law will succumb to pure mathematics and physics, which will not spell the end to big gains in computing power. Hardware architecture will keep getting cleverer, even as its individual building blocks bump up against natural physical limits. And then there is quantum computing, which I discuss near the end of this chapter.

When it comes to being able to do tasks demanded by your personal life, and for all but the most computing-intensive professions, you needn't worry yourself about the demise of Moore's Law at some future date. I expect you think about the computer chips that are entwined with so much of your day-to-day experience about as much as you think about the electric motors that surround you.

In a 2012 article published in the *New York Times*, Abraham Verghese, the popular physician/author, describes the huge black doctor's bag that his uncle carried with him when he practiced in Madras (now Chennai), India, stuffed full of medicines, syringes, needles and medical instruments. When the author sees patients, he carries a small bag, which contains a handheld ultrasound* machine, that can be used to peer through the skin and see the moving heart, blood vessels, abscesses, etc., a PanOptic ophthalmoscope that gives a beautiful view of the retina, which is the one place in the body where you can see arteries, veins and nerves directly, and an iPad, which comes in especially handy for sharing anatomy pictures with patients and educational materials with students and residents. As his hearing ages, Dr. Verghese might want to add an electronic stethoscope.[6]

The Office of Naval Research has produced the Automated Critical Care System, which fits in a backpack. The system monitors vital signs. A fluid pump will deliver IV fluids at the rate it calculates as well as administer precise quantities of intravenous drugs it determines are indicated. A local medic or telemedicine caregiver can over-ride these orders. For the soldier who is not medically trained and out of touch with help, the contents of the backpack can autopilot care of a critically injured comrade for hours.[7]

Image quality and reliability on mobile devices are much higher than they used to be. Images transmitted to mobile devices by one imaging system tested in 2014 by 19 clinicians, including 9 radiologists and 4 neurologists, was rated superior to the desktop viewers that were deployed throughout the enterprise.[8] A study of MRIs of the knee found no difference in radiologists' accuracy of interpretation, whether they had viewed the study on a radiology workstation or on the screen of an iPhone equipped with standard software for displaying radiologic studies.

---

* A recent version of the handheld ultrasound can, thanks to sophisticated software, make hitting a tumor or abscess with a needle, for biopsy or drainage, a surer thing. The device senses the angle and position on the skin of a needle and indicates the path of the needle through the underlying tissue. The operator can then adjust the position and angle of insertion without ever breaking the skin until she sees a straight path to the lump or abscess she's aiming for and can go right to it. (NIH Supports New Ultrasound System. *Federal Telemedicine News.* May 18, 2014.)

Because of the small size of the screen, readings did take about four minutes longer using the iPhone.[9]

If you're old enough you probably remember the iconic Apple Computer screen-saver, "Flying Toasters," released in 1989. Though toasters still don't fly, today you can purchase for $130, a Breville brand toaster in which, "A microchip delivers precise browning control and regulates a lift-and-look button, which lets you check the toast without canceling the cycle." No doubt the cost of smart toasters will plummet while they learn to do even more amazing things (whatever those might be).

If it is not already enabled by at least one computer chip, virtually every electronic device in your home and office soon will be. And these gizmos will be able to "talk" to each other. (Imagine the potential strength of an alliance between the freezer and the microwave once they can really converse!) Of course, you will still have the option to choose old-fashioned devices like wind-up clocks and unamplified musical instruments. What may be lost when you digitize is a theme that runs through this book.[10]

The "internet of things" already makes some homes' lighting, heating and security more efficient, and even manageable from out of town by smartphone. Embedded chips enhance vehicle safety, whether driven by humans or by computers. Automated digital positioning devices keep track of and dispatch millions of taxis and gig-company passenger vehicles, alerting drivers along the way of traffic jams and alternate routes.

Thanks to the internet of things, cardiologists monitor and adjust pacemakers remotely. Sensors in orthotics and prosthetics (braces and artificial parts) continuously monitor and report information on a patient's length of use, strides, range of motion, muscular force and cadence. These data, properly analyzed, can be enormously valuable to the individual patient in rehabilitation and maintaining function, as well as to the medical researcher and device designer.[11]

On a less serious note, you can buy today: RollScout, a toilet paper holder that alerts you when the roll is empty; Egg Minder, which holds 14 eggs and signals your phone how many eggs are in the tray and which ones are going bad; and 24eight, a diaper that texts the caretaker's phone when it's wet.[*,12]

The National Science Foundation estimated that there were nearly 6.4 billion connected objects in 2017, up 30 percent from 2015 and expected to reach 20.8 billion by 2020.[13] A significant share of these things will be serious medical devices.

There are hazards. What if the software is wrong just 0.01% of the time in predicting that it is safe to change lanes on the highway? What if a malicious hacker

---

* The 24eight product got me to thinking about raising my own children. It didn't take long before, with each of them, I could distinguish among their hungry, tired, pained and wet cries. It was a visceral connection, rooted I'm sure, in a good dose of instinct that resides in some deeper brain structures. Might there have been something of this human connection lost if my children's needs had been interpreted for me by an AI-driven system that I had trained initially by pushing a button that said "hungry," "tired," "pained" or "wet" every time I responded to one of their cries?

gets into a cardiac pacemaker and just turns it off? (This happened in an episode of "Homeland." Terrorists hack into the Vice-President's pacemaker, provoking a heart attack that kills him.) Experts say uninvited entry into the workings of a pacemaker, insulin pump or narcotic delivery device is quite possible in real life. In fact, the internet of things is considered much less secure even than the numerous electronic medical record systems that have been broken into in recent years. (See Chapter 7, "Security and Privacy.")

The main point here is to say that computing devices will continue their march to ubiquity and that, as they do, we will become less aware of them. Already we're doing less on computers and more on smartphones and other gadgets that we may not even recognize as computers. Operating these tools will become more intuitive. When I started out with my first computer, I had to learn some commands in MS-DOS, the disk operating system that put Bill Gates and Microsoft on the map. Today the only thing I usually need to know about an operating system is its name and version number before I download software.

3-D Printing

This information-heavy technology is just coming into its own. Layer after layer of one or more substrate substances is laid down by a 3-D printer according to a plan dictated by a computer. In healthcare, the layers have usually been generated from data captured by three-dimensional medical imaging studies like ultrasounds, CT and MRI scans.

The thinner each layer, the smoother, more detailed and truer to the original is the built-up solid object. Depending on the substrate, as of 2017, the lower end for layer thickness is about 0.1 mm. Today's most sophisticated 3-D printers can construct objects, using up to six different substrates simultaneously, as well as dyes, to create 360,000 different colors and textures.

This technology is already being used to make individually customized, and therefore more comfortable and functional, pieces for hearing aids, dental implants, artificial joints, prosthetic hands and legs, and even plain-old orthopedic splints. Printed human skin has been successfully employed to treat burn victims. We're not far from printing heart valves and ears. Developers are still a long way off, though, from the holy grail of printing whole new organs, like livers and kidneys.

Detailed 3-D models of individual patients are regularly probed and sliced by physicians who need to strategize and practice highly complicated surgeries before performing them on the actual persons.

The Gartner Consulting Group predicted in 2017 that, by 2019, one third of all medical implant procedures will include parts produced with 3-D printer technology. Another research firm, IndustryARC, forecasts that the market for 3-D printed technologies in healthcare will have almost doubled from $660 million in 2016 to $1.21 billion in 2020.[14] The cost of 3-D printing outfits is plummeting, making it ever more practical, even for smaller healthcare systems, to custom-make just what their patients need, bypassing the myriad middlemen who inhabit the medical marketplace, and maybe even reducing some costs to patients.

Interoperability and Standards

When you go to most any ATM most anywhere in the world you can hook into your own bank's account to accomplish certain transactions, using only a plastic card and a four-digit password. Compare that to getting your own medical information. Each practice and institution that holds a piece of your data requires its own registration, login and password (assuming it has a secure portal that gives patients access to their own data, which is far from universal). Likely as not, the portal will not be easy to use. In 2015, just 15% of patients who had been recently hospitalized accessed their medical records, in spite of 88% of hospitals offering that service.[15] A 2017 survey of patients who had used a portal to view their lab results found that nearly two thirds of them had received the results with no explanation, leading almost half of them to search for more information online.[16]

Not only is it a chore to access your own medical information, but the barriers to sharing that information among your healthcare providers, who ought to inform and collaborate with each other (as you permit) as a matter of course, are enormous. Things may be better if you receive all of your health services at one integrated system. Even within a single system, a hospital's business and medical records information systems may not be on speaking terms with its clinics' systems, requiring you, for example, to register again at the hospital radiology department after having just given all your information to the business associate in the doctor's office in the same medical center.

The Veterans Administration has launched an effort, based on open access software, called Blue Button. By clicking on a prominent blue button on the VA website screen, a veteran is supposed to be able to access a whole range of her personal health information held by the VA. The VA says, "Patients and their delegates had predominantly positive experiences with health record transparency." (That sounds like faint praise to me.[17])

HIPAAnoia, exaggerated fear of getting in trouble with the feds (leading even to possible jail time) over the Health Insurance Portability and Accountability Act (HIPAA), is one huge impediment to free flow of patient information. In 2015, Congress even passed a law meant to reduce HIPAAnoia, making "information blocking" an offense, punishable by up to $10,000 per occurrence.

Though the law clearly states it is okay to share data for legitimate clinical reasons, especially in acute medical situations, too many institutions still maintain a paranoid mindset about releasing medical information. Every clinician will have stories similar to one of mine, in which I had to wait nearly an hour for a medical records department supervisor at another hospital to okay releasing an old electrocardiogram of a patient who had presented with acute chest pain to me at my hospital's emergency room; all the while the clock was ticking on heart muscle possibly being lost to a heart attack.

I will say much more in Chapter 6 about how misalignment of financial with clinical incentives is the single most important reason for the inefficiency of medical care in comparison to other service businesses like banks, airlines and hotels. For now, I will stick to discussing the technological barriers to free flow of medical data.

Very few medical institutions have the chance to reset their information systems all at once. Most started their computerization journey decades ago when they installed business systems to manage functions like purchasing, billing and accounts receivable. Eventually, they graduated to an integrated business suite. Clinical functions, like dictation and laboratory reporting systems, were added later. Finally, the institution purchased a larger suite of clinical functionalities and then (especially once Meaningful Use came into play in 2009) an electronic medical record, either incorporated into the existing clinical system or from another vendor.* Between 2008 and 2014, digital medical record use by hospitals increased from less than one in ten to more than three in four.[18] Medical practices have climbed a similarly steep slope of computerization.

In the ensuing scramble to get in on the gigabucks offered by the feds for complying with the Meaningful Use Program, too many vendor promises about system integration turned out to be vaporware. Functionalities that may have looked fully grown in the demos used to sell systems were, in reality, barely in development.

Chaos still reigns in many information technology departments, furiously working to tie their disparate systems together, even among the various parts of so-called integrated systems. Tasks that seem like they ought to be simple, such as pairing radiology images with reports, present big challenges to many electronic medical information systems.[19]

When it comes to integration of functions, some comprehensive systems are better than others. A few big institutions, like Kaiser-Permanente and Mayo Clinic (both use the Epic electronic health record), have allied closely with vendors, while creating a corporate-wide culture of consistent use of their systems. Some smaller operations manage to get their informatics acts together too. But once anybody ventures outside the home system's walls, it's anarchy. The prestigious *Milbank Quarterly* reported in 2017, on a survey of 60 US leaders in health information technology, that 50% of the respondents felt EMR vendors were routinely guilty of designing information blocking into their systems, as well as 25% of hospitals and health systems.[20]

---

* Meaningful Use got its start in 2009 with enactment of the American Reinvestment and Recovery Act (ARRA) and the accompanying Health Information Technology for Economic and Clinical Health (HITECH) Act. These provisions specified escalating monetary incentives and penalties for computerizing medical institutions and practices. Since then, many billions of dollars (I cannot find a single number) have been spent by government and by the healthcare industry to computerize clinical care.

Regional health information organizations (RHIO—pronounced ree-oh) have stepped in to provide data exchange services within a defined area. RHIOs started out as a first crack at meeting the interoperability provisions of the 2009 Health Information Technology for Economic & Clinical Health (HITECH) Act, the ultimate goal of which was to develop a National Health Information Network. The ability to exchange clinical data electronically is a key item in one of the stages of Meaningful Use.

A RHIO may serve a single borough (e.g. Bronx), city (e.g. Buffalo, Memphis), region (e.g. Hudson Valley and Catskills), or state (e.g. Colorado, Indiana). There are almost as many sub-types of RHIO architecture as there are RHIOs. They all converge on the concept of creating a shared data repository through use of a common data model for things like registration information, laboratory results, written reports, diagnosis and procedure codes. Each of these fields already has a well-established and widely-accepted indexing system. A standard health data interchange model, HL7, is employed when moving data between computers. The next generation of HL7, Fast Healthcare Internet Interoperability Resources (FHIR, pronounced "fire") promises to unlock a fair share of the interoperability challenges by starting out with a logical model that is consistent, intuitive and flexible.

The biggest chore in founding a RHIO is grinding out an administrative and regulatory structure, which leaves the leaders of competing organizations feeling secure enough that, by sharing information, they're not giving away business. Once again, the roadblocks to information system advancement are people, politics and money, not technology.

RHIO medical records provide far from a comprehensive picture of a patient. These electronic documents capture and make available just a slice of what's been learned about the patient during at an emergency room visit or hospital stay. According to a government report released in 2015, only 56% of hospitals had attempted to get information electronically from other providers, and just 40% of those had successfully merged the information into their own databases. In other words, just 24% of hospitals (40% of 56%) had succeeded in incorporating *even one* external patient record into their own.[21]

Nevertheless, analysis of 2000 emergency department visits to 3 western New York hospitals that were tied to the same regional Health Information Exchange (HIE) in 2014 showed that patients whose ER doctors referred to the information that was available in the HIE record, received up to 50% fewer laboratory tests and 26% to 47% fewer radiology studies. This study also found that, without a scribe to navigate the user-unfriendly information systems, most doctors would probably not have bothered to obtain the old data.[22]

A study of the health information exchange in Rochester, New York, found that the HIE system was accessed during 2.4% of emergency room encounters. Still, for these few patients whose information someone had taken the trouble to look up, the odds of their being admitted to the hospital from the ER were 30% lower.[23]

A survey of accountable care organization managers that was reported in 2015 found that only 3% of them believed a publicly-run health information exchange could provide the information their organizations needed to best manage their patients' medical needs. Ninety-eight percent would prefer to participate in a private, community based exchange.[24]

In 2015, twelve leading EHR vendors formed the CommonWell Health Alliance Partnership. The Alliance issued a consensus statement by which they agreed to a set of "objective measures of interoperability and ongoing reporting." Notably, Epic Systems—the market leader in electronic health records, with $1.75 billion in revenue in 2016—refused to join. Epic was roundly criticized in 2014 by US Representative Phil Gingrey (R-Ga.), a physician, who cited a RAND Corporation report that asserted Epic's electronic health record was deliberately designed to be closed.

Hegemonic healthcare institutions might well, for the time being, perceive a competitive advantage to using patient records that are available only to its own people.[25] Sooner or later (by my reckoning, unconscionably later), health data interchange standards will be as ubiquitous as financial transaction standards have been for decades. Once this is accomplished, competition will have to be on the basis of service to patients and system users, not on the basis of cornering a set of data or technologies.

The Cloud

Microsoft's big break came when its founder, Bill Gates, figured out ahead of his rivals that it was the software that ran computers, not the hardware itself, which had the most value. In 1980, he made a deal with IBM, the undisputed gorilla in the computer world at that time, to license Microsoft's Disk Operating System, MS-DOS, for use in all of IBM's personal computers. In 2005, IBM sold its personal computer manufacturing business to Lenovo. PCs had become a low profit margin commodity. The market was flooded with cheap machines, produced by the likes of Dell and Hewlett-Packard; and Bill Gates became the richest person in the world.

Though still a giant, Microsoft has been eclipsed by other giants, including Apple, Facebook, Google and Amazon. The seeds of Microsoft's slide from the top of the heap were planted in the early sixties, when some dreamers imagined that computing itself would become a public utility, available to everybody, just like electricity, telephone service and television signals. With the rise of the internet and of the World Wide Web over the past decade and a half, connectedness has come to the fore. Microsoft sort of missed that boat. Their efforts at dominating the web via their browser, Internet Explorer and their search engine, Bing, have not met with nearly the success that the dominance of MS-DOS brought to the operating system space.

The internet, plus ultra-cheap, easily accessible information storage, are the technologies that made the cloud a reality. Pennies or less per gigabyte (1000 megabytes) per month was the bulk rate for cloud-based memory in 2016.

The simplest definition of cloud computing is storage of data and programs on remote machines that are accessed over the internet. There are various broad categories of services, including: virtual machines, software that resides with the host cloud and does the work that the computer on your desktop would do (Infrastructure as a Service, IaaS); computing environments for developing applications (Platform as a Service, PaaS); and access to software when you need it (Software as a Service, SaaS). Cloud-based resources are accessed with a client, which can be a desktop computer, a dumb terminal, a laptop, tablet or smartphone.

Doing computing on a cloud has the same advantages as renting a small earth mover for the weekend to build berms in your backyard. You pay for just what you need when you need it, and an expert maintains the machine.

The equipment rental company no doubt purchased the earth mover wholesale. Similarly, a cloud service provider can offer a low price because it buys in bulk too, up to terabytes (a million megabytes) or exabytes (a thousand terabytes) of capacity. In 2016, Google was estimated to hold 10-15 exabytes of data, the equivalent of 30 million personal computers.[26]

The downside is that the implement is not yours. You have to trust that the rental company has maintained it well enough that you don't have to worry that the engine will seize mid-job for lack of lubrication.

The added worry for people in healthcare, where HIPAA rules both business procedures and psyches, is that once you have passed protected health information over your own firewall, you have lost some control. Standards, contracts and procedures have to be very carefully constructed in order to protect patients, practices and institutions from the practical and legal consequences of a breech.

When it comes to cloud computing, IBM and Microsoft have not been caught so flatfooted as they had been by unanticipated leverage (and profits) generated by operating systems and the internet, respectively. In 2016, these corporations were ranked two and three, after Amazon, as cloud service providers, a $70 billion business in 2015 that is estimated to double by 2019. On the other hand, cloud computing services are probably on the way to becoming yet another commodity, with fierce competition and low profit margins.

The delay in communicating with distant cloud computers, even at the speed of light, is proving to be too much for fully autonomous vehicles that need to gather, process and act on a huge and varied array of data in the blink of an eye. We will probably soon see smaller computers all over the place, sort of like cell phone towers, processing at least a share of the data that are currently sent to remote server farms.[27]

Collaborative Tools and Patient Portals

How many email messages do you get per day? How about tweets? How often do you check Facebook? Can you imagine life without them? "Wistfully," is a likely answer to the last question. No matter how cleverly we set automatic filters, we are all bombarded by too many messages.

On the other hand, think about what a hassle it used to be in olden days to schedule a meeting, get a simple question answered or share and review a document with workmates, when your main tools were telephone, mail, Nike net, and later on, fax machine. Telephone tag was the order of the day.

Now, thanks to communication technologies developed in the last couple of decades, we think nothing of scheduling a meeting, complete with audiovisuals and talking heads, with colleagues who are located across the continent or the ocean. We produce documents collaboratively. We effortlessly poll co-workers, customers and board members.

There is not that much to say about this ever-richer tool set except, perhaps, to urge you to think hard about how accessible you wish to be. In 2015, the average office worker received 121 emails per day and opened 34% of them. Forty-two percent of Americans check their email in the bathroom and eighteen percent do it while driving.[28] Be parsimonious with your contact information. I learned that lesson the hard way back in 1976, when I was one of two doctors in a town of 2000, and I agreed to having my home phone number published.

If you are lucky enough to have the support of a trusted assistant who can filter your messages, all the better. Filtering is the beauty that a well-designed patient portal provides for a medical practice. Frontline staff can handle the large majority of messages themselves, taking care of things like appointments (assuming online scheduling is not already a feature of the system), referrals, test result reports, medication refills, etc., forwarding on the relatively small number of messages that require a clinician's touch. Collaboration among team members is facilitated. Clinician, diabetes educator, dietician and behaviorist can all easily get their two cents in, with the patient and with each other.

Some very creative people are designing systems that provide a better framework for connecting patients and caregivers. For example, TapCloud software obtains from patients who may be located anywhere, employing an easy-to-use electronic format, information about their well-being, symptoms, pain, medications and vital signs. Clinicians and staff can monitor day-to-day how a patient is doing by viewing her information, clearly presented on a dashboard. The crucial step of closing the loop with the patient is up to the practice, whether by phone call, video check-in, email message, home visit or office visit.

This particular system has been used successfully to: track health parameters and accomplish preoperative routines prior to elective surgical procedures; follow post-surgery recovery; help manage pain and other symptoms for homecare hospice patients; remind patients to take medications, get follow-up tests and exercise; and check on medication side effects. Studies have shown improvements in patient health and satisfaction and decreases in overall cost. Practices that use TapCloud have documented a remarkable decrease in hospital readmission and post-operative complication rates.

In general, patients are happy to receive routine communication by secure email. A report published in the *Journal of the American Board of Family Medicine* in 2015 learned from polling 409 patients that fax was their least favorite way to receive medical results. Personal voicemail and letter were okay. Password protected email was favored by over half of respondents for receiving highly sensitive medical information.[29]

TechnologyAdvice surveyed 406 US adults in 2014, asking them what online services they would like to see their primary care physician offer. Sixty-four percent of respondents said they wanted their provider to offer some sort of digital tools: health resources, education materials, secure messaging scheduling, access to test results or diagnoses.[30]

On the other hand, as of a review article published in 2012 (there were only five good studies on the subject then), patients who used a portal, when compared to a control group that did not access their provider's practice electronically, showed no decrease in frequency of office visits or phone contacts, nor was adherence to their medication regimen any better.[31]

One of today's most popular buzzwords is "patient engagement." When it comes to an electronic patient portal, engagement means more than just pushing out unexplained lab results or fielding requests for medication refills. It means conversation.

Every serious electronic medical record offers a patient portal. Seeing this feature as a tool for patient engagement and collaboration is key to its effective use. The other key is a well-designed backend process that routes the right information to the right people in a timely manner and makes it easy for them to act on it. Sooner or later, the majority of physicians wind up liking their patient portals.

Artificial Intelligence

In this context, "artificial" implies smarts that are housed in a non-biologic system, which means that its opposite ("natural intelligence?") would allow for the sorts of cleverness encountered in dolphins and chimpanzees. The word "intelligence" is really hard to define. Are computers intelligent? Or dogs? Or ravens? How about the wily octopus, with two thirds of its nervous system located in its limbs?

There is no need to venture a comprehensive definition of intelligence here. For the sake of this work, by "artificial intelligence" I mean a computing machine that either makes recommendations to a human decision-maker or makes decisions itself and acts on them.

One camp of the artificial intelligence (AI) community, the so-called automation camp, has, as its primary goal, to build machines that can replace human beings. These are the groups that are busy designing things like vehicles that are truly self-driving. When not building things, the more theoretical and philosophical members of this crowd busy themselves with figuring out if it is possible to make a conscious machine and, if the answer is "yes," how such a device might work and how it would be controlled.

Consciousness is an even slipperier concept than intelligence, fascinating stuff, but not within the scope of this edition. (Perhaps "Machines That Think" will be a chapter in the fifth edition of *Digital Healing*, due out in 2038.)

An interesting way to think about intelligence is to blur its boundaries. I am not as intelligent as I plus my smartphone databases are. My phone and I would not be as intelligent as we plus our reminder-filled EHR, which are not as intelligent as our whole practice, peopled as it is with smart and empowered staff dedicated to caring for our patients and supported by a well-organized information and communication system. The quality and safety literature make it clear that the great majority of errors in any field, including in healthcare, occur because of system breakdowns, not because just one link that is not intelligent enough.

The augmentation camp is the other main artificial intelligence faction. It seeks to blur the boundaries between human and machine intelligence, aiming to enhance human intelligence with computing machines, an extension of the sort of *homo sapiens* ingenuity that replaced flint blades with metal ones with power saws with computer-controlled laser cutters. The newer model vehicles we drive today, loaded with features like hazard warnings, parking assist, cruise control and route selectors, are examples of the gradualist ways of the augmentation camp.

A middle-of-the road strategy taken by some in the driverless vehicle movement is to hand off tasks between machine and human, letting machines navigate divided highways and such, where traffic is generally orderly and surprises are few, while leaving more challenging tasks, such as congested urban streets, winding dirt roads and snowy conditions, to human drivers.

The handoff problem remains, though. What if the human is daydreaming or dozing? How does the vehicle get her attention within a few seconds? The Audi A8 watches its human with a camera backed by facial recognition software. It knows when its steering wheel is being touched. If the car can tell the human is not paying attention it can flash visual cues, make warning sounds, and even tighten the seatbelt and pump the brakes. If there is still no response, the car turns on its flashers, slows to a stop, unlocks the doors and sends a distress signal.

A collaborative project by two dozen automakers builds crash dummies, in multiple sizes, and sexes, that are anatomically much more realistic and, thanks to information technology, loaded with more sensors than you could shake a stick shift at. Engineers have imagined a small army of these sorts of sensors, hooked into autos that could, in real time, determine the mechanism of a crash and predict injuries to driver and passengers even before emergency medical services arrive.[32]

For the purposes of this book on healthcare, a life-or-death enterprise, it still makes sense nearly always to settle for the humbler goals of the augmentation AI camp.

Things are moving really fast in the realm of assisting clinicians to do their work, for example in natural language processing (NLP), which is what computer people call making sense out of human language, spoken or written. Like biological species, every language and dialect grew up in a specific environment, serving the specific needs of the humans in that niche. Languages are evolved things, which, like creatures, are hugely diverse, idiosyncratic and changeable, reflecting the environments that spawned them.

Thanks to artificial neural networks, a computing technique first conceived in the 1940s but only coming to fruition in the last decade or so, Google, Apple, Facebook, Amazon, Microsoft, Baidu (a Chinese company) and many, many others have been able to make an exponential leap in their systems' ability to turn the spoken word into written text, translate between languages and index the text so it can be input as data.

Over the course of nine months of 2016, Google Translate was able to improve its accuracy in translating between English and Japanese as much as it had in the previous ten years. The Google system learned, for example, to return "minister of agriculture," when that phrase was translated into Japanese and then back into English, rather than spitting out "priest of farming," as earlier versions had done.[33] Google let on that their remarkable system was the result of a switch from a rule-based system to a neural network-based one.*

Rule-based systems do just what they say. They accumulate and tie together axioms that tell the calculating machine what to do. Realms like chess and geometry, which are governed by unbendable rules, are ideal for this sort of approach. In 1997, Deep Blue, an IBM supercomputer, beat the world's top chess player, Gary Kasparov, at his own game. The machine used rules that had been supplied by chess mavens to calculate the strategic value of 200,000 possible positions per second and then chose the move with the highest value. Needless to say, humans play the game very differently than Deep Blue. Parenthetically, a computer teamed with an adept human chess player can still beat the most powerful computer that is not partnered with a *homo sapiens*.

Relatively well-defined medical fields, like cancer chemotherapy, matching antibiotics to infections and medical therapy of glaucoma, succumbed early to codification. Rules of practice were derived by reviewing the medical literature, interviewing medical experts and sometimes taking notes while following them around in their practice. Once these formulas had been encoded into a software program, a patient's data could be input and a reliable therapeutic recommendation would come out. The narrower the field, the easier to capture it in a rule-based system.

Between 2007 and 2009, a Dutch rule-based system significantly outperformed experienced radiation oncologists in predicting two-year survival, shortness of breath and swallowing difficulty in 155 lung cancer patients.[34] A review of studies of EHR-based decision support systems for help in ordering radiologic procedures, reported in 2015 that use of such systems improved appropriateness of ordering as well as showed a small decrease of use.[35]

In 2017, an AI system designed by Exsientia, a UK startup, beat 9 of 10 experienced drug chemists in selecting molecules likely to have biological effects, a first stage in most drug development. There are an estimated 10^{60} different possible

---

* Just for fun, see how many different meanings you can get out of this six-word sentence, "I didn't say you stole my car." It will still be a while, I think, before Google can get all six of them.

compounds that are likely to have drug-like effects, more than the number of atoms in the solar system.[36]

Making sense of what the average four-year old knows is a much bigger challenge. Think of the quantity of contextual rules that would have to be anticipated for a computer to "understand" this instruction to a toddler, "Go get Herbie's chair." The child knows Herbie is the dog and that Dad is calling down to the basement to ask his daughter to drag the chair that Herbie sleeps in to the foot of the stairs so Dad can schlep the big object up to the kitchen where Herbie hangs out and watches the house while the family leaves for a day at the beach. Once the task is understood, a whole different set of challenging problems will need to be solved before a helper robot would be able to navigate the basement, stairs and kitchen, and autonomously carry the chair to where Dad wants it.

Artificial neural networks take a completely different tack than rule-based systems. They mimic biology, not reasoning. The human nervous system grows and learns by selectively reinforcing and pruning the million billion (10^{15}) connections among about hundred billion (10^{11}) brain neurons.* Inputs from senses, thoughts and feelings "groove" neural pathways that lead to feelings, thoughts and actions. What exactly happens between input and output is almost totally a mystery. (Just ask a behaviorist.)

In 2017, a neural network-based program beat the world's best poker players.[37] Though Texas Hold 'Em may not represent the pinnacle of human culture, learning to play a game that is not deterministic, like chess or go, is a big leap forward for a computer. Getting a machine to beat humans in a contest that encompasses the randomness of the deal and the psychology of betting and bluffing is no small thing. The program, named Libratus, did not include facial expression recognition software that might uncover its opponents' tells. It just found a way to learn as it played, including how to throw random bets into its game in ways that had never been done before, confounding its human adversaries.[38]

Artificial neural networks do the same thing as the human brain, on a much smaller scale. Layers of virtual neurons—software structures expressed by electrical signals among silicon-based circuits—recursively adjust their connections until they consistently pair the right outputs with mountains of inputs. Google Translate was initially trained, for example, on millions of documents translated or revised by humans, including records kept by the European Union, the United Nations, and its agencies. "Trainers" continue to expose the system to all sorts of documents written in more than one language, from company reports to bilingual books.[39]

Lately, self-training programs that bootstrap machine learning without depending on human input, like AlphaGo Zero, which, after three days of playing

---

* It is predicted that we'll soon be able to connect up 50 to 75 billion artificial neurons, nearly equal to a human brain. The artificial neurons will be much less richly connected than in the biological brain. Besides, recent neuroscience research has revealed that the human brain employs both rule-based and neural net strategies to produce intelligent behavior.[39]

4.9 million training games with itself, was able to beat its champion predecessor, AlphaGo (Classic?) in 100 of 100 games.[40] The rate of machine learning is accelerating, while decreasing drastically the amount of information that costly humans have to hand-feed the systems. Google even offers a software program, called AutoML that builds machine learning software. (Do you feel as if you're sitting between wall mirrors in the barber shop?[41])

In 2017, a machine learning program trained on the records of 172, 726 emergency department visits, using only vital signs, chief complaint and active medical history, bested the usual triage system, which was based on scoring and human intuition, in predicting which patients would need critical care, an emergency procedure or inpatient hospitalization. The program was even able to provide a rationale for its assessments of high risk 65% of the time, a notable feat for a system based on neural network technology, which tends to be notoriously opaque when it comes to explaining how it does what it does. This was a retrospective study that paired patients' presentation with their outcome, meaning that, before people are willing to trust it, it will need to be tested in a prospective fashion, on patients as they arrive at the ED.[42]

Developers of Mindstrong, an AI algorithm, which turned machine learning loose on 54 million messages sent to the Crisis Text line, claim their system is able, after analyzing just three texts by a single client, to accurately decide if her suicidal talk ought to be taken seriously and referred to a counselor. If it really works, this system could be a real boon in heading off the second leading cause of death (after unintentional injury) in Americans between 15 and 34 years old. As you'd want it to, the system generates a large number of false positives, that is people who are judged to be at higher risk than they really are. Anyone would gladly trade having to screen too many people who are not so distressed so as not to miss even one who is really in danger of harming herself.[43] You may be interested to learn that "ibuprofen" and "bridge" are more heavily weighted as trigger words for suicidality than is "suicide."

Word anticipation when writing text messages on a smartphone is one of the most familiar functions driven by an artificial neural net. No matter how amazing a job your gadget does at guessing the next word or two of a text message you're writing, it does not actually "understand" one bit of what you mean to say.

Getting devices to talk back to you in a human voice is another task that has made great strides thanks to machine learning. It started with those messages composed of machinelike-sounding strings of phone number digits you got when you dialed a number no longer in service or information (remember 411?). Now, thanks to AI, the mechanical voices are being humanized, with more natural rhythms and inflections, which means, with more perceived emotional content. Critics worry that big business will introduce us to a host of brothers and sisters of Amazon's Alexa and Apple's Siri who, armed with AI-driven language recognition software that measures and can respond to the subtle emotional qualities of a customer's speech, will sincerely try to talk us into buying stuff.*,44

No matter how good machines are today at turning spoken language into text, there are still a few jobs in the health information systems department (it used to be called "medical records") for people who once had careers as medical transcriptionists, turning dictation into written documents. Now they can work as auditors and analysts, providing the human eye and oversight to what's in the record, assuring that it says what it really means and that it makes sense.

In 2012, Google computer vision engineers trained a computer system to recognize human faces and cats, not by inputting rules that specified checking for things like number of legs, pointiness of ears, furriness, tail, pupil shape, whiskers, etc. Rather, they programed a neural network consisting of 16,000 processors to review 10 million randomly-selected YouTube videos, some of which contained humans and some of which contained cats. After three days of processing, the system detected human faces with 81.7% accuracy and cats at 74.8%.

Since that time, artificial neural networks have gotten a whole lot better at identifying all sorts of things, including individual faces, stop signs and suspicious mammogram shadows. One program, called Face2Gene, developed by programmers who had taught Facebook to find a particular face in a group of photos, does a remarkably accurate job of identifying congenital syndromes based on images of patients' faces. Using AI, RightEye Geo Pref Autism Test correctly identified autism spectrum disorder 86% of the time in over 400 toddlers by measuring children's eye movements as they watched videos of people and faces on one half of a split screen and moving geometric shapes on the other. Winterlight has employed AI to process recorded speech in order to identify and track cognitive function of people with Alzheimer's disease.[45]

A study published in the journal, *Schizophrenia*, in 2015, claimed that a speech analysis program predicted development of psychosis with *100% accuracy* in 34 at-risk youths, outperforming clinical interviews.[46]

In 2017, the inventors and trainers of a deep neural network declared that their had developed a system that rivaled 21 board-certified dermatologists at distinguishing malignant from non-malignant conditions, based on images of the skin lesions.[47]

If I were a young radiologist or a pathologist, or maybe a dermatologist, I might worry that a good deal of what I do for a living could eventually be taken over by AI-driven systems that do pattern recognition. In 2017, computer scientists and

---

* On the other side of the argument are those people who are already tired of virtual assistants that sound either like chatty perky females or Victorian butlers, their language seasoned with all those nice little extra words that make them seem sort of human. These humanized voices are called by detractors, "skeumorphs," meaning useless holdovers from a previous era, like the buggy whip holders that were placed within reach of the driver on some early automobiles. Skeumorphs have a place, though, when it comes to reassuring people that a new technology is really okay. (Thompson, C. Stop the chitchat. Bots don't need to sound like us. *Wired* [online]. November/16, 2017.)

radiologists announced that they had developed CheXNet, an AI program trained on a database of 100,000 chest films that beat the average radiologist in diagnosing pneumonia.[48]

An article entitled "Radiologists struggle to ID gorilla on a CT lung scan" might make a radiologist uncomfortable about her career prospects. You have probably seen the video clip in which people pass a basketball back and forth. Viewers are tasked with counting the number of passes. In the meantime, a person dressed in a gorilla suit wanders through the frame. Most people never see the animal. The same thing happened to 24 radiologists who were asked to note the abnormalities in five chest CT scans. They identified about 55% of the nodules. Twenty out of twenty-four of them scrolled by, on average more than four times, the image of a dancing gorilla that was forty-eight times the size of a typical nodule. If it makes you feel better, not one of 25 lay readers saw the gorilla and they succeeded in identifying only 12% of the nodules after 10 minutes of training. We would expect a really smart computer, on the other hand, to see every abnormality, including the gorilla.[49]

The kicker is that nobody knows how these networks do it. Rules for pruning and strengthening connections between artificial neurons are constantly being tweaked by software engineers. But the actual pathways by which a system delivers sentences that make sense across languages, anticipates words in a text message, distinguishes a benign from a malignant breast tumor, or a Manx from a tabby, are completely opaque. There is no visible rule that says if the feline creature in the picture has no tail it is likely to be a Manx cat.

What about computers that don't just analyze data and make decisions but actually operate things in the world, like truly autonomous vehicles? What sorts of rules will they come up with that will decide, in a split second, when faced with an unforeseen set of dangerous circumstances, whether to swerve into a ditch with a car full of passengers or to strike a woman pushing a baby carriage across the highway?*,[50]

---

* It will be interesting to see how a fleet of semi-autonomous Chevrolet Bolts, which are scheduled to be unleashed on lower Manhattan in 2018, will do there. You can bet that a significant share of New York pedestrians and drivers will quickly learn to take advantage of the AI-driven vehicles' built-in default to always cede the right-of-way, no matter who really has it. (Stewart, J. In New York self-driving cars get ready to face the bullies. *Wired* [online]. October 22, 2017.) A reviewer of a 3-mile trip in a self-driven vehicle in San Francisco had this to say about the over-cautious, herky-jerky driving style of his autonomous Bolt. "If the Silicon Valley motto is 'move fast and break things,' Detroit's seems to be 'move below the speed limit and ensure you don't kill anyone.'" (Marshall, A. My herky-jerky ride in General Motors' ultra-cautious self driving car. *Wired* [online]. November/29, 2017.) The RAND Corporation issued a report in 2017 of calculations they ran on 3 scenarios, in which autonomous vehicles get on the road when they are 10% safer than human-driven ones, 75% better, and 90% better. The 10% scenario looked best, as it would save up to 3000 lives per year from the outset. Currently, they say you're better off in a self-driving vehicle than in one driven by a 16-year-old or a 90-year-old. (Marshall, A. To save the most lives, deploy [imperfect] self-driving cars ASAP. *Wired* [online]. November 7, 2017.)

We (especially scientists, technologists and lawyers) are immersed in the Western way of thinking that the world is reducible to logical rules and that the way to understand it is to learn all the rules and how to apply them (see Chapter 1, "Logical Conclusions–How Medicine Fits into Western Culture"). It can be hard to accept that we now make mind-bogglingly competent machines that defy our understanding of just how they do what they do.

Besides the psychological challenge posed by turning things over to machines that we do not fully understand, there is the very real threat of letting things run without injecting human values into the process. The august Institute of Electrical and Electronics Engineers (IEEE) Standards Association created the Global Initiative for Ethical Considerations in Artificial Intelligence and Autonomous Systems, which produced in 2016 the first of a number of planned versions of "Ethically Aligned Design: A Vision for Prioritizing Human Wellbeing with Artificial Intelligence and Autonomous Systems."[51]

The sort of AI that drives language translation and computer vision is being used extensively by businesses to shape all sorts of decisions, including: whom to try to sell what to; whom to interview for a job; where to locate a business; etc. After parsing reams of data, a machine may well report that: people who happen to be white do best at a certain job; that mortgages for properties in certain neighborhoods have a higher failure rate; that people who have a particular Christian name or buy a certain brand of toilet paper are at higher risk for home fires. It takes a human being to step in to stand up for values such as fairness.[52]

There is a move afoot in the United States to require government agencies, such as those dealing with criminal justice, health and welfare, to reveal the algorithms that they use in decision-making. As one activist put it, "We should have equivalent due-process protections for algorithmic decisions as for human decisions."[53]

A group at the University of Chicago has demonstrated an AI program that beats Yelp's own AI, as well as human reviewers, at getting fake restaurant reviews placed on the Yelp website. It is not a large leap to automating the generation of fake news and even scientific papers. So far, human reviewers have mostly been able to stay ahead of the machines in these realms.[54]

The people who set up the training of facial recognition programs must even be reminded to include non-white faces in the inputs. Google was embarrassed in June 2015 when its highly-touted photo categorization system identified two African Americans as gorillas.[55]

Smart humans can devise ambiguous adversarial examples designed to trick machine-learning systems into misclassifying data. The Massachusetts Institute of Technology's Computer Science and Artificial Intelligence Laboratory demonstrated just how easy it was to trip up Google's hotshot Inception V3 image classifier by inputting adversarial examples that caused it, for example, to mistake a panda for a gibbon, a turtle for a rifle (or most anything else non-turtle-like) and a row of machine guns for a helicopter, all distinctions that a human viewer had not an iota of trouble in discerning. We need to give this fact a lot of thought before we turn over control of our vehicles and all sorts of other stuff that ill-intentioned humans can so easily trick.[56]

Unseen biases inherent in the culture that is shared by everyone, including the people who devise AI-driven systems, can be magnified once those systems are turned loose. A program, based on reams of real data, designed by well-meaning penologists and computer scientists, mistakenly flagged twice the number of black as white prisoners as being at high risk for re-offending.[57] Even good AI can amplify bad data and biased assumptions.

Neural network-powered AI, with all its attendant benefits and risks, will be insinuating itself more and more into the healthcare endeavor. There is a growing library of off-the-shelf software for doing machine learning. Here is a short list of where machine learning will be found, at ever higher levels of sophistication: direct voice-to-machine transcription; translation of patient information documents;* navigating the insurance coverage quagmire; allocating professional staff; identifying dangerous combinations of drugs and laboratory findings; providing early notification of impending medical crises; recognizing abnormalities in radiologic studies; assisting decision-making for therapy of diseases like prostate and breast cancer; guiding driverless carts to deliver food trays and medical supplies to hospital patients; powering companion dolls, in the shape of babies or cuddly animals, for children and for the demented; interpreting electrocardiograms electroencephalograms, and all sorts of other -grams; instructing an "artificial pancreas" when to deliver insulin, and how much; directing drones to pick up and deliver laboratory samples and medical supplies out in the community, etc. The sky is the limit. As always, it will take human intelligence to understand how best to use artificial intelligence.

Robots

As a little boy, I loved the television show, "Captain Video and His Video Rangers," which ran from 1949 until 1955. It was certainly not the subtlety of his gestures that made the robot, I Tobor, my favorite character. My young scientist mind was turned on by the idea of a machine that was smart and could do human stuff. I dimly recall an episode in which a scientist installed into a slot behind a door in I Tobor's trunk, a single piece, about the size of a can of tomato paste, that made the metal humanoid conscious and intelligent. (Note: I have chosen to use masculine pronouns when referring to this robot because there is no doubt in my mind

---

* AI can have a powerful impact on how non-English speakers experience healthcare through more accurate translations on signage and medication labels. A study that appeared in the journal *Pediatrics* in 2010 of medication labels generated by a computer translator into Spanish had an overall error rate of over 50%. Some of these errors could have had significant potential negative effects on the patients taking the drugs. (Sharif, I, Tse, J. Accuracy of computer-generated, Spanish-language medicine labels. *Pediatrics*. 2008;125(5), 960–965.)

that that's what Tobor was, in spite, as far as I know, of a total lack of that sort of plumbing.)

Unfortunately, nobody has yet devised a single piece that will make robots smart and able. Today, the robot you are most liable to encounter in a healthcare setting is Tug, a self-driving cart that navigates hospital hallways and elevators to deliver food trays, supplies and medicines. Tug looks just like what it is, a cart—one that, nonetheless, shows significant abilities in all three of the basic categories of robot function, sensing, analyzing and acting. Notice how these three categories apply just as well to a rat, an octopus or a human who is faced with a task.

* * * * * * *

Thanks to relentless mechanization of agricultural, in 1988, the United States had the lowest number of farmers since 1850. In that 138-year interval, the population to be fed increased more than tenfold. And there was still enough product to ship huge quantities of foodstuffs overseas.[58] In the old days, it took nearly two thirds of the workforce to feed the American populace. Today, just 2% of American families live on farms and ranches (a proxy for the number of people actually employed in agriculture).

What happened to all those displaced farmworkers? They moved to cities where many of them found work in manufacturing. The orders of magnitude boost in productivity that mostly urban-based workers were able to achieve, thanks to the machines of the industrial revolution, turned out unimaginable quantities of manufactured goods. But it took plenty of suffering and bloodshed before most of the people who produced the wares received wages that allowed them to afford a reasonable share of the goods they manufactured, as well as the time off to enjoy them.

The ongoing mechanization of factories has been doing to the manufacturing work force what mechanization of the farm did to the agricultural employment. In 2017, a plant that produces 500,000 tons of steel wire per year opened in Donawitz, Austria, with just 14 employees. In the 1960s, a similar mill would have required 1000 workers.[59] In one amazing video of a highly automated Daimler factory,[60] the majority of the humans one sees in the course of putting together a Mercedes-Benz 2014 S-Class vehicle are sweeping the floors. Never mind exporting jobs to countries with cheaper labor. Machine labor is now or soon will be cheaper yet.

Powerful information systems are causing many service jobs to bite the dust too. In the face of online booking systems, travel agents are becoming things of the past. Remember record stores and video stores and the clerks who served you? How many department stores have closed and how many clerks and managers have been let go because people shop online now? Estimates of job loss to automation have run from 5% to 50% of the US workforce by the early 2030s. The consulting firm, PricewaterhouseCoopers, predicts that 17% of jobs in human health and social work will be at risk, while only 8% or 9% will be for domestic and education personnel, respectively. This compares to a whopping 56% for transportation and storage and 46% for manufacturing, 32% for financial and insurance sectors, and 27% for communications.[61]

Few healthcare workers have felt yet the brunt of automation. It will be a while before a robot can make a bed, let alone one with a debilitated patient in it. Though a patient may fill out a questionnaire detailing symptoms and history before seeing me, she still needs me, as a physician, to make sense of it. Even if the electronic record suggests, based upon these data, what diagnoses to consider, what tests to order next or what medication to prescribe, it is still up to me to decide how to proceed. Neither my job nor that of the nurse aide I work with is jeopardized by imminent automation.

In a robot, sensing is done with optics, radar, touch, sound, accelerometer, etc. Analysis is performed by computers. Motors and hydraulic systems move the unit to act. Put these pieces together and you can construct a machine that does perfectly the exact same weld on the same place on every automobile chassis that passes it on the assembly line, without ever tiring or needing a break for food or a cigarette.

It takes a lot more sensors and actuators, plus a big slice of artificial intelligence, to build one of those laughably clumsy robots that competes in the annual Defense Advanced Research Projects Agency (DARPA) robotics challenge, where a machine is expected to: drive a vehicle to the site of the test; traverse rubble on foot (or on whatever); remove debris that blocks an entryway; open a door and enter a building; climb a ladder; drill a hole in a concrete wall; locate and close a valve on a leaky pipe; connect a fire hose and turn it on.[62]

These generalized tasks strike me as the material world version of the linguistic challenge "Go get Herbie's chair," mentioned earlier. A competent, fit human ought to be able to complete all of these assignments lickety-split, with little or no special training. Such simple chores present a huge challenge, however, to a machine controlled by a computer.

As with language, it is much easier to construct a device to do one hard thing very well than it is to build a machine that is capable of doing a number of not very hard, but not very well specified tasks well enough. Check out videos of recent Robot Challenges. If you're like me, you will want to jump up and help these big clumsy machines. In 2016, Hubo, a humanoid robot produced in Korea, did successfully complete all eight tasks in 44.5 minutes, a huge step up from how the entries stumbled and bumbled their way to ignominious ends in the 2015 event.[63]

I predict we will see autonomous vehicles on American roadways before we see robots doing surgery without a surgeon in the room or computers writing prescriptions or making radiologic diagnoses without being signed off by a human with the appropriate license.

The US Army Telemedicine and Advanced Technology Research Center has been experimenting with a robot called The Bear that will pick up wounded soldiers from the battlefield and carry them to safety. The device got its name from its sweet bear-like face, considered important to gain trust, even of battle-hardened fighters. The Bear is controlled remotely by a joystick-wielding operator, which makes its deployment much more likely in the near future than an autonomous device.[64]

Socially assistive robots already provide guidance and companionship to people who are post-stroke, demented, or autistic. There is an ever-growing list of diagnoses and uses for such devices.

Virtual Reality

Mirrors changed how human beings look at and think of ourselves. Photographs altered our perceptions of the whole world. Then came sound recording and moving pictures. Then talkies. Clever technologists have made continuous enhancements to reflected and reconstructed realities. Today, workshops all over the world are adding features like three-dimensional scenes that change with head and body movements, as well as touch sensors that not only respond to the user's movements (a simple computer mouse does that), but supply resistance when you push something in the virtual world and texture when you touch it. Touch sensation is called haptic feedback. Virtual reality seeks to best the old Kodak (R.I.P.) slogan, "The next best thing to being there," with "At least as good as being there." That is what theme park operators strive for. And training simulators. We are just scratching the surface in employing VR to help patients get better.

With a little imagination, avid electronic gamers already feel as if they walk, swim and fly around in simulated cities or on foreign planets. These higher-level manufactured experiences are designed to immerse the user in a more vivid and engaging virtual world than most of us have yet experienced. "Virtual reality" (VR) is the term used to describe the state that these enhanced sensory technologies strive for.

The Moovel Lab, an offspring of the German car company, Daimler, has created a virtual reality headset to be worn while you're lying on your stomach and sort of experiencing the world as an autonomous version of the Rover, Daimler's electric car, would "see" it, via its 3-D camera, lidar (Light Detection And Ranging device, sort of a radar that operates with a laser) and onboard computer. The idea is to research the human/machine interface by giving people the "feel" of what the device is "experiencing."[65]

VR is in its infancy. It has been used to help veterans diagnosed with PTSD to gradually re-experience the sort of trauma that originated their suffering in a way that enhances desensitization to the offending stimuli. Automated social encounters, via VR technology that also measures reactions, have been used to help diagnose autism, and then as a means to teach people on the autism spectrum how to respond to others in a way that smooths a person's way in society.

VR headsets have also been used with some success to distract patients undergoing painful procedures.[66]

Quantum Computing

It may be extremely challenging to ace a course in classical electrodynamics, but the four Maxwell's Equations on which it is based are essentially no harder to grasp intuitively than it is to see how waves work in the ocean. Quantum mechanics, on the other hand, is a wholly different beast. Even the great Einstein was never able to reconcile himself fully to some of the strangest features of the quantum world, such as the connection between pairs of particles, the states of which remain synchronized even when they are separated by a distance too great for a light signal to pass the state information from one to the other. Einstein, whose theories of relativity were anchored in the fact that nothing travels faster than the speed of light, called this phenomenon, officially labeled "entanglement," "spooky action at a distance."

No physicist or philosopher has arrived at an intuitively satisfying explanation of entanglement. Science, based as it sometimes is on unvisualizable mathematical constructs like imaginary numbers and dimensions higher than three, can baffle brains that evolved over eons to negotiate the day-to-day challenges of life on Earth. Technologies that derive from such esoteric constructs are living proof that, if the current scientific theory does not represent ultimate truth, it at least informs us enough about how things work to spawn concrete new ways to bend the world of matter and energy to meet human needs and desires.

Quantum computing exploits some of the strange properties of quantum physics. Whereas classical digital computers are based on the simple idea that a switch is either on or off, allowing an electrical signal to pass or not, corresponding to a one or a zero (called a bit of binary information), quantum computers are based on qbits, which can be either ones or zeroes, tangled up with other qbits, which are also in an indeterminate state. A web of entangled qbits can "stack" quantum states to represent the programmed "question," then calculate the answer all at once.

This whole new way of computing is, theoretically, orders of magnitude more powerful and faster than classical computing. A perfectly functioning 50 qbit computer would be equivalent to an impossible 10 quadrillion (10 followed by 12 zeros) -bit classical computer. Heretofore, unbreakable encryption codes, based on the high computational cost of finding prime factors of large numbers, would dissolve before the power of a quantum-computing device. Weather systems and airflow over flying machines, now studied with supercomputers, would give up unheard of levels of detail and prediction to the new computers. The three-dimensional structure of complex proteins would be calculated down to their nuts and bolts. Subtleties of disease patterns would be uncovered.

The trouble is that quantum states are very fragile. These days, qbits are usually electrons, which have "up," "down," "neither" or "both" spins. Scientists are testing machines built on tiny agglomerations of atoms, called "condensed matter," which feature states that may be a bit more stable than the spin of a single electron. All quantum computers must be cooled to near absolute zero so the jiggling induced by heat does not disturb the states of the qbits. Just look at a qbit (literally by bouncing a photon off of it) and it changes unpredictably.

Needless to say, building a quantum computer is quite a challenge. In 2017, IBM announced a quantum computer boasting 5 qbits, with the goal of a 50 qbit computer within a few years. That same year, D-Wave, the self-proclaimed leader in quantum computers and the software to run them, announced it had actually sold a 2000 qbit computer to its first customer. Their corporate propaganda touts plans to double the number of qbits in their machines every two years. (Move over, Moore's Law!)

Without getting into the specifics of the hype, realistically, I suspect it will take five or ten years before quantum computers are cheap, reliable and flexible enough to have much of an impact on the world, including the world of healthcare. Keep an eye on this technology.

Summary

This chapter is the longest in the book and the most technical. So let me summarize the most important points in the form of predictions about the short- and intermediate-term future.

- Lack of bandwidth is rapidly disappearing as a limiting factor in efforts to link information and communication systems, even in remote areas of the United States and the world.
- More and more tools will be fitted with ever tinier and more powerful computer chips, turning them into "smart devices," many of them portable, capable of higher levels of performance and of communicating via internet protocols.
- The array of products manufactured by 3-D printers—from splints to implants, and, eventually artificial tissues and even organs–will grow dramatically, producing more functional and comfortable and maybe even less expensive medical items, as well as a panoply of training devices for health professionals.
- Interoperability will slowly increase, allowing systems to exchange data and share resources. Healthcare systems and the technology vendors that supply them will be dragged into sharing, kicking and screaming.
- Files, software and virtual computers will continue their migration to the cloud, lowering costs but increasing worries about privacy and safety of protected health information.
- Artificial intelligence will rely ever more heavily on artificial neural nets rather than on rule-based systems to perform complicated tasks like: translating natural language; turning language into data; and recognizing patterns to aid in complex tasks like diagnosis, disease course prediction and diagnostic image interpretation. The need to make AI systems more transparent to their human users will become more acute.

- Computing devices powered by artificial intelligence will displace white-collar workers in every sector of the economy, including healthcare.
- Robots, enabled by artificial intelligence, will take over some tasks from humans in healthcare, such as delivering goods and even providing companionship. For a long time to come, robots will mostly serve to enhance jobs that require human abilities, not to replace them.
- Virtual reality will continue on its course of becoming more "realistic." Its immersiveness will be extensively exploited by and for patients in pursuit of diagnostic and therapeutic goals, as well as by health professionals for education and practice enhancements.
- Though as yet unproven as a practical technology, quantum computing should eventually result in (pardon the expression) a quantum leap in computing power, tackling problems that are beyond the reach of classical computing.
- The biggest challenge to making information technology serve the needs of patient care will continue to be to align economic realities with patient care needs.
- Every aspect of information and communication, technology will sooner or later succumb to commodification. As bandwidth, electronic medical records, helper robots, machine intelligence and virtual reality become cheap and ubiquitous, gaining a competitive edge with technology will lie in how well the system is used to foster and maintain relationships among patients and staff.
- Getting people onboard and keeping them there, not the technology itself, will continue to be the biggest challenge by far to making a new device or system work.

Chapter 4

What Humans Do Better Than Computers

The clinician cannot begin to improve these functions [ability to make observations that no inanimate instrument is capable of]...until he recognizes himself as a unique and powerful piece of scientific equipment.

—Alvan R. Feinstein and Ralph I. Horowitz[1]

We thought we could cure everything, but it turns out we can only cure a small amount of human suffering. The rest of it needs to be healed.

—Rachel Naomi Remen[2]

So how do doctors heal themselves?....Doctors need to recover the doctor's way of knowing.

—Daniel S. Passerman and James P.Meza[3]

Technology is a way of organizing the universe so that man doesn't have to experience it.

—Max Frisch, Swiss playwright and novelist

Take the universe of things to be done. Narrow the focus to just the universe of things to be done to address the health of human beings. Subtract Chapter 2, "What Computers Do Better Than Humans," from the total, and you've got the contents of this chapter, "What Humans Do Better than Computers."

Think about it. Or rather, feel about it. What is it that we do better than the machines we have built to serve us?

That's right. We feel. There is this embodied self, dating its evolutionary history back to when the first living cells appeared 4.1 billion years ago, less than half a billion years after the Earth coalesced out of the cloud of matter that orbited the sun. By trial and error, in countless creatures through billions of years, the evolutionary process has filled every nook and cranny of the Earth with resilient life, from ecosystems that thrive on hot sulfurous plumes in ocean trenches seven miles deep to blooms on polar ice caps. All the while, Nature ceaselessly shuffles life's circumstances and re-deals.

Living things have mastered the process of using energy to snatch order out of chaos. As time goes by, things get more complex. The most complex thing Nature has served up so far, at least so far as our earthbound understanding goes, is the human brain.

There are about 85 billion neurons packed into the three-pound human brain. Each nerve cell makes an estimated 10,000 connections with other neurons. Jeff Lichtman, the Harvard neuroscientist who heads the Human Connectome Project, has estimated that it would take 1000 petabytes (10^{18}) to fully index a single human brain, far and away the most complex structure in the known Universe.[4]

By comparison, in 2013 the internet was estimated to contain 5 petabytes, of which Google had indexed 0.2 petabytes, or just 0.04%.[5] So you can see how far, far away our microtomes, microscopes, microelectrodes, functional MRI scans, integrated circuits, super-computers and server farms are from capturing the complexity of what a single human brain can do.

There is talk about how quantum computers, which, by exploiting spooky properties of quantum physics such as entanglement and superposition, could solve calculating problems that there are not enough time nor silicon atoms in the Universe for a binary computer to crack. (See "Quantum Computing" in Chapter 3, "Technology.") This technology is in its infancy. Impressive though the hype about quantum computing may be, it still only means that computers will be able to perform the operations they already do now, only blindingly faster, on datasets that are orders of magnitude bigger. Computers that manifest what we call intelligence, feelings, or consciousness, all concepts whose definitions remain unsettled after millennia of philosophical debate, still exist mostly in the imaginations of computer scientists and writers of science fiction.

Intelligence

There is room here to write several books about intelligence and consciousness. I'm afraid we're mostly stuck with meanings for these human characteristics that are akin to the definition of pornography stated in 1964 by Supreme Court Justice Potter Stuart in his opinion in the case Jacobellis vs. Ohio.[6] Stuart wrote "I know it when I see it."

In 1980, the renowned American philosopher of mind, John Searle, proposed a Potter Stewart sort of definition of intelligence, his Chinese Room Argument. A device would be deemed intelligent if it were able to carry on a conversation, via messages in Chinese slipped under the door of a room with an unseen person within. The person behind the door may be a Chinese speaker who responds to the messages, passing the responses back out under the door. Alternatively, if she does not speak the language, she passes the messages to a computer that reads them and prints responses, which the human slides back out. If the person outside cannot tell if it is a Chinese speaker or a computer carrying on the dialog from the other side of the door, the machine is deemed to be intelligent. By the way, Searle did not believe that a computer could ever manifest human intelligence.

A down-and-dirty definition of intelligence might be to decide things in a way that produces the best outcomes. Does that make intelligent Deep Blue, the IBM super-computer that in 1997 beat Gary Kasparov, the world champ in chess, or AlphaGo, the Google-sponsored computer program that trounced Lee Sedol, the world's best Go player in 2016? Perhaps, but something is missing. It's the inability of these amazing calculating machines to do anything else. If you teach them to play chess well, even to learn from playing humans and/or simulated games within their own "electronic brains," they can get great at that thing only. You might say that these computers manifest chess-intelligence or go-intelligence.

How about Watson, the IBM super-computer that in 2011 went head-to-head with the greatest champions of game show "Jeopardy" and beat them all?[7] I find that a way more impressive feat than mastering a game that has just a few rules on how to move pieces, even though those rules lead to more possible games than any conceivable machine could ever exhaustively search. To play "Jeopardy", you have to know a lot about things like Harry Potter, airport names and one-armed gymnasts, all referred to in standard American English.

Watson's apparent prodigious ability to turn millions of factoids into usable information has been harnessed by IBM to do medicine. In 2014, an article in *Business Insider* even declared, "IBM's Watson Supercomputer May Soon Be The Best Doctor In The World."[8] In 2016, IBM proudly proclaimed that Watson, which included an exponentially growing database of millions of documents, was able to "read" 40 million documents in 15 seconds. IBM purchased Merge Healthcare in 2015 for $1 billion in order to add medical image processing to Watson's arsenal. Combine the one million gigabytes of medical data that a person is said to generate in a lifetime with the medical database and image processing power that Watson is amassing and maybe the corporation will birth "The Best Doctor In The World." Who knows exactly when that will be. And how will we know? Perhaps, when Watson defeats human contestants on "Beat the Reaper",[9] the gameshow introduced by the comedy group, Firesign Theater on their 1968 record album, *Waiting for the Electrician or Someone Like Him*.

I was about to say that no computer is going to write and tell its own jokes. This is not a trivial thing. Philosophers, linguists, anthropologists and psychologists have had a lot to say over the ages about this most human of linguistic acts. I must admit to being a bit horrified to learn, thanks to Google,[10] that there actually is a sub-field of computational linguistics called "computational humor." (For obvious reasons, how to recognize knock-knock jokes was one of the first humor problems solved by computers and their masters.)

Perhaps during the lifetime of at least some of you readers, IBM's Watson will reach its potential as world's greatest doctor. Maybe Watson will even make it as a stand-up comic.

In an article that appeared in Health Affairs in 2013, the authors estimated that if health IT, in its current state of development, were fully implemented in 30% of community-based physician offices, including IT-supported delegation of care to NPs and PAs, demand for physicians could be reduced by 8% to 16%. Empowering generalist doctors with IT information could also reduce the demand for specialists by 2% to 5%. Were real functional IT systems to be implemented in 70% of practices, these numbers could double. Regional physician shortages could be addressed by delivering 12% of care remotely or asynchronously.[11] You will see in subsequent chapters that, as things currently stand, this is a pipedream.

Someone to Talk to

What will there be for my junior colleagues of today to do tomorrow? Plenty. In fact, the not-too-distant future could be a golden time to practice if we do things right, which means freeing human beings to do what we do best when we provide healthcare.

A healthy, well-fed human laborer can put out 75 watts, about one-tenth of a horsepower, over an eight-hour work shift. That comes to a little over 2 million joules of energy. A gallon of gasoline contains about 120 million joules. A modern gasoline engine can reach an efficiency of 30%, which means that, burning a gallon of gasoline, the machine can do 36 million joules of work, the equivalent of eighteen men laboring for eight hours. Luddites destroyed cloth mill machinery in the early 19th century England, grasping very well how the steam power obtained from burning coal, the carbon-based fuel that powered the Industrial Revolution, was changing their traditional way of life.

In their day, Luddites were harassed and even killed for their militant challenge to the brave new Victorian world. The group's greatest heritage is their name. "Luddite" remains a disparaging term, applied to someone who opposes technological progress.

There is a whole lot to be said for the improvements that the energy concentrated in fossil fuels has wrought in the life of the average worker, in terms of reduced drudgery and, for the consumer, in terms of affordable goods and services. Hopefully, there is still enough time to mitigate the harm we've done to our atmosphere over the last couple of centuries by burning coal, petroleum products and wood. The challenge is to learn to exploit more dilute renewable resources, store and transmit the harvested energy.

Today's Luddites want to roll the clock back on electronic media. They see the real disruption that things like texting, Facebook, internet surfing and video games have wrought on attention span, privacy and family life.

That's not going to happen. The electrons are out of the virtual toothpaste tube.

One frustration for everybody, Luddite or not, is voice message hell. We've all craved the opportunity to talk to a reasonable human being so we can work out some misunderstanding with the bank, insurance company, cable company, or airline. Such a person may lurk behind several levels of hell (I mean selections, spoken or keyed) featuring generous doses of time on hold, seasoned with bad music and repetitive, maddeningly cheerful messages. If you are lucky, the person you finally reach (whose conversation with you, you've been informed, might be recorded for the sake of better serving you in the future, i.e. auditing her adherence to the company's performance standards) has been given the latitude to make decisions, rather than just to read you options off the screen of her computer-generated problem-solving flowchart.

Why do you crave a person to talk to? Because if given some latitude, a person can still solve problems that a computer cannot anticipate. Just as importantly, because a person can, in the space of a few sentences, form an idea of who you are and respond to *you*. That interpersonal connection is one of the things that makes us human beings tick.

Interpersonal connection is, in itself, healing. A study that analyzed communication styles, based on audiotapes of doctor-patient office visits, published in the journal *Medical Care* in 1989, reported on the analysis of two hundred and fifty-two encounters that were recorded in four widely-different practice settings with patients who had been diagnosed with ulcers, hypertension, diabetes or breast cancers. As they revealed themselves on the tapes, moment-to-moment communication behaviors were coded and analyzed by experts. The researchers concluded that objective measures of how well patient and doctor interact correlate strongly with patients' estimates of their own wellbeing and even, on follow-up, with the number of days' work they had lost to illness since the last visit. The doctor's communication behavior that best predicted patient well-being was the physician's ability to follow a patient's lead, to listen rather than interrupt with questions, comments and directions. Patients who exerted more control over the conversation and who more freely expressed their feelings, both positive and negative, did better.[*,12]

---

* As anybody who has ever been to the doctor (which is just about everybody) knows, odds are that the next physician you consult will not let you take the lead in the conversation. She is liable to seem rushed and preoccupied with her own agenda. Long before we had computers to contend with in consultation rooms, I observed that physicians seem to leave training as worse listeners than we were when we entered. We start out on our long career path not that much weirder nor less in touch with normal human interaction than everybody else. The hidden curriculum, gleaned from superiors who serve as role models—when you're a medical student, everybody is a superior—trains us to be rushed and distant. My impressions are borne out by a review of 18 studies published in the medical literature between 1990 and 2010 entitled, "Empathy Decline and Its Reasons…." that appeared in the journal, *Academic Medicine*. [Neumann, M et al. Empathy decline and its reasons: A systematic review of studies with medical students and residents. *Academic Medicine*. 2011:86(8), 996–1009.]

If you want to read an interesting (and depressing) analysis of this process, try *Getting Rid of Patients* by sociologist Terry Mizrahi, who followed around a cohort of interns and residents in an internal medicine training program for three years before publishing her book in 1986.

I like to think that human-to-human contact accounts for at least some of why a study published in *Health Affairs in* 2014 found that practices with one or two physicians had 33% fewer preventable hospital admissions than practices with 10 to 19 doctors. No matter that larger practices could probably afford fancier information systems and the staff to maintain them, I suspect it was the intimate understanding between patients and doctors in one- or two-provider practices that helped to keep patients out of the hospital (and probably helped the doctors to be happier in their job).[13]

When I was hospitalized recently for a joint replacement, the nurse who admitted me asked, as she'd been trained to do, what was my definition of excellent care? I responded, "To be related to by the staff, as well as they can ascertain, as who I really am." The nurse duly paraphrased my words and wrote them on the white board at the foot of my bed.

I had a great surgical result and excellent patient care. Of all the encounters I had with myriad staff (including too many from supervisors and managers who stopped in my room to ask if I was truly having an excellent hospital experience), the interaction that sticks out most in my mind was with a woman who delivered a meal tray. She asked me for my birthdate, as everybody had been trained to do, so as to deliver the right procedures, drugs and meals to the right patients. I asked her, "What do you do with patients who are demented or delirious?" She replied, "Oh. We just don't feed 'em."

This woman had understood who I am and responded to it. (Some would say, as I deserved.) No automated meal delivery robot, not even *Star Wars'* R2D2 or *The Jetsons'* Rosie, could have produced that memorable interaction.

Chapter 5

Data versus Story

It is much more important to know what sort of a patient has a disease than what sort of a disease a patient has.

—William Osler, MD, American physician, educator and writer

No hay enfermedades, sino enfermos. (There is no such thing as illness, only sick people.)

—Gregorio Marañón, MD, Spanish physician, historian and philosopher

...I want to note especially the importance of the resource that is most often under-utilized in our information systems – our patients.

—Charles Safran, MD[1], physician and medical informaticist

...patients are not only texts read by their physicians but also the author of their bodies' stories.

—Paul C. Sorum, MD[2]

Data are just summaries of thousands of stories – tell a few of those stories to help make the data meaningful.

—Dan Heath, author and business educator

At one time we might have turned to an old-timer to explain the world. Now we consult Google and if we have any trouble with the computer we ask a teenager.

—Atul Gawande, MD, physician and author[3]

In the mid 1990s, I was asked to join a small group of physicians who were to advise the large healthcare system we worked for on choosing an outpatient medical record for its many practices. We held meetings where we experienced vendor demos and sometimes even got to put our hands on a keyboard. Before we made our final recommendation to the corporate powers who would pull the trigger on this megabuck purchase, we made a site visit to a practice that actually used the record we had liked best. Everybody we talked to there was enthusiastic about their electronic medical record (EMR). So that's the one we recommended and that's the one our health system bought.

What the users and we visitors liked best about this particular product was that it appeared to combine seamlessly all the data a clinician would want on a patient—vital signs, allergies, past problems, hospitalizations and surgeries, medications, laboratory and imaging results, consultant reports, etc.—with the ability to dictate a narrative of the patient encounter as it occurred.

Automated language recognition and transcription were not very good in those days. But with one click of the mouse, a clinician could access the dictation system, where human transcriptionists would turn out and in short order insert into the electronic record the kind of note we all had been generating for about as long as we had practiced. (I did handwrite doctor progress notes in my first practice, 1976–78, and for many years after that in hospital charts.)

To the detriment of everybody except the bean counters, the storytelling part of that EMR got ignored pretty quickly. Most practices stopped paying for transcription. Now, if a clinician wanted to include a narrative of a patient encounter, she had to make a few extra clicks and then hand-type the text. We were all encouraged by the business folks, for the sake of billing, to document as much of each encounter as we could using the templated problem-associated checklists of symptoms and observed physical findings that the record system provided. Improving the quality of care or of clinicians' work life got unconvincing lip service.

As Beaumont Hospital in Royal Oak, Michigan changed over to an EMR in 2011 to 2013 they found, when they compared 500 doctors' progress notes on hospitalized patients with five diagnoses that present with invariable physical findings (such as paralysis in certain types of strokes or a missing leg after an amputation), inaccurate documentation occurred significantly more frequently in electronic records than in paper ones (24% versus 4%). Not surprisingly, resident physicians-in-training had lower rates of inaccuracies and omissions than did full-fledged attending physicians.[4]

Checklists are meant to jog the clinician's memory about things to look for or to do as they relate to each particular complaint, diagnosis and treatment. After all, would you set foot on an airplane whose pilot did not believe in checklists?

In 2008 and 2009, the World Health Organization pilot tested its nineteen-item surgical safety checklist. The list included actions like: confirming the patient's identity before surgery; marking the skin over the surgical site; taking a time out before beginning the procedure during which all staff introduce themselves and their roles to each other; etc. The results were amazing. Complications such as infections and excess bleeding fell by a third and intra- and post-operative death rates by almost half. The checklist was adopted by surgical teams all over the world.

Unfortunately, these spectacular results have been difficult to duplicate. An analysis of 200,000 procedures performed at 101 hospitals in Ontario, Canada showed no reduction in complications and death after introduction of the checklist. The same sorts of negative results have cropped up in studies of other promising safety programs based on checklists.

Researchers have found, you guessed it, that the problem is not with the lists themselves, but with the people who use them. It takes an extra effort to keep complacency and short-cutting at bay. No matter the high stakes in the operating room, checking boxes without thinking can occur for the same reasons that you check the boxes without reading the terms you are agreeing to when you download new software. It is just too easy. Doesn't everybody already know my name? Don't I know this patient? Didn't I just do a history and physical exam on her? As always, getting something to work and keep working is a matter of having the right systems, the right training, the right data and the right people. Finding or writing the right checklist and even incorporating it into the electronic medical record are the easy parts.[5]

For a number of years I worked for an organization whose mission was to assess doctors who'd gotten in trouble, with their hospital's medical staff, with an insurance company, with their state licensing board, etc. My job was to develop an education plan for those clients who appeared to be "fixable." To be sure, the two-day evaluation revealed deficits in many of my charges' fund of medical knowledge, which, in itself, should not have been so hard to address. I could assign continuing medical education courses and directed reading. The bigger problem was that many of the clients had a hard time accepting when they didn't know something, no matter how good the evidence. Multiple studies have shown in multiple ways that doctors tend to overestimate what we know and what we do well. Generally speaking, the less competent the doctor, the bigger the discrepancy between self-assessment and objective performance.[6]

I came to understand that an underlying problem to most all of the doctors who came within our education organization's grasp (which is how they often saw it because usually they had been forced to consult us by the agency with whom they'd gotten in trouble) was isolation. Even if they belonged to a large medical group, these physicians had arrived at a place where they didn't receive the feedback—from colleagues, patients, the literature, the quality improvement department—that they needed to stay on-track in their professional practice. Their problems went much deeper, having to do more with how they related to the world than with how firm their grasp was of the medical knowledge they needed to perform well. Checklists wouldn't have helped them much.

The big limitation of checklists is that they are too much like telegrams and not enough like conversations. Patient handoff between shifts or services is one of the activities most fraught with medical error. Handoffs have been implicated in 28% of surgical errors and 20% to 24% of malpractice claims. One-way transmission of facts just doesn't do it. Humans need context, a very brief overview of the patient and her medical situation. We need to hear what can go wrong and what to watch for, not just a list of diagnoses, medications, laboratory values and pending procedures and tests. To be sure, a well-constructed summary on a sheet of paper or on a computer screen that clearly presents this information is invaluable. But studies have shown that if you are serious about reducing errors generated during handoffs, you need a real conversation with room for questions.[*,7]

Physicians working over a four-month period in a weekly general medical clinic in England were asked to record two lists of up to three suspected diagnoses for each new patient they saw. The first list was recorded after reading a letter from the referring general practitioner and taking a history from the patient and the second after also performing a physical exam. These early guesses were then compared to the working diagnoses that had been arrived at after two months of testing and ongoing medical care. In 66 of 80 patients, the doctor had gotten the agreed-upon diagnosis right after just reading the referral note and taking the patient's history herself. That number went up to 73 out of 80 with a physical exam too. This means that it took time and more testing to arrive at the correct diagnosis in fewer than 10% of the patients. My own experience as a clinician, which began about the time of that study and has continued for another four decades, tells me that I can still rely on the initial history and physical to get the diagnosis right most of the time.[8]

What Checklists Don't Tell You

A 2013 study of a wide variety of 190 diagnostic errors made by clinicians who worked at two large veterans care facilities found that of 79% of the errors that had occurred in the course of the patient-provider encounter at the office or urgent care center, 53% percent were attributable to breakdown in communication between patient and provider resulting in flaws in the medical history that was obtained and 47% due to missed findings on physical examination. I doubt that many of those booboos that started out with the patient in the room could have been avoided if the provider had just had a bigger checklist.[9]

To the delight of business people, encounter checklists automatically tabulate: how many history items the clinician reviewed; how many organ systems she examined; how many diagnoses she arrived at; and the complexity of the case, thus allowing for more accurate and usually higher charges via billing codes. Many a doctor who has billed the lion's share of patient visits as routine has found that a large proportion of encounters have been up-coded by a new electronic record

---

* Researchers who observed 23 shift handoffs of 262 patients between doctors at a Canadian hospital found that they spent 50% more time discussing the first patient on their list than the last. The list was usually ordered according to room number, not patient acuity or need. (Preidt, R. Some patients may be shortchanged during hospital shift changes. *HealthDay*, November 12, 2012.)

system to the category of complex or even extensive service, paving the way for higher charges to patients, insurance companies and government agencies and for collecting a chunk more money. Studies have shown that installing an EMR results in seeing fewer patients per day but making more money, the opposite of the intended purpose of government programs to encourage EMR use.[10]

Theoretically, with so much more of the data quantified and recorded by standardized electronic checkmarks, it should have been easier to do real, statistically valid, quality improvement projects within and across practices. It might even have been possible to do actual medical research by querying the database. (see Chapter 12, "Research")

Being able to trend and understand individuals and populations is the beauty of having a good handle on patient data. The promise of a bottom-up approach to turning raw medical data into actionable insights for practice improvement was largely unrealized by the big healthcare organization I worked for in the years following the switch to this outpatient EMR. After about 15 years, they purchased a different product, one that finally will be able to share data with their inpatient systems. We will see how well the new system does at turning data into information.

In many medical settings, database query is still a finicky operation, requiring highly skilled staff to formulate and troubleshoot each individual non-routine inquiry. Database technologies, data mining methods and solid ontologies (bedrock concepts that lead to robust data structures) are making great strides in realizing the promise that patient databases hold for answering questions about disease incidence and course, variation among individuals, approaches to treatment, quality of outcomes, etc. But, we are still far from where we ought to be.

Let's look at what discrete data, no matter how well organized and interrogatable, leave behind. They lose the story. The record of a child's sore throat, run through the pharyngitis template in my EMR, might note that: symptoms have been present for three days; the child has felt warm to the parents' touch; the child has missed three days of school; her ears don't hurt; her two siblings do not have similar symptoms; she looks sick; she has a fever; the throat is red but not pussy; she has a slight dry cough; the lungs are clear; and so on. The checklist will also remind me to: check for a stiff neck, which helps to rule out meningitis; look for asymmetry in the tonsils, which can indicate the rare but potentially life-threatening complication of an abscess lurking behind one of them; and to see if I can feel her spleen, which would count toward a diagnosis of mononucleosis. But the checklist would have generated no trace that reflects the fatigue on the child's mother's face; her worry about missing a couple of days of work; or her concern over her daughter slipping further behind in her schoolwork, all exceedingly important information when it comes to treating this particular child of this particular family on this particular day.

My first encounter with templates was in a rural hospital where I worked for a number of years. The hospital purchased a paper-based emergency medicine documentation product called the T-System. The system is still around today, in original paper and a new improved electronic format. I don't know how successful the electronic product has been. That depends largely, I suppose, on how well the T-System meshes with other hospital and emergency room information systems.

In its day, the T-System was terrific. I could pull from a rack the single two-sided template sheet for sore throat, chest pain or laceration and begin checking boxes and filling in blanks as soon as I saw the patient. The template constantly reminded me of questions I might have forgotten to ask, body parts I might have overlooked examining and tests I ought to order. At the end of the encounter, I could usually check off one or more of the diagnoses that was already listed. Most elements of plans for treatment and follow up could also be found on the form, waiting for me to check them off.

If a patient did not have a local doctor and needed medical follow-up, I could mark the box on the T-Sheet and on the pre-printed discharge instructions that asked her to make an appointment to see me at the office. If she didn't show, I had the copy of the record to remind me to call and check on her.

With just a copy of the T-Sheet record that had been faxed from the emergency room to go by, when a patient whom I hadn't known before our ER encounter arrived at my office for follow-up, I found sometimes that I could not remember her at all, even if it had been just a week since I'd seen her. Demographic data were the only items on the record that told who she was.

These sorts of amnesiac spells were much rarer when I wrote or dictated emergency room notes. Even a few brief prose sentences, composed after a single ER visit, could capture enough of the person for me to have some idea of who that patient was the next time I saw her.

Data and story. When it comes to caring for human beings, both are important.

The Politics of Communication

Thanks in large part to their use of numerous well-constructed procedural checklists, commercial pilots rarely make dangerous mistakes. They do their work in cockpits that are sealed off from passengers. I am sure that flight attendants, whose job it is to interact directly with the people in the cabin, return daily to their homes or hotel rooms chock full of passenger stories. Pilots probably have a lot less to talk about after work.

For the purpose of getting us where we need to go efficiently and safely, the division of labor between pilot and flight attendant, between data and story, works just fine. Pilots still need to know something about human language and interaction when they talk to the control tower and crew, especially in an emergency.* For

---

* Safety research did lead to extensive training on communication within the cockpit. When I flew on a flight-for-life medical helicopter, I, a mere passenger, was told to watch for possible obstructions on takeoff and landing and to report what I saw to the pilot, *immediately*. The same sort of message has been late in arriving in the medical workplace. Flattening the hierarchy by making everybody responsible is a critical part of any safety or quality program. Merely putting information into people's hands does not mean much if they have no authority to act on it.

their part, underneath the stylish uniform and the prescribed politeness of flight attendants, lies a professional who has been extensively trained in the minutiae of handling every imaginable sort of in-flight incident.

Can you imagine ever saying "no" to a direct safety-related "request" from a flight attendant? A social psychology experiment found that 70% of total strangers who were approached in person and asked to complete a survey, for no compensation, said "yes," while just 2% agreed to do so when the request was put to them via email.[11]

Every clinician has to be good at collecting data and using it to address patients' problems. We also ought to know how to elicit stories and how to converse. Even pathologists and radiologists, who respectively spend most of their professional time in laboratories or in front of monitor screens that display medical images, are called upon to talk to colleagues and sometimes to patients.

A fascinating study of 15 radiologists, reported in 2008,[12] found that, if the monitor displayed a small color photo of the patient in the corner of the screen, the resulting interpretations were significantly more meticulous than if the doctors did not have a picture in their mind's eye of the person who was associated with the x-ray image.

Progressive thinkers have added to the standard equipment in the endoscopy suite a small simple video camera focused on the patient's face, with a monitor that the operating doctor can see while performing a colonoscopy from the other end. There's nothing like watching a person's facial expression and hearing the tone of her voice when it comes to assessing her comfort level.

Data and story interact in subtle ways. The crux challenge of medical practice, and of the information systems that support it, lies in how to balance data and story, encapsulated in the tension between watching the computer monitor or the patient's face while recording a medical history in an electronic medical record. (I will have much more to say about this matter in Chapter 8, "The Electronic Health Record.")

Thanks to rapid advances made in natural language processing, we are heading toward some resolution of this tension. Clinicians already do some dictation that goes directly from microphone to text without passing through the ears, fingers (and everything in between) of a human transcriptionist. The next step is to turn this prose into usable data, a movement being led from outside the health industry. Businesses are learning to tease data out of huge quantities of spoken and written prose and turn it into information that targets marketing for every sort of product (including political candidates) to every sort of customer. Intelligence agencies have pioneered using AI techniques to extract machine-usable information from billions of messages that are expressed in natural human languages. (See "Artificial Intelligence" in Chapter 3, "Technology.")

Excellent patient care requires doing justice to both data and story. It becomes harder to give story its due when providers spend more time with computers than with patients. In 2017, Project HOPE of the People-to-People Health Foundation reported in the journal *Health Affairs* a study of the electronic medical records of 765,129 people that automatically logged the time that their office-based primary care physicians had spent at computer terminals and the time that they had been with patients. On average, the doctors had spent 3.17 hours with their computers and 3.08 hours with their patients on a clinic day.[13]

Based on my study, as well as on my own experience, I can say unequivocally that the pendulum has, for quite a while, been swinging away from story and toward data, accelerating in the past few decades in large part under the influence of electronic information technology. The centuries-old Western cultural trend of valuing scientific ways of knowing above all others (see Chapter 1, "Logical Conclusions, How Medicine Fits Into Western Culture") has lately been given added impetus by Meaningful Use incentives, which have induced virtually the whole medical marketplace to rush head-long into using half-baked electronic medical records that strive to record patient information as digital data. Promises that we would all be able to make good use of the data that reside in the EMR remain largely unfulfilled, while barriers that these records pose to communication between patient and provider remain high.

We will never go back to paper-based medical data systems. They were not such great shakes. Even the multi-page comprehensive patient history and physical, which every medical student strives to learn to accomplish in under two hours, paints an imperfect picture of the patient. The mandated review-of-systems portion of the history, for example, amounts to extensive memory-based, thoughtlessly applied checklists of every conceivable symptom.

Left-Handed Pregnant Women

With experience, one learns how to customize the review-of-systems, based on an overall sense of the patient's problem and where one needs to probe more or less deeply. It probably suffices for a 20-year-old man whom one is admitting to the hospital with pneumonia to pose only one question on the urinary system portion of the checklist, "Does it burn when you pee?" If that same patient were 60 years old, the likelihood of prostate disease in this age group would lead you to throw in at least one screening question for urinary outlet obstruction like, "Can you still write your name in the snow?"

For gathering this sort of discrete data, computerized checklists with branching logic are much better than relying on unaided memory. Letting the patient complete the checklist, with a summary available at the time of the encounter, can free up the clinician to do what a human does best, which is to elicit the story. This is standard procedure already at some practices.

Every specialist does her own version of the complete history and physical. A neurologist's narrative will begin, "This 34-year-old left-handed woman...." An obstetrician would say, "This 34-year-old $G_3 P_2$..." (gravida 3 means she has had three pregnancies, para 2 means two deliveries). And so on. It is probably not important at the outset for the neurologist to know how many pregnancies her patient had. I cannot conceive why an obstetrician would need to know her patient's handedness, except perhaps to anticipate in which direction to duck if the mother takes a swing at her in the throes of labor.

Sir William Osler, the renowned diagnostician, notoriously did not allow leaving out one single tidbit from any patient's history, including probably the handedness of a woman with a normal pregnancy. From his base at Johns Hopkins medical school, he literally created the modern American medical training curriculum in the late 19th and early 20th centuries, rooted in basic science learned in the classroom and laboratory, followed by clinical science learned in the clinics and wards. He advocated extremely careful observation when caring for patients. Osler famously said, "Listen to your patient, he *[sic]* is telling you the diagnosis."

Osler's bedside diagnostic method required that every patient be approached as a *tabula rasa*, which meant that the doctor (there were no physician assistants or nurse-practitioners in his day) must personally begin at square one with each subject, acquiring a completely fresh comprehensive history directly from the patient, then performing his (female physicians were nearly unheard of) own physical examination. Nothing was to be taken for granted. At the outset, the data collected and impressions of previous physicians were not to be allowed to bias a fresh pair of eyes, ears, hands and nostrils.

Sir William's total dedication to each patient was laudable. His knowledge and observational powers were legendary, leading him to make diagnoses nobody else could. But there are some problems here. In his idealization of doctor as lone-wolf diagnostician, which carried through the medical education methods he created, Osler de-emphasized cooperation among the people caring for a patient. Every doctor was emperor of his own case. We still pay dearly for this concept so deeply embedded in our fragmented medical culture.

Second, performing a comprehensive history and physical takes a long time. It is not practical. Nobody but medical students and an occasional sub-specialist really does such an exam. Information that is available from other sources, accurate or not, is read or copied and pasted into the record and presented as newly acquired. Large areas are glossed over. "WNL," "Within Normal Limits," is a common abbreviation used to indicate that a particular item on the physical exam was okay. Doctors learn in the course of our training that "WNL" also means, "We Never Looked."

Because medical histories are sequential, not cumulative, errors get repeated. In keeping with the governing principle of the party game telephone, misstatements multiply and morph as they are retold, until large parts of the story may not resemble the correct and original facts. This is the third and most serious shortcoming of William Osler's *tabula rasa* method for obtaining a medical history. If each version of a patient's life story must stand on its own, as the product of a single doctor, the story does not ever get corrected or corroborated, nor does it get much wider and deeper.

No matter how repetitive or time-inefficient, a narrative, composed of real English, dictated or keyboarded into the record, can capture so much more of the story than the best-designed checklist. It is how you tell a story. Trouble is, in the interest of saving time, so many narratives are copied from previous notes that cutting-and-pasting has itself becomes an issue in some malpractice cases, calling into question whether the writer actually obtained or reviewed the re-recorded information. During an eight-month period in 2016, of 23,630 notes entered by 460 clinicians regarding patients on the general medicine inpatient service of the University of California, San Francisco, 46% were copied from elsewhere in the record, 36% imported from other records, and only 18% actually written by the person actually caring for the patient.[14]

The personal health record (PHR), about which I will have a good deal more to say in Chapter 14, "The Connected World of Patients," is the answer to problems posed by sequential histories. Rather than belonging to the institution that created it, a PHR belongs to the patient. She can correct it and add to it. Each clinician who has a hand in caring for the patient can contribute to a comprehensive, accurate, emminently usable story. Progressive healthcare organizations are experimenting now with the PHR.

Electronic data systems are critical to the future of cumulative comprehensive medical records. Half-baked or not, they are here to stay. Here is that same question I imply near the end of most every chapter. What are we to do in the meantime?

In the meantime, clinicians, patients and the institutions meant to serve all of us have to figure out how to swing the pendulum back in the direction of real human interaction. We must devise ways to value the stories in which our humanness resides. We need to figure out how to insert stories and display them prominently in medical records, even in the absence of the software that can extract data from these narratives. Since the dawn of time, way before the advent of electronic technology, we humans have been turning stories into information.

Remember those radiologists who were motivated to do better at their highly technical job of CT interpretation after exposure to just the trace of patients' stories that they could glean from a picture of their faces. After the study, all 15 of those doctors reported feeling more empathy for the patients whose pictures they got to see. Not only did that tiny human touch help the radiologists do their jobs a little better, I imagine it helped them like their jobs a little better too. All of us depend on human contact for our wellbeing, even radiologists and airplane pilots.

Chapter 6

Economics

America's health care system is neither healthy, caring, nor a system.

—**Walter Cronkite**

Healthcare is the only civil system where new technology makes prices go up instead of down.

—**Jaan Tallinn, Estonian programmer**

As grandmothers used to say, "Better to pay the grocer than the doctor."

—**Michael Pollan,** *Food Rules: An Eater's Manual*

The Gartner Group estimated that worldwide healthcare IT spending would reach $3.5 trillion in 2017, up 3% from the year before. Cognitive Medical Systems reckoned the US would devote about $100 billion to healthcare IT in 2017 and that spending would increase at a compounded annual growth rate of 13.5%.[1]

If information technology can do so many wonderful things for patients, clinicians and healthcare institutions, and we're spending so much money on it, why aren't we better at it, at least in the United States? Why is it so much harder to check into a hospital than into a hotel? To understand a health insurance policy than a mortgage contract? For your surgeon to learn what she needs to about your medical history before replacing your hip than for your accountant to have all the information she needs to do your taxes?

It seems that good management of healthcare, the most information-intensive endeavor I can think of outside of nuclear physics and astronomy, ought to dictate employing the most advanced information technologies. A 2015 paper published by the McKinsey Global Institute, entitled "Digital America: A Tale of the Haves and

Have-Mores," ranks healthcare digitization 19th out of 22 economic sectors. This came to about $40 billion, a little over 4% of revenue, a third less than the finance and media sectors spend on digital technology, but still a respectable amount. It is interesting to note that less than half of that total, $15.6 billion, went to clinical uses. The rest, presumably, was spent on business[2] functions. Shouldn't we still be able to do pretty well with that much money?

The answer came to me as I contemplated how I might organize a course to familiarize MBA students with healthcare. The over-arching principle I arrived at was misalignment of incentives. Despite decades of tireless efforts at reform, which are endlessly gamed by the targets of reform, the American healthcare non-system still struggles to reward efficiency and quality. No matter how hard we try to get beyond the fragmented fee-for-service model we grew up with, under which the more service you provide the more you get paid, healthcare just gets more expensive while the population gets marginally healthier at best and healthcare workers get more alienated.

JAMA reported in 2017 that, between 1996 and 2013, spending for healthcare increased 75%, from $1.2 trillion to $2.1 trillion. Changes in service price and intensity accounted for 50% of the increase in spending, 23% was due to population growth and 11.5% resulted from aging of the population. Decreases in disease prevalence actually reduced spending by 2.4%. In other words, half of the $900 billion annual spending increase that happened over 17 years was because more medical care was delivered at a higher cost to a population that was overall a little healthier.[*,3]

The Centers for Medicare and Medicaid Services predicted that, in 2017, healthcare spending would rise 5.4% to $3.5 trillion, which amounts to 18.3% of the GDP, $10,832 per capita. By comparison, this is about 20% more per capita than the next most expensive, Luxembourg, one third more than Switzerland and Norway, the countries with the third and fourth most costly healthcare, and about double what Canadians pay. Healthcare spending is predicted to increase by about 5.8% per year between now and 2025, 1.3% faster than GDP growth, topping $5.5 trillion. Large employers project that healthcare benefits will cost them over $14,000 per insured employee in 2018.[4]

For all this money spent, in 2015, the US ranked 29th worst out of 35 Organization for Economic and Co-operative Development (OCED) countries in infant mortality and 26th in life expectancy at birth.[5] Pretty close to all of our health statistics look this bad.

I have read a number of books, and could write several myself, that attempt to explain how this country came to spend by far the most money for far from the best healthcare in the world. I am not about to prescribe any general remedies,

---

[*] I am aware that one could make the argument that the 2.4% decline in disease incidence and prevalence was the result of $450 billion extra spending. If so, the question still remains whether the American people were getting their money's worth.

not even for the IT sector. Instead, let me start with the case of electronic fetal monitoring in the labor and delivery suite, a great example of misaligned medical, financial and legal incentives.

The Case of Fetal Monitoring

When it comes to birthing babies, "natural is better" is about as true as you can get. Over the last century or so, medical science has provided a host of technologies that have saved the lives of countless newborns and mothers. Nevertheless, when possible, normal spontaneous vaginal delivery (NSVD) is best. It took the women's movement of the sixties and seventies to remind us of that. Birthing suites, fathers in the delivery room and prepared childbirth classes are a few of the tangible outcomes. Every medical intervention, from episiotomy to anesthesia to forceps to cesarean section, has its attendant complications and costs.

Fetal monitoring, on its surface non-invasive and pretty benign, is one of those interventions. For several decades, it has been part of standard operating procedure on just about every obstetrics ward in the country.

In the 1890s, midwives and physicians learned that a fetus' heart rate could serve as a measure of its wellbeing. Protocols that had doctors recording the fetal heart rate at every prenatal visit and labor deck nurses checking babies' pulses at regular intervals became the norm.

In the early 1960s, devices appeared that could continuously monitor and record a fetus' heart rate.[6] This was considered a quantum leap in the ability of doctors and staff to assess a baby's wellbeing during the course of labor. By 1975, the heart rate of one out of five fetuses was being continuously monitored during labor, employing an ultrasound device to detect motion of the baby's heart valves and recording a graph of that pulse on a continuous paper strip.[7] On my medical school obstetrics rotation in 1973, 100% of labors were continuously monitored.

An ultrasound transducer is held against the laboring mother's abdomen by an elastic belt that goes all the way around her. If she moves, the transducer is liable to be displaced and the baby's heart signal lost. At best, a silent alarm alerts a nurse to come check the patient. At worst, the machine beeps an audible alert in the patient's room, a sound that is sure to increase the mother's anxiety. As a medical student, I spent a lot of my time on the labor deck adjusting fetal monitor belts.

Keeping a transducer in place effectively ties a laboring woman to her bed. Until the final stages of labor, mother mammals (including humans) tend to get restless. They walk around. Mothers' movement and vertical position are thought to help a baby achieve a lie that will facilitate its passage down the birth canal. A laboring mother's loss of mobility appeared to be a small price to pay, though, for early warning that a baby was in trouble. Eventually, most every woman was lying in bed with a monitor strapped to her through most of her in-hospital labor.

Because timely forceps extraction or cesarean section can be life saving, decision pathways around fetal monitor strip interpretation were generally weighted in a direction that led away from NSVD at the first suggestion of fetal distress. Besides, insurance pays more to the doctor and hospital for an instrumented or operative delivery and postpartum care than for a normal spontaneous vaginal delivery. The doctor gets to intervene, produce a baby, sew up the mom and go home, rather than wait through stressful hours or days more of labor, possibly hazardous to mother and child and definitely wearying to physician and staff.

Trouble is, when they look at outcomes, researchers repeatedly find that if the mother had a normal pregnancy and no risk factors for complicated delivery, fetal monitoring yielded no improvement in newborn health.[8] The only change in outcomes was that mothers whose labors had been monitored received more interventions—including forceps and C-section deliveries, with their attendant risks, complications and cost—than unmonitored patients.

Still, the reasoning goes, definitive intervention looks better in court. If the result of a delivery is an unhealthy baby, the doctor's decision to apply forceps or perform a C-section shows that she did everything possible to avert a bad outcome. This has provided a strong incentive for doctors and birthing centers to monitor labors, assuring themselves they would not miss signs of fetal distress and fail to act aggressively in their goal to turn every threatened fetus into a healthy newborn.*

Unfortunately, electronic fetal monitoring is very imprecise. No matter how exactly the criteria for diagnosing fetal distress are stated, there remains a huge margin for interpretation and error. The technology serves up a significant number of babies who appear in trouble on the monitor but are not so at delivery (false positives) as well as a smaller number whose monitor strips appear okay but the newborn is not (false negatives).

False positives and false negatives are reciprocal. The more of the one, the less of the other. How data are interpreted, where thresholds are set for intervention, not the data or the technology themselves, make the tradeoff of false positives for false negatives. In American healthcare, as a matter of course, we are mostly willing to accept a lot of false positives in order to minimize false negatives.

After all, we get paid for doing the testing needed to chase down false positives and sued for overlooking false negatives. But in the process of assuring that we miss

---

* Studies show that the vast majority of newborn complications are attributable to maternal or fetal problems that have nothing to do with the labor and delivery process. Nevertheless, many blameless defendants in obstetrics malpractice cases end up either paying huge awards once the jury has laid eyes on the poor child or settling out of court for fear of what a jury would do if they saw the child. If one delivers babies, fear of lawsuits is not irrational. Universal fetal monitoring is.

very few patients who really have a certain disease, we mistakenly hang the diagnosis on a lot of people who don't have it, ignoring the cost in worry, pain, complications and dollars that false positives lay on patient and society.* Indiscriminate electronic monitoring produces a lot of false positives for fetal distress.

Thanks in part to this technology, cesarean section rates have climbed. More babies are labeled distressed and delivered through a surgical incision in the abdomen instead of vaginally, the way Nature designed. Between 1975 and 2007, C-section rates tripled in the United States, from 10.4% to 31.3%.[9] The World Health Organization estimates that a 10–15% C-section rate is the sweet spot where the most lives are saved and complications avoided.[†,10]

Never mind evidence that ought to discourage routine fetal monitoring for women at low risk for complications of labor or delivery, in 2013, 89% of labors in the United States were monitored, 80% of those continuously.[11] In a nod to women's demands for less intervention, many birthing facilities will perform on admission a "baseline monitor strip" for 30 minutes or so "to make sure that the baby is starting out okay," before a woman is turned loose to move about her room, wander the halls or thrash in their bed, unencumbered by a monitor belt.

For low-risk pregnancies, baseline monitor strips have yielded the same results as continuous fetal monitoring did: no better outcomes for babies; higher levels of intervention and complication for moms; and higher expenses for payers. Still, doctors fear that if they do not monitor labors at least a little bit, an attorney might ask them in court, "How did you know, *doctor*, that this fetus was healthy when the mother came to the labor unit?" The irony is that when electronic fetal monitor

---

* Routine prostate-specific antigen (PSA) screening for early diagnosis of prostate cancer is a prime example of the hazards of false-positives. Asymptomatic middle-aged men whose routine PSAs are found to be elevated are on their way down a slippery slope of procedures and interventions that have not been shown to improve the longevity nor the quality of life of this group. Their life tends to be, in fact, worse overall, with more urinary incontinence, erectile dysfunction and worry. It took years, but even the American Urological Association (AUA), whose doctors make a large share of their living finding and treating prostate cancer, came around in 2013 to recommending against routine screening for men younger than 55. The AUA suggests that men between the ages of 55 and 69 discuss the matter of PSA screening with their health care provider, "weighing the benefits of preventing prostate cancer mortality in one man for every 1,000 men screened over a decade against the known potential harms associated with screening and treatment." I don't get routine PSA tests myself, nor do I recommend them for my asymptomatic patients.

† Thanks to quality improvement efforts targeted to reduce surgical deliveries, C-section rates peaked in 2009 and have come down a down a bit since. (http://www.cesareanrates.com/p/history-of-united-states-cesarean-rates.html) It turns out that the most effective intervention for a birthing center to reduce its C-section numbers is to get its doctors on board with this goal and then post a chart at regular intervals that lists and ranks each physician's operative delivery rate. Ending routine fetal monitoring for low-risk mothers and babies would be another useful strategy. I don't know that anybody has tried it.

records are introduced into evidence at malpractice trials, they are as likely to hurt as to help the defense.*

In the case of electronic fetal monitoring, we have a great example of misalignment of incentives. On one hand, there is the desire to produce the best outcome, which ideally means just the right amount of intervention to yield the maximum of healthy babies and mothers. On the other hand, there are the rewards of better reimbursement for more intervention, a less stressful schedule and the irrational fear of being less able to attest under oath to the fetus' health.

Here is more to think about. The quality of relationship with the patient, not competence, is by far the most important factor in determining who gets sued for malpractice and who does not. One study of 353 physicians at a large teaching hospital found that those in the highest third of patient satisfaction rankings were sued for malpractice 26% less than those in the middle third and 110% less than those in the lowest third.[12]

When I taught obstetrics to family medicine residents, I often observed the doctor-in-training, upon entering the room of a woman in labor, walk straight to the fetal monitor and begin pouring over its paper output strip before she had even said "hello" to the patient. Whether or not the monitoring was indicated, a machine had been interposed between doctor and patient. I needed to remind those callow trainees that their attention really should be focused first and foremost on the mother, from whom they could learn so many things that the fetal monitor would not tell them.

Too often, in too many locations besides the obstetrical ward, novice and seasoned doctors alike allow technology to come between themselves and their patients, to the detriment of both. Electronic fetal monitoring is just one example. I will have a lot more to say about this topic in Chapter 8, "Electronic Health Record."

Before I move on, though, I need to come back to where I started with this story. Electronic fetal monitoring saves lives. In high risk pregnancy or in the midst of a labor that manifests dangerous signs like vaginal bleeding or elevated maternal blood pressure, the data generated by this simple, non-invasive device can mean the difference between a baby living or dying. As usual, the undesirable outcomes

---

* By contrast, a study reported in *JAMA* in 1997 that when videotaped patient encounters with family doctors who had been sued at least twice were compared to tapes of doctors who had never been the target of a malpractice investigation, the doctors with unblemished records had done a better job of explaining to patients what they were doing, asking their opinions more, laughing more, as well as spending more time with patients. Interestingly, these findings did not hold for surgeons, presumably because their patients expected less "hand-holding" from procedure-oriented specialists. (Levinson, W, Roter, DL, Mullooly, JP et al. Physician-patient communication: The relationship with malpractice claims among primary care physicians and surgeons. *JAMA*. 1977:277(7), 553–559.) Another study that analyzed surgeons' tone of voice in two 10-second clips, one from the first minute of a patient-doctor encounter and one from the last minute, could predict with some accuracy which ones had been sued. (Ambady, N, Laplante, D, Nguyen, T et al. Surgeons' tone of voice: A clue to malpractice history. *Surgery*. 2002:132(1), 5–9.)

related to fetal monitoring lie not with the technology itself but with how we choose to use it. And how we choose to use it is influenced by incentives—such as financial, provider convenience and fear of lawsuit—that do not align with the mother's and the baby's best interests.

Distorted Incentives

The National Health Service in England started measuring and financially rewarding the performance of general practitioners in 2004 under its Quality of Outcomes Framework (QOF). They budgeted for 75% of GPs to meet the standards. Ninety-seven percent did. GPs diverted attention to those items they were being paid extra for. And their morale declined.[13]

An English friend, a health policy wonk who had helped to design the QOF, told me that doctors came to prefer using the old blood pressure devices in their offices because there was some imprecision inherent in reading the analog dial. For a diastolic blood pressure, the dropping needle could easily be seen as pointing to 92, 90 or 88. The readout of a digital machine offers no room to fudge. If the cutoff point for rewarding doctors for blood pressure management is 90 diastolic, and if you make it a point not to lie in your professional life (which, thank goodness, is still the case for the vast majority of practitioners), which kind of blood pressure device would you prefer?

Under fee-for-service arrangements, financial incentives are especially perverse. It is generally much easier and more lucrative to get a new head CT on a drunk (with Medicaid to pay for it) who was found unconscious and brought to the emergency room than to try to ascertain if there had been any other recent medical encounters, let alone wrest the results of a scan that was done just a week before from the medical records department of a different hospital. If both organizations get paid for doing the same service, why should the staff at hospital number two go through the hassle and contend with the HIPAAnoia of the staff at hospital number one in order to obtain a recent scan report, let alone have the actual images themselves sent by electronic means? Here's why: A) It's incredibly wasteful. Somebody pays. In this case, it's not the patient, doctors or hospital, but probably, ultimately, the taxpayer; and B) CT scans expose a person to a lot of radiation.

Even in the case of organizations like Kaiser-Permanente, which has replaced uncoordinated fee-for-service with a well-oiled integrated care machine that puts the patient information its own clinicians need at their fingertips, playing too well with others does not make financial sense. As it is for any other business, an integrated healthcare system's incentive is to keep as much business as it can within its own network. Making a patient's information too portable means losing some control. Information is power and power is money. (See "Interoperability" in Chapter 3, "Technology.")

There are those who argue that the structure of healthcare data is not that different than that of any other industry whose successful automation provides interoperability and usability based upon the sorts of universal standards that healthcare can only dream about. Information systems in the healthcare sector could operate just as smoothly as they do in finance and transportation in putting crucial information at the fingertips of those who need it to take care of a patient. The difference, they assert, between healthcare and everybody else is that in healthcare the financial incentives for good information systems are not only not there, but that they are often perverse.

There are standards for billing data interchange; a good thing, since the average medical practice communicates with 17–20 payers per week. Nevertheless, 90% of providers and 68% of health plans consider the telephone to be their primary form of communication with each other.[14] At the expense of everybody, except of the insurance companies that skim an estimated 20% of profits off the top of the $3 trillion-plus healthcare economy, inefficiency pays.

As I discuss in Chapter 3, "Technology," healthcare organizations, along with the information technology companies they depend on, are, nevertheless, moving (some more quickly than others) in the direction of universal standards for health data interchange. Once it doesn't pay to erect barriers to free exchange of data, we will really start to tap the power of information technology to improve health and healthcare. We may even be able to shop intelligently for medical services on the basis of quality and cost.

Funding Telehealth

I co-wrote a book, *Telemedicine and the Reinvention of Healthcare*, published in 1999. Telemedicine was then, and is even more so now, a set of technologies ripe for implementation. As I will elucidate in Chapter 10, "Telehealth," these technologies can offer innumerable services with the efficiencies gained by moving electrons (information) rather than molecules (people and things).

Nearly two decades after my book came out, though everybody is talking about it now and even dipping their toes in the water, telemedicine still has not caught on that well, except in a few forward-thinking corners of the healthcare industry. Why not? It is not the technology, which has become more available, standardized, user-friendly and affordable; but the financial incentives for telehealth do not often align with the service incentives. As of 2014, 0.2% of Medicare beneficiaries had received services via telehealth.[15]

There are multiple administrative impediments to telehealth, one of the biggest of which is the requirement that every provider hold a state medical license from every state in which she consults.* State medical boards, which by and large are

---

* I recently applied for licenses to practice medicine in two states where I do some consulting. The process cost six months, hundreds of dollars and many gray hairs. Among the pieces of information required of me were my fingerprints, the dollar amount of a malpractice case settled thirty years ago, and discharge papers from 1978, when I finished my tour of duty with the National Health Service Corps. It felt like they had stopped just short of requiring a note from my mother's obstetrician. State licensing boards are controlled by physicians, bureaucrats and attorneys whose incentives do not align with the sometimes dire need to bring more medical practitioners into their states.

controlled by physicians, have little incentive to lower barriers for out-of-state doctors to practice medicine-at-a-distance on their turf. Medicare has recently made some piecemeal reforms aimed at loosening licensing requirements for practicing telemedicine across state lines. Defending business too often trumps patient interest in this realm too. These barriers would fall in a bureaucratic heartbeat (measured in years) if the incentives were to line up.

Over the course of my career, I must have saved patients and insurance companies hundreds of thousands of dollars in unmade trips to offices and emergency rooms with the hours I spent on the phone following up on patients' problems and answering their questions. I never once was paid a penny for this telephone time, only for face-to-face time. Under the fee-for-service system, there was no reward to my hospital or to me for keeping patients from using expensive in-person services.* I took the time and trouble to offer real medical service remotely because it was the right thing to do, certainly not out of any financial incentive to my employers or to me.

Medicine practiced by phone is, by definition, telemedicine. It was only in 2001 that Congress authorized payment, via Section 1834(m) of the Social Security Act, for what we traditionally think of as telehealth services, real time video consultations. Because they were afraid of adding a deluge of new spending to the bloated Medicare program, lawmakers filled the legislation with restrictions and limitations that made it widely cumbersome and narrowly practical. Under fee-for-service Medicare rightly saw, through its payer goggles, that telehealth services were just more services that could cost them more money. Most insurance companies followed Medicare's miserly payment formulas for telemedicine services.

Payers worry, as one would expect, that telehealth services will add to total healthcare costs by increasing utilization, rather than supplanting more expensive face-to-face services. One study, released in 2017 by the RAND Corporation, of data generated from 300,000 beneficiaries of the California Public Employees Retirement System found that, thanks to telemedicine, the total cost of care for upper respiratory infections increased a little. The average charge for a telehealth visit was $79, for an office visit $146, and for an emergency room visit $1,734. The authors estimated that 88% of telehealth consultations for colds came from people who otherwise would not have sought any care at all for these minor maladies. Keep in mind that this is one study, a big one to be sure, of one medical problem in one population.[16] It is unimaginable that, on the whole, intervening early with low cost telemedicine services doesn't save lots of suffering and money.

---

* I've experienced this myself recently as a patient. Under Medicare rules, I had to schedule a face-to-face appointment with my doctor so he could sign the order for continuing use of the CPAP device that has treated my sleep apnea for 20 years. We had forgotten to have him mention the sleep apnea and CPAP when I had seen him for a physical exam earlier in the year. I needed nothing more from him at this encounter than for the doctor to be able to attest in a progress note that the word "CPAP" had been uttered so he could sign the Medicare paperwork. He was paid $118 by Medicare plus my supplemental insurance for this wholly unnecessary service.

Healthcare institutions often have little reason to be gung-ho about telemedicine. For instance, when a hospital and cardiologist get paid a certain amount for performing coronary artery stent placement plus follow-up care, it's easiest and cheapest for the doctor and hospital to leave it up to the patient or caregiver to address the transportation, time away from home and work, comfort, childcare and chaperoning issues that need to be negotiated before the patient can attend a follow-up appointment at her doctor's office. News that a competing cardiac program has gained market share among homebound and rural patients by offering clinical visits via interactive video may be what it takes to make hospital administration, medical staff and marketers see their incentives align with providing this telehealth service. These sorts of marketing incentives, unfortunately, apply much better to narrowly-focused high-margin services than to broad low-margin ones.

Here is an example of a telehealth program that was targeted to reduce losses on low-margin services rather than to promote high-margin ones. I dreamed it up some years ago with a couple of co-conspirators. The program was designed to align financial and service incentives on chronically ill patients with poor resources, the sorts of patients most likely to be overlooked.

"Frequent fliers"* is a pejorative term used to describe people who spend the most time in the emergency room and hospital. For many of them, their problems could largely be managed at home. They have chronic diseases they don't take care of for lack of: money to purchase their medicines; access to regular medical care; physical or mental ability to care for themselves; understanding of their disease, etc. Some people just panic easily and call the ambulance every time they feel short of breath. These patients show up in the ER over and over. Sometimes they are admitted to the hospital.

People who are incessantly found either on gurneys in the emergency room or in hospital beds are some of the most frustrating patients and some of the costliest to care for. Any intervention that will help them to stay away from acute care medicine will improve the quality of their lives and save payers and hospitals big chunks of cash.

Our little telehealth group asked the hospital data folks to get us a list of patients who had had a high number of ER and inpatient admissions in the past year, along

---

* Let me insert an ethical note here. Gallows humor has forever been one way to cope with the stresses inherent in dealing with the high stakes of caring for critically ill people, often with too little time, information or sleep to be sure one is making the best decisions. Unfortunately, some of this "humor" comes at the expense of very sad patients and their situations. I am not about to wag my finger and turn my back on a strategy that has helped me through many overwrought situations in the course of my training and career. However, I do need to caution that computerized systems make it easier than ever to label patients: as non-compliant, psychotic, drug using, abusive, or frequent fliers. It is of utmost importance that we guard against enshrining and communicating prejudices in our records, whether electronic or paper-based. (Joy, M., Clement, T., Sisti, D. The ethics of behavioral health information technology: Frequent flyer icons and implicit bias. *JAMA*. 2016:316(15), 1539–1540.)

with how much money the institution had lost in caring for each of them. We chose to pilot our program with patients whose acute care had been most costly to the hospital's bottom line. Then we asked the hospital's case managers, whose job it was to coordinate care for these very challenging patients, to narrow our choices to twelve, based on the managers' sense of who would be able to go along with the program.

The plan was to set up little more than a simple interactive link, over a plain old twisted pair telephone landline. Daily check-ins were to include a brief face-to-face low-bandwidth video chat with the case manager, a few simple standardized questions about symptoms to be answered on a keypad, and possibly, automated measurement of things like pulse and blood oxygen saturation, tailored to the individual's medical condition.

Based on what we saw in the telehealth literature of the time, we estimated that the hospital would see a return on its investment in the program within three to six months. (With the falling cost of these technologies, the payback today would be nearly instantaneous.) Unfortunately, this innovative, simple program never happened. Though the financial and patient care incentives appeared to be well aligned, the project languished for lack of vision and leadership in the management bureaucracy that stood above us. Once again, the barrier to improving service through technology was not the technology itself but the people who could have made it work.

Costly Technology

Robotic surgery is yet another place where economic incentives trump rational planning. A 2016 article in *JAMA Surgery* demonstrated that the decision by a hospital to add expensive (both in terms of investment and in terms of cost to insurers and patients) robotic surgery was based much more on the perceived need to offer this service in the face of local competitors than its actual value to patients. In general, neither patient outcomes nor profit margins improved after introduction of robotic surgery. This sort of "technological arms race" is one of the biggest drivers of inflation of healthcare cost.[17]

How about all those gizmos that people purchase to monitor heart rate, steps taken, sleep time, distance run or cycled, calories consumed or burned, and so on? Some medical practices have made efforts to collect these data. But nobody knows very well how to use them. Research on interpreting and acting on self-monitoring data is still in its infancy. Why then, organizations ask themselves, should they go to the trouble and expense of incorporating big blobs of marginally useful patient-generated data into their medical records? To harried clinicians, adding these data to the medical record may appear to be just another technology learning curve to climb, with little payoff at the summit.

Here's why they should do it anyway: Because more and more patients expect it. I predict that a large share of technological innovation in the clinical realm will be patient-driven. Imperfect though the science behind it may be, patients will want their providers to accept their monitoring data and help them make sense of it.

Practices will be pushed by their patients into doing more remote consultation, via phone, video and patient portal. Studies show patients like it that way; so do doctors, once they get used to the idea. Satisfaction goes up when patients can quickly get answers out of a practice. Even paying a reasonable fee for a consultation via an internet portal can beat the heck out of the old way of having to go through a nurse who takes way too seriously her role of protecting "her" doctor from undesired intrusions, then having to wait hours or days or forever for the doctor to call back. With or without standardized report cards, patient satisfaction is critical to the long-term success of any type of medical practice. (See Chapter 14, "The Connected World of Patients," for a fuller discussion.)

Pity the Healthcare Executive

I have declared to many a healthcare executive that I was glad to have an easy job. "I'm just a doctor," I'd say. "My job is to take care of people. Yours is to figure out how to pay for it." I mean it. Every manager in the business of healthcare daily makes compromises between what patients really need and what the organization will get paid for. Every time I gaze upwards in the lobby of the dear local hospital where, for decades, I've been a doctor, a teacher and a patient, it makes me furious to see five stories of dramatic open space. I think about how much extra it must have cost to construct the building that way and imagine how those dollars could have been put to use to meet real medical needs in our community. Not surprisingly, that vacant expanse opens out onto the cardiology, orthopedics and other high-margin units that compete for patients with too many other hospitals in our region that provide these same lucrative services.

If they are to survive for the foreseeable future, healthcare institutions will have to keep playing the hands of the misaligned incentives that they are dealt. Until information technology marks the cards by putting the right information and power transparently into all the players' hands, expensive lobbies (and lobbyists) will continue to figure way too prominently in the ultra-complex economic equations that govern today's healthcare.

Sooner or later, though, providers will compete on the basis of quality and value. Healthcare will catch up with most every other industry, from earth moving to entertainment, in making information technology a cornerstone of delivering a quality product at a good price in a way that pleases its customers (the Triple Aim).

Just one more word about the economics of HIT. As I've said, it is way less expensive to move electrons than atoms. Thanks to these many electronic technologies, we should see some greening of the healthcare business, with less use of paper, less travel of patients and professionals and fewer large energy-hogging computing devices. However, I wouldn't sell my stock in paper products, transportation, or energy companies just yet.[18]

Chapter 7

Security and Privacy

People ask me all the time, "What keeps you up at night?" And I say, "Spicy Mexican food, weapons of mass destruction, and cyber attacks."

—Dutch Ruppersberger, US Congressional Representative

When it comes to privacy and accountability, people always demand the former for themselves and the latter for everyone else.

—David Brin, American scientist and author

To be left alone is the most precious thing one can ask of the modern world.

—Anthony Burgess, *Homage to Qwert Yuiop: Essays*

I imagine that by this point, in the course of discussions about sending patient data all over the place and massaging it in myriad ways, you have asked yourself at least several times, "But what about privacy?" When it comes to personal health data, security and privacy are among everybody's foremost concerns. They ought to be. According to a survey done in 2017 by the business consulting firm, Accenture, the healthcare data of one in four US consumers had been breached.[1] Another survey from 2017 revealed that 49% of healthcare organizations had experienced at least one data breach in the previous two years.[2] 2017 was the first year when the number of security compromises in health information systems that came from outsiders exceeded the number of inside jobs.[3] The world is full of evil, greedy hackers.

Personal health information makes an especially fat target because: a single system may hold the records of hundreds, thousands or millions of people. These records often contain lots of financial data, like social security and credit card numbers. Certain diagnoses can open the way to scams for scoring drugs or expensive medical equipment; and most of all, healthcare has in general been way less focused on security than other industries.

Security versus Privacy

"Security" and "privacy" do not mean the same thing. The former is the broader term. "Security" is the ability of a system to protect information and system resources with respect to confidentiality and integrity. Computer security is comprised of three core areas, summarized by the acronym "CIA":

Confidentiality—Ensuring that information is not accessed by unauthorized persons.

Integrity—Ensuring that information is not altered by unauthorized persons in a way that is not detectable by authorized users.

Authentication—Ensuring that users are the persons they claim to be.[4]

"Privacy" simply means control over who has access to information. Security does not assure privacy. A system may have its data locked down tight and a flawless authentication system to see to it that each datum gets only into the specific hands of those who have the right to see it. Still, a clever snoop may find out what she wants to know by making multiple queries to multiple databases, even public ones.

Take the work of Latanya Sweeney, currently Director of the Data Privacy Laboratory at Harvard. When she was a graduate student in the mid-1990s, she massaged a database of all hospital admissions of Massachusetts state employees. In order to provide safe raw material for the medical, public health and policy the researchers that state is crawling with, the data had been anonymized by removing all obvious identifiers, including name, birthdate, address, phone number, social security number, insurance policy numbers, etc. Sweeney purchased, for $20, the complete voter registration rolls for the 54,000 residents of the City of Cambridge, where the Governor resided. Combining these data with anonymized hospital admission data, she was able to obtain Massachusetts Governor Weld's complete medical record, including diagnoses and prescriptions, which she forwarded, with much publicity, to his office.[5]

Identity scrubber software that reviews records and automatically recognizes and removes identifying data via natural language processing works quite well (though not flawlessly), thereby allowing research to proceed at a fraction of what it costs to employ humans to de-identify personal medical information.[6]

Autonomy, a core American value, dictates that as much control as possible of our personal health information should rest in the hands of the patient or legal guardian. The word "privacy" never appears in the US Constitution. Nevertheless, as a key component of the Enlightenment ideal of individual freedom that was so tightly embraced by our forefathers, the right to privacy undergirds our law and our culture. Keeping one's personal life out of view is one important strategy for remaining free. Ironically, until the concept of the personal health record recently appeared on the scene, nobody questioned the fact that it was healthcare providers who were the actual proprietors, each of their own piece, of a person's medical record.

I need not elaborate the myriad good reasons to keep personal medical information private. Trouble is, in this electronic age, that's getting harder to do. Supposedly de-identified data have been harvested and processed by data brokers to collect people, along with their address, phone number or email, on lists with titles like: "People with Cancer by State;" "Booming Boomers with Erectile Dysfunction;" "Bladder Control Product Buyers;" "Heart Disease Sufferers;" and "STD Mater" (mature singles who have a sexually transmitted disease).[7]

The Wall Street Journal reported in 2013 that Equifax, one of the big three consumer credit reporting agencies kept a database that included women's gynecologist visits over the previous year. (We all know now just how safe Equifax's data have been. Notoriously, in 2017, the company allowed the largest single breech of private consumer data in history, affecting 143 million people.) Executive director of the World Privacy Forum alleged in the same article that "at least one data broker sells lists of rape victims."[8]

It was reported in the early 2000s that 15%–17% of US adults had changed doctors, paid expenses out of pocket, given inaccurate or incomplete medical history, self-treated or asked a doctor not to record a medical problem in order to keep embarrassing or costly health information from being discovered.[9]

People's desires for privacy of their personal medical information has been described as "granular." There are way more variations among people about what sorts of information they want shared with whom under what circumstances for what purposes than can be easily summarized on a checklist. I expect we will be struggling with how to accommodate such nuanced notions of privacy for a long time.[10]

Blockchain,* a technology that securely manages a distributed database, may be a solution to the problem of keeping track of the widely-dispersed pieces of a personal health record while maintaining control of who gets to see which pieces. At least one company, MedRec, has developed and is marketing a medical record management system based on blockchain technology.[11] Trouble is, because every transaction is vetted and recorded simultaneously in a slew of distributed computers, each of which uses energy in the process, blockchain is very, very energy inefficient. For each transaction, Bitcoin, the most widely known of the blockchain companies, consumes the same amount of energy as is needed to power nine US

---

* Blockchain software is open source. Bitcoin, founded in 2009, the most famous and biggest user of blockchain, bills itself as an "alternative currency" that provides secure transactions outside of the usual state-controlled currency systems. A number of other organizations, from startups to staid old banks to black marketers, eager to profit from sexy, innovative, private and secure new ways of doing business, have taken up this technology. There have already been a number of high-profile busts of criminal organizations that employed the so-called Dark Web, modeled on Bitcoin, to accomplish communications and transactions.

homes for a day. Bitcoin's activity causes 17.7 million tons of CO_2 to be added to the atmosphere in a year. Clearly, this will be unsustainable when it comes to encrypting and exchanging gobs of medical records.[12]

Privacy issues can extend to whole communities. There is the notorious example of the Havasupai, a small Native American tribe that lives in the deepest part of the Grand Canyon. Because of the group's longtime isolation, in 1990, geneticists from Arizona State University hooked up with the tribe, eager to learn all they could from members' DNA. The stated goal of the study was to shed light on the extremely high rate of diabetes among the Havasupai.

Once the scientists had collected the blood, they also searched the DNA to study other problems, including alcoholism and schizophrenia, as well as to uncover tribal roots that were at odds with the Native Americans' own origin stories. Years after the study began, the Havasupai sued. ASU received a lot of bad press, returned the blood, and paid $700,000 to the tribe, which banished all university employees from the reservation.

* * * * * *

A word on disparities in different generations' views on privacy. Stories abound of young people who have not been hired for jobs thanks to pictures of them naked, drunk, stoned (or all three) that have been posted on their social media pages. We have all seen these same folks snap pictures of the meal we are sharing with them and posting the images before dessert arrives. We older folks assume that digital natives don't care as much as we do about privacy. Careful studies have shown that there is not such a great disparity of attitudes toward privacy among the generations, as there is a simple lack of knowledge of the rules and understanding of the consequences among the younger set.[13]

Security Threats

Let's start with broader security issues. There is a ferocious, never-ending war out there between the hackers in black outfits, who spend their lives figuring out how to break into computer systems that contain every sort of information that is meant to stay private, and the security experts, dressed in white, who are constantly on the alert for hacker attacks and how to thwart them. Some of the best white-clad guys and gals learned their chops wearing black outfits. (The zany "Spy vs. Spy" cartoons that run along the margins of *Mad Magazine* come to mind.)

Cyberspace is awash in viruses, worms, Trojan horses, and the like, either residing in the hundreds of millions of computing devices out there or trying to get in. The exponentially growing internet of things is providing that many more entrance points for evil code. That machine intelligence-powered interactive teddy bear that you bought for your child's last birthday and promptly connected to the internet could provide especially easy access to your personal computer and all the information it contains. After all, who'd suspect a cute little cuddly thing like that of being a spy?[14]

Healthcare has been especially hard hit by cybercriminals. Major cyberattacks on healthcare data increased 63% from 2015 to 2016, amounting to over 12 million records breached.[15] Today 60% of healthcare organizations have a senior executive with a title like Chief Information Security Officer.[16]

Many years ago, I would pooh-pooh security concerns over electronic patient data. My patients' electronic records were much more secure behind the password-protected electronic firewalls in my office system, I would say, than paper records ever had been, scattered as they were among inboxes, outboxes, desktops and open shelves in the clinic. The difference is, of course, that a miscreant with a wheelbarrow might be able to steal 50 hard copies of patient records; but with the right hacking tools, she might hijack millions. In 2016, a breach at Banner Health compromised 3.6 million patient records in one fell swoop.

Installing software updates as soon as they become available is the single most important step you can take to deflect cyberattacks. A large share of these updates are patches to the vulnerabilities to security breaches that are always cropping up. WannaCry, the notorious ransomware that affected 230,000 computers worldwide in May 2017, was wholly frustrated in machines that had installed a critical software patch to the Microsoft Windows operating system that had been released, for free, two months before the attack.

Cybersecurity is a highly technical game of Spy vs. Spy, played from both sides of the ball by experts who are very smart and very devious. I recommend that you get the best advice, hire the best people, purchase and maintain the best systems and pray to your Higher Power.

Getting fallible humans to follow the best advice is not to be taken for granted. In 2017, only 48% of 778 providers who answered a survey said they encrypted medical orders before texting them.[17] Just seeing that system users select strong passwords and don't share them or write them down on Post-It notes stuck somewhere on their desk can be a huge challenge.[18] Health Informatics Research reported in 2017 the results of a survey administered via Google Forms and Facebook. Of 299 medical practitioners who responded, 220 (74%) admitted to having shared their EHR password at least once.[19] Perhaps a new ultrasound device that identifies an individual by the shape and dynamic performance of her heart will be the answer. So far it has shown 98% accuracy.[20]

If you are a clinician, your practice may want to purchase cyber liability and data breach insurance on top of your usual professional and business liability insurance products. Policies typically cover multimedia goofs, security and privacy breaches, network asset protection, cyber extortion and terrorism. One handout from a medical and dental malpractice company asked the FAQ, "Is cyber liability insurance expensive?" and answered, "Not when compared to the potential cost of a breach…" Of course, that's the seller talking.

I have a good deal to say about privacy, a basic value for most Americans. We all know our privacy has been under attack. For years, I forewent some pretty significant savings at the supermarket where I shopped by not signing up for their preferred shopper program. I did not want them tracking what I bought. I gave in a long time ago, taking my discounts in the knowledge that, one way or another, everybody knows everything anyway about what I purchase everywhere. I understand that the purchases I make online are being tracked, as well as all those I make in person with a credit card, which I almost always use. Though my conscience is clear, I suspect that multiple agencies concerned with national security hold information about me, some of it private, somewhere in their vast electronic vaults.*

I have not messed with Facebook, Twitter, or other social media sites at all, in part because it would make that much more of me public, accessible and, I fear, manipulable. (See "Social media" in Chapter 14, "The Connected World of Patients.")

There is a lot of handwringing going on these days about the ubiquitous loss of privacy. Customers demand that permission to share their personal data be an opt-in, not an opt-out function, on business websites. They want Facebook to reform what data it collects and how the company uses it. So does Congress. The European Union has come down on Google for how it handles and sell the personal information of its users, which is just about everybody.

People may defend themselves by signing up for email services and choose search engines that anonymize their internet presence. The National Institutes of Health sets standards for obtaining patient permission to use their genome data, even in studies that will fully anonymize and meld their data into a large group. Experts are even figuring out how, borrowing techniques derived from a field called public key cryptography, to compare a person's genome with others in a database without putting her identity at risk.[21]

Everybody Wants Your Data

23andMe announced in 2017 a new financing round of $1.75 billion. Rest assured that smart venture capitalists are not expecting big returns on their investments based on a $99 analysis of the DNA extracted from cells in customers' spit. Pharma giant Genentech has already forked over $60 million to 23andMe for rights to mine

---

* This example, from a May 14, 2017 article in *The New York Times*, strengthened my resolve not to participate in Facebook. "Digital companies are capable of targeting audiences so narrow that they can pinpoint, say, Idaho residents in long-distance relationships who are contemplating buying a minivan. (Facebook's ads manager says that description matches 3100 people.)" My kids will just have to keep sending me images of their kids by email. P.S. Do you really believe that there could be that many Idahoans in long distance relationships who are in the market for a minivan? (Koblin, J et al. My kids will just have to send keep sending me images of their kids by email. As viewers drift online, advertisers hold fast to broadcast TV. *The New York Times*. May 14, 2017.)

the company's database of two million customer genomes in search of clues for developing new lucrative drugs. Eighty-five percent of those customers have given 23andMe the right to use their data for research.[22]

How's this for bizarre and chilling? A group from the University of Washington has shown that is possible to insert a set of nucleotides into a strand of DNA that, when decoded, will translate into a malicious bit of software code that will disrupt the sequencer.[23]

Many people do opt-in to sharing their personal health information. CVS pharmacy has offered a $5 rebate for every 10 prescription refills if the customer waives HIPAA privacy rights. Walgreens has awarded discounts to customers via a smartphone application that syncs with health tracking devices.[24]

A poll of 3010 participants conducted by Truven Health Analytics-NPR in December 2014 found that 53% of respondents were willing to share their health information anonymously for the purpose of research. Millennials (born early 1980s to mid 1990s) were most likely to say "yes," at 61%, members of the Silent Generation (born 1925–1945) were least likely, at 43%. There was a small, not statistically significant trend toward sharing with increased education and no trend with respect to income.[25]

In the long run, attempts to preserve privacy will mostly be losing efforts. In 2000, Dr. Sweeney, mentioned above, demonstrated that 87% of Americans could be uniquely identified by just three pieces of information, their zip code, birthdate and sex.[26] In 2017, seven out of ten smartphone apps shared users' data with third party information services.[27]

It is possible to de-identify data to a desired level of privacy by doing things like: specifying an age range instead of a birthdate; not checking a box for sex; or giving a range of zip codes. There are protocols for doing so. However, with every step taken to unfocus the data, they become a bit fuzzier and perhaps a bit less useful to a public health worker or a researcher.[28]

Particularly in the medical realm, we need to protect privacy as much as possible. We do not want the parents of a pregnant teen learning of her condition because of an unencrypted message from her family doctor about her next prenatal visit. We also do not want them suspecting their daughter's delicate condition, as one shocked set of parents did in 2012, when she received by mail sent to their home, coupons for baby clothes and cribs. Data miners at Target had uncovered a purchasing pattern of women in early pregnancy that not only identified their condition, but could even predict their due date with some accuracy.[29]

Target and plenty of other retailers have done some backpedaling since that story broke. I'll bet, though, that their big data departments have only increased in size and power (and maybe in subtlety) since then. Businesses will just have to be smarter about how they use what they know about us. It will take people, not machines, to decide how these data are employed. As of now, only human beings *understand* the cultural conventions that surround privacy.

The whole notion around what ought to be private has long been in flux. Privacy standards started loosening way before the electronics revolution, as buttoned-up Victorian maidens of late nineteenth and early twentieth century gave way to the scantily-dressed flappers of the Roaring Twenties. Electronic media have accelerated the trend of bringing more personal information and body parts out in the open.

Millennials, who were born between the mid-1990s and mid-2000s, are the first generation to come of age with the cloud, where most data will eventually reside and where those data are potentially much more shareable. Not surprisingly, based on the savvy of these computer "natives," they are more concerned about protecting their online identity and privacy than the generations that precede them. These young folks are collaborative by nature, but they want to be able to control what they share, as well as with whom and when they share it.

Some say that privacy, including of personal health data, is becoming a thing of the past. Soon we will hardly have any, they contend. Cardiac pacemaker data have already been used in court to discredit an arsonist's alibi that he was asleep when the fire that burned down his home and killed his cat started. A dead woman's Fitbit data were used to establish the real time of her death, throwing her husband's alibi[30] into question.

China has developed a sort of credit score, similar to the FICO score we Americans have been labeled with since 1956. A few years ago, eight financial institutions were granted permission by the People's Bank of China to create a system that not only tracks how promptly you pay your bills, but how much energy you use and whether you belong to the Communist Party. All of this information already resided on large databases that are controlled by the government. People with higher scores get more perks. I imagine there will plenty of room in these scoring systems for health data points too, like smoking and exercise, paired with social engineering nudges of rewards and penalties. So far, the Chinese "Social Credit Score" system has been voluntary, with ample benefits for participating.[31]

In case there is still a shred of information about you that is not in the public domain, there is a movement afoot to donate all your medical data to medical science, just as you can your cadaver, in the hopes that the information will contribute to research that helps someone else.[32] There could be a whole lot of useful scientific information unlocked by unfettered access to every bit of medical data of people who have died, more than medical students and others ever get from unfettered access to actual bodies of dead people in the morgue or the gross anatomy lab. In either case, after all, what's left to feel embarrassed about?

Chapter 8

Electronic Health Record

EHRs are both microcosms and shapers of medical care.

—Sean W. Smith, computer scientist and Ross Koppel, sociologist

The EHR is not a direct reflection of the patient and physiology, but a reflection of the recording process inherent in healthcare with noise and feedback loops.

—George Hripcsak, MD and David Albers, PhD, informaticists[1]

"My hospital will be paperless at the same time as your bathroom is."

—Overheard at an American Medical Association meeting, 2003.

One weekend in the mid-1980s, I filled in at a medical practice in a town of under 2000 inhabitants. The doctors did something unheard of. They all left town at the same time. The hospital board and administration had scheduled a retreat to do long-range planning. For the few days I spent there, the whole shebang—office practice, inpatients, emergency room, nursing home and pregnant women—was mine.

It was fun because: I love rural practice and rural people; these were good doctors; and it was only for two days. Let me describe the private practice's outpatient records, which were kept on open shelves in a closet behind the reception desk. Information was hand-written on 5" × 8" lined index cards. At the top went the patient's name and birthdate. Visits were recorded sequentially. Most encounters took up one line. A typical encounter note might read:

2-18-86   Strep.   1.2m units Bicillin. $15—pd.

(That is $8 for the office visit and $7 for the injection, not the exact figures, but close enough to give you some idea of where inflation has taken the cost of medical care since then.) The cards were stowed in manila sleeves bearing the patient name, birthdate, address and phone number on the front. When the sleeve got full, a new one was started and filed on the shelf next to the bulging old one.

These doctors had practiced together forever. They knew well not only just about every patient they saw, but the children, parents, grandparents, aunts, uncles and cousins of these people, who were their neighbors. The doctors' home phone numbers were all in the phone book. Pagers had not yet reached the hinterland. Cell phones were science fiction. When a doctor went out for dinner or to the movie theater, he told the hospital where he could be reached. Unless he was out of town or on his deathbed, each physician always took calls from his own patients. If these guys were sued for malpractice at all, it was hardly ever.

The doctors obviously believed they did not need to have much patient information written down. They kept in their heads most of what they thought they needed to know about the people in their practice. As a person who had to pick up caring for these patients, I disagreed with this laissez faire attitude toward recordkeeping. And as a normal human being, I mistrusted that their memories could be *that* good.

I am still in touch with the inheritors of that practice. Though the population of their service area has not increased much in the last three decades, there are now twice as many providers in town. All of them are employed by the hospital. They have pagers, cell phones, unpublished personal phone numbers and an electronic health record that they struggle with, as well as a rotating on-call system. When I checked in with them a few years ago, some of the providers still handwrote at least some of their encounter notes, which were scanned into the electronic record, and also filed in the old paper chart system that was maintained in parallel with the electronic one. If I were to try to cover their practice single-handedly today, I expect I would be significantly better informed about the patients than I was when I took the reins 30 years ago. Though I might have to untangle some of the information that had been recorded by analog and/or digital means, there would have to be a whole lot more data than what those 5" × 8" index cards held.

One study has estimated that 29% of errors in family medicine practice are the result of faulty information handling.[2] In a 2003 survey of 32 Colorado primary care clinics, 253 clinicians were asked to record, immediately after each of 1614 patient encounters, whether there had been any information missing in the medical record that the clinician considered important in caring for the patient that day. Overall, 13.8% of records were judged to be without crucial data: 6.1% were laboratory test results, 5.4% letters or dictated encounter notes, 3.8% radiology reports, 3.7% history and physical reports and 3.2% a list of medications. Only 20% of the practices had full or partial EHRs. Those with electronic medical records were missing significantly less important data.[3]

Problem-Oriented Medical Record

Long before we were computerizing medical records, we were organizing them. In 1964, Dr. Larry Weed planted a seed that led to a revolution in medical informatics when he published an article in the *New Irish Journal of Medical Science* entitled "Medical Records, Medical Care and Patient Education." That was the first appearance in print of the concept of the problem-oriented medical record. In 1968, the *New England Journal of Medicine* picked up on Weed's ideas when they ran his article, "Medical records that guide and teach." And the revolution was underway.

The problem-oriented medical record (POMR) has at its center a problem list, one prominent place in the patient's chart that holds a continuously updated inventory of all the important issues that anybody providing medical care to a patient ought to keep in mind. An accurate problem list would have helped me enormously when I covered that rural practice. I would have killed for a good problem list. (A pessimist would wonder if I might have killed someone for lack of one.) That one page could have told me not to worry about appendicitis in a patient with belly pain if "Appendectomy" appeared on the list and reminded me to look for pancreatitis if "Alcoholism" was there. This is the permanent problem list.

Weed's record system also features a temporary problem list where acute, transitory afflictions like ear infection or a single elevated blood sugar are noted. Recurring or persisting problems can move from the temporary to the permanent list. "Acute otitis media" (middle ear infection) can become "Chronic otitis media." "Elevated blood sugar" can morph into "Diabetes mellitus."

Problems are revised to reflect new understanding as it unfolds. "Chronic otitis media" could be amended to reflect "Chronic otitis media with right tympanosotomy tube (which goes through the ear drum to ventilate and drain it)." Down the road, "Diabetes" might be listed as "Insulin-dependent, type II diabetes mellitus." Each of these one-line problem titles carries a big load of important information for the clinician. Applying a standard diagnostic code to every item is a giant step toward turning a medical record, even a paper-based one, into a searchable medical record system.

You can see the advantages of recording a problem list electronically. Diagnoses are easily updated. The system can also track when revisions were made and by whom, as well as interrogate and sort problem lists for the purposes of population management and quality improvement.

As Weed designed his POMR, all progress notes were to be keyed to items on the temporary or permanent problem list, even "Health Maintenance," which in some systems is the default Permanent Problem #1. There are lots of other standards and rules for maintaining a truly problem-oriented medical record. But the problem list, especially the permanent problem list, is the axis around which it all revolves.

Studies have shown that practices that maintain a higher-quality problem list tend to provide higher-quality care.[4] In olden days (1976), patients from practices with a problem list at the front of the chart were found to receive better follow-up for their medical problems.*,5

Every electronic health record purports to have a problem list. The list may not be very valuable if it is not being kept up to date by the clinicians who use it. Too often, what passes for a problem list is a chronological index of encounters and the diagnoses they generated, extracted directly from the codes that were used to bill for those services. A good deal of important information is liable to be missing from such a list.

A good measure of the usefulness of an EHR is how well it generates and maintains a permanent problem list. Once an important medical problem or significant procedure has been recorded, does it appear in a prominent place whenever a clinician opens a patient record? Is there a method for revising and updating the master list, rather than just tacking more stuff on at the end?

Everybody in a practice should keep an eye out for omissions and inaccuracies on the problem list of every patient they see. There must be an agreed-upon mechanism for revising the list. Generally, only clinicians should be able to make the changes. The problem list can provide a forum for valuable patient care discussions as well as a jumping off point for population management and quality improvement.

Financial and Human Costs of EHRs

In 2008, just 9% of hospitals and 17% of physicians used EHRs.[6] By 2016, 96% of hospitals and 78% of physicians had electronic health records certified under the auspices of the Health Information Technology for Economic and Clinical Health (HITECH) portion of the 2009 American Recovery and Reinvestment Act (ARRA). For each new system, computerization cost an estimated $163,765 per physician. As of 2015, it was estimated that Centers for Medicare and Medicaid Services had paid more than $30 billion in incentives to install EHR systems, amounting to about $65,000 per provider.[7] Sixty-four percent of skilled nursing facilities used EHRs in 2016.[8]

The overall cost to a practice to install, maintain and manage an EHR, came to $32,500 per physician per year in 2016.[9] EHRs may be a contributing factor to the rapid decline in independent private practices. The Medical Group Management

---

* There is room here, of course, to argue cause and effect. It is an open question whether physicians who are more conscientious about maintaining good medical records are, in general, more conscientious in the care they provide.

A study published in 2013 appears to contradict the correlation that I suggested between quality of documentation and quality of care. A review of 239 doctors' clinic notes of encounters with patients who had diabetes or coronary artery disease, at no less than the exalted Brigham and Women's Hospital, a part of the Harvard medical Mecca, found lots of documentation missing in lots of notes, as well as about 10% of content copied and pasted. There was no correlation from chart to chart nor from doctor to doctor between how well the care actually given met quality standards and how well the note documented the encounter.

Association estimated in 2017 that privately owned practices spent on IT, above EHR outfitting expenses, between $14,000 and $19,000 per full-time physician per year, depending on specialty. Hospitals forked out $5,400–$8,200 less to purchase the same services for the physicians[10] they employed.

It's not like things are so great for hospitals either. Moody's Investors Service said in 2017 that a hospital system could expect a 10% decline in operating cash and a 6% falloff in days' cash on hand in the year following installing a new EHR system.[11]

In 2013, the magazine, *Medical Economics*, reported on a survey of nearly 1000 physicians about their practice's EHR. Here's what they learned: 73% of practices would not purchase their current EHR system again; 67% did not like their system's functionality; 65% felt they had lost money on the deal; nearly 50% thought the system had cost too much; 45% felt patient care had suffered and 38% doubted that their current system would be viable in five years.[12] Only 31% thought that the EHR had helped them to coordinate care with hospitals.

In 2014, a majority of surveyed providers responded to a query by the AmericanEHR Partners and the American Medical Association that they were very dissatisfied with their medical record systems.[13]

2015 was the first year in which practices' purchasing replacement EHRs exceeded first-time buyers. Twenty-five percent of them cited "clumsiness/faulty" as the primary reason for changing horses. Billing was still the top-requested application.[14]

In 2016, Black Book Market Research found that 87% of financially threatened hospitals that had replaced their systems in the previous several years regretted having made that decision. Sixty-two percent of non-managerial IT staff felt the change had negatively affected patient care, including 90% of nurses, 95% of whom reported they had had no input into EHR replacement activities. On the one hand, only 5% of hospital leaders assessed that the replacement process had an unfavorable effect on patient care. On the other hand, 66% of the people who actually used the new systems said that patient data exchange functionality had *declined* since the install.[15]

It could be worse. In 2013, it was estimated that the British National Health Service had wasted 10.1 billion pounds ($15.5 billion) on a national EHR system that didn't work.[16]

A study of internal medicine interns in two training programs in Baltimore that was conducted in 2012 reported that the doctors spent 12% of their work hours with patients and 40% in front of computer screens.[17] A 2016 time and motion study of 57 US physicians in 4 specialties, funded by the American Medical Association, reported that for every hour physicians spent caring for patients face-to-face they spent 2 hours doing desk work while in clinic plus an additional 1–2 hours at home on clerical work.[18]

Though a good share of work time is now spent with keyboard and mouse, rather than with pen and paper, it is still called "paperwork," and still pronounced with the same disdain. When I was in practice, I used to say that I had a plan to handle accumulated paperwork based on a leaf blower. Today that plan would employ a large glass of water, to be emptied into a strategic piece or two of electronic hardware.

A survey of Rhode Island physicians performed in 2014 came to the interesting conclusion, reported in an article with the wonderful title, "It is like texting at the dinner table," that physicians who practiced in the hospital and those who practiced in outpatient clinics were about equally unhappy with their EHRs (i.e. plenty unhappy). The hospital-based doctors' number one complaint was that the EHR took them away from the bedside. Office-based doctors were most unhappy in their perception that the record decreased the quality of their interactions with patients.[19]

A survey of Veterans Administration physicians reported in 2014 that frustration with EHR-based clinical alerting systems strongly correlated with doctors' intentions to quit and find another job.[20] A report that appeared in *Mayo Clinic Proceedings* in 2016 found, among the 6375 physicians studied, a strong correlation between computerized physician order entry use and dissatisfaction with amount of time devoted to clerical tasks as well as the risk of physician burnout.[21] In 2015, researchers reported that 54% of physicians experienced some sign of burnout, up from 46% just two years prior.[22] Unhappiness with the busywork engendered by widespread adoption of EHRs was cited as a main cause.

A central goal for the government's huge expensive push for EHR adoption is the opportunity that electronic data provide to monitor, address and report quality in healthcare. A poll performed by the Medical Group Management Association in 2017 found that 31% of medical practices with EHRs said they used all of their record's analytic capabilities. The rest fell somewhere between "some and none."[23]

An article in *Health Affairs* reported that, as of 2015, that there were at least 159 publicly available measures of outpatient physician care and that physicians spent 2.6 hours per week and staff 12.5 hours attending to required quality reporting to multiple agencies and insurance companies. This translates to a cost of $15.4 billion, $40,000 per physician per year. The authors detail that insurers and government massage clinical and billing data in order to assess practices against over 500 insurer-supplied quality measures and 1700 government ones. The measures themselves are far from consistent with each other.[24]

Worse yet, all this extra paper/computer work may be for naught. The medical literature has shown that pay-for-performance programs, which depend to such a large extent on EHRs in outpatient settings, may result in a handful of improvements in narrowly-defined care processes (such as, at least for a while, more diabetic patients getting foot exams) but that the truly desired outcome (in this case, reducing limb amputations) has hardly ever been demonstrated.[25]

Healthcare worker discontent has provided the impetus to morph the Triple Aim—improving the patient experience of care (including quality and satisfaction);

improving the health of populations; and reducing the per capita cost of health care—into the Quadruple Aim, which is the Triple Aim plus the goal of improving the work life of clinicians and staff.[26]

In 2015, the American Medical Informatics Association suggested these priorities for EHR development over the next five years:

- Simplify and speed documentation
- Refocus regulation
- Increase transparency and streamline certification
- Foster innovation
- Support person-centered care delivery

I would like to see bullet points four and five above moved to numbers two and one, respectively. The primary goal of an EHR ought not to be to improve documentation or even to reduce errors. It should be to facilitate work processes and systems that enhance care of the individual and health of the population.

A rule of thumb for installing a new outpatient EHR is to decrease the patient load for each provider by at least 50% and have lots of technical help immediately available for at least a month. No matter how much training everyone has received before the go-live day (referred to by some as the "drop-dead" day) and how user-friendly the new system is purported to be, expect loads of chaos, frustration and anger and that, eventually, hopefully, things will settle down.*

If a practice is lucky, it will experience only a 20–30% reduction long-term in the maximum number of patients that its providers can see in a given time period. However, if the EHR product chosen helps to document better-paying encounter codes (see Chapter 6, "Economics"), there may still be a gain in overall productivity (number of patient encounters times average charge per encounter). One pediatric primary care network, consisting of 260 providers in 42 practices, found that, between 2008 and 2013, their EHR resulted in an $11.09 increase in average per-visit charges and an $11.49 increase in collections.[27]

At a most basic level, the problem with the EHR is that it is rooted in hardcopy thinking. It is primarily data-oriented, a repository for recording and recalling information, still modeled on the paper patient charts that were divided into sections that held notes, lab results, radiology results, old records, orders, medications, etc.

I can only imagine what an electronic medical record system would look like if it were truly designed around assisting caregivers to do their job. It would have explicit representations of workflow, patient state, temporal progression and other concepts crucial for doing clinical care, the sorts of integrative functions that human professionals still have to depend too much on our unaided brains to accomplish.

---

* Which reminds me of the one of the fundamental principles of general surgery as taught to me by a resident when I was a medical student. "All bleeding stops. Eventually."

We need tools that combine and display disparate data as they change over time to help us think outside the examination or hospital room to which we've confined ourselves for so long.[28]

Even shuffling the order in which information is presented can help. Just shifting the traditional problem-oriented SOAP (subjective, objective, assessment, plan) note to an APSO (assessment, plan, subjective, objective) format, with collapsible categories that allow the clinician to dig deeper only if she wants to, can make a big difference in the usability of and satisfaction with the record.[29]

Poor usability is the biggest complaint of today's EHR users. How many screens, how many drop-down menus, how many clicks does it take to look up or to record something about a patient? A study entitled "4000 Clicks," reported in the *American Journal of Emergency Medicine* in 2013, that emergency room resident physicians clicked a mouse on average 4000 times in the course of a 10-hour shift.[30] At one second per click, that comes out to over an hour per shift. Clicking is not why I, nor anybody else I know, went to medical school.

Add on top of that the observation in a 2017 study that emergency physicians at three large urban emergency departments were interrupted by people an average of 12.5 times per hour, most often while working at a computer, and you get some idea of just how difficult it can be for a clinician to maintain a coherent train of thought, let alone have a satisfying human interaction.[31]

Following are a few more than half of the quotations from an article that ran in *Becker's Hospital Review* in 2015, entitled "25 quotes that show just how fed up physicians are with EHRs."

- Imagine, in a world where a 2-year-old can operate an iPhone, you have graduate-educated physicians brought to their knees by electronic medical records.
- Too often I pull up a record…and it's almost impossible to really get an understanding of the story line.
- We do not select the electronic record or pay for it, the hospital does. But we pay for it in other ways: lost productivity, workflow interruptions, usability frustrations. That is our investment, and we deserve a return on that investment.
- Most of our consultants or people we communicate with have their own EHR systems, and unfortunately the way we get their reports is they fax them. We then print them and scan them, so they're not searchable.
- The patients definitely sense that we're a lot more stressed now. We're spending three hours per day—and that's no exaggeration—just trying to get caught up.
- It's very easy to record large amounts of data and click-off boxes. So the emphasis is really on data collection, but what physicians ought to be doing is data synthesis.

- ...this is an impediment of access to safe, quality patient care...Most systems today are not [designed around clinical care]. They are set up to comply with the federal regulations and with policymakers...[who]...spend all of our time and effort on documentation as opposed to the key issue of medical decision-making.
- Our PA quit because she typed with two fingers...For me to review one note of hers, it was 38 clicks.
- I noticed that my patients noticed that I was trying to talk to them and enter their history and put orders in as I was going—I could tell they felt I was very detached and more focused on this....I just knew it wasn't the right thing. I personally had to hire a scribe, but that's now at a cost of $25,000 and $30,000 out of my pocket.
- When I'm in the ICU...I could write a bunch of orders saying 'If this, do this, if this, do this'—you can't do that....There are so many orders you can't [write]. It only leads to harm for patient care, more medical errors, not less.
- I just think that giving up 10 hours of my time a week [to navigating the EHR] is significant.
- I can tell you that over the last three months, since EHR implementation, my clinical productivity—my ability to take care of patients—has dropped by about a third. People's health is endangered.
- The designers of the EHR software seem to labor under the delusion that to have more data is equivalent to having more useful and actionable information. For instance, the first data field I see should be the patient's chief complaint, not how they arrived or whether or not they have a primary doctor.
- [Time spent on documentation] has resulted in a choice I must make between direct care for sick, needy, dying, suffering patients, and the need to satisfy the many EHR requirements to complete the visit.[32]

And if you think doctors are unhappy about the EHRs they use, just ask nurses. In Black Book's Q3 2014 EHR Loyalty survey of 14,000 registered nurses working in hospitals in 40 states, 90% attested that their current EHR had not improved communication among members of the care team and 94% did not believe it improved nurse-patient communication. Only 26% said they believed that the EHR had improved the quality of patient information.[33]

Usability is a whole field unto its own. Healthcare could learn a lot from the aviation industry about human factors in system design, where they have nearly a century-long lead in addressing quality and safety-related matters. There are strong parallels between the aviation and healthcare, with high levels of expertise needed for professional decision-making, customer safety risks, high use of technology, strong professional culture and plenty of regulatory oversight.

When it comes to safety, separate competing aviation businesses have still been able, by mandate of the Federal Aviation Commission, to agree on a host of industry-wide standards for things like graphical design of human-computer interfaces, quality management in software design, evaluation methods to measure system usability and standardized investigative procedures for adverse events.

Three-quarters of aircraft crashes are caused by flawed communication, which means that someone knew something that, had it gotten through to the person who could have acted on it, would have averted the disaster. The aircraft industry has put its intelligence and resources into developing a culture that promotes good information flow, as well as the technology to support it. Healthcare is just getting around to these all-important tasks, with little evidence yet of collaboration among the competition-obsessed players.[34]

The Healthcare Information and Management and Systems Society (HIMSS) defines usability with these nine attributes: simplicity, naturalness, consistency, forgiveness and feedback, effective use of language, efficient transactions, effective information presentation, preservation of context and minimization of cognitive load. A simpler and more intuitive (sort of circular) definition by Zhang and Walji refers to how useful, usable and satisfying a system is for users to accomplish their goals.[35]

The steep learning curve that even today's best electronic health records present to a clinician is less vertical for "digital natives." If digital technology has always been a part of your life, electronic devices make a sort of visceral sense to you in the same way that operating vehicles with manual transmissions did to our foremothers. Though there is not an exact cutoff birth year that distinguishes digital natives from digital immigrants, I imagine a hazy boundary lies somewhere in the 1990s. A poll of internal medicine residents, mostly millennials, found in 2015 that texting was their preferred method for in-hospital communication because of its efficiency and ease of use.[36] Digital natives or not, in 2016 it was estimated that resident physicians-in-training spent 25–60% of their work time doing documentation.[37]

In the course of teaching health science students in my practice, I learned that, among the many enrichments that hosting a student brings to a practice, is the knowhow of a digital native. Within a couple of weeks of using our EHR, many of these students were able to teach my digital immigrant partners and me shortcuts that we had not figured out in the course of several years' experience with the system.

There are diverse reasons why electronic health records receive mostly horrible grades for usability. Here are some of the barriers to designing and selling an easy-to-use EHR.

■ Clinical practice is about as complex an endeavor as there is. Designing and manufacturing a 7.2 billion transistor computer chip (the record as of 2016 for a commercially available unit) is certainly exceedingly complex.[38] But it's just about fabricating things with silicon and a few other elements, employing principles of physics and chemistry. Biological systems, especially human beings, are orders-of-magnitude more complex, with enormous variability among individuals on top of that.

■ Many EHRs started out as additions to well-established business systems, which had been optimized to meet the needs of the people who deal with money, operations and such. Sifting priorities in the direction of clinical information presents enormous challenges, both technical and cultural.

■ In general, the technical people who design systems get a large share of their instructions from the business people who make purchase decisions, not from clinicians. Too often healthcare management practice gives little more than lip service to bringing front-line clinicians in on technology and process development. Involving providers in anything but seeing patients (and thereby generating revenue) costs money in the short run, especially if you have to pay clinicians for their time. Though there are not studies to prove it, I have no doubt that reimbursing clinician time upfront will generally show a nice return on investment for new provider information technology, measured in efficiency and effectiveness of care, as well as in dollars.

■ Techies and clinicians don't speak the same language. They need to learn to talk to each other and collaborate. Such a cultural shift did happen in the wake of the 1962 Kefauver-Harris Amendments to the Federal Food, Drug, and Cosmetic Act, which mandated solid statistical scientific evidence of effectiveness prior to new drug approval. As a result, pharmaceutical houses were more than happy to pay whatever it took for biostatisticians and clinicians to learn to speak each other's language. They have been collaborating ever since.[39] This is a great example of aligned incentives.

■ Health care data are encoded in multiple different formats. There are simple systems of measurement that generate a single number, like blood sugar or pain scales from one to ten; checklists of symptoms and signs that may or may not refer to a shared standardized vocabulary; images; and narrative notes and reports entered as free-form text.

■ Though there have been notable efforts to create standardized ontologies, taxonomies and vocabularies for use in EHRs, so that a datum means the same thing from platform to platform, we are nowhere near to arriving at the uniformity that would make one system feel familiar if you have learned a different one.

■ Making an EHR system easy to modify has not been a high priority. There is enormous variability in how medicine is practiced, which means there is a great need for customization.* However, revisions drive the higher maintenance costs that come with loss of standardization. The manufacturer loses some control over its product as well. After all is said and done, a record system that cannot adjust gracefully to enough local needs will rapidly become an impediment to efficiency and effectiveness, a square peg that requires clinicians and staff to waste too much of their time on whittling instead of caring for patients.†

■ The Meaningful Use Program incentivized vendors to push too many half-baked, vaporware-filled products to the market and purchasers to buy them.

The American Medical Association issued in 2014 an eight-point framework for improving usability:

■ Enhance physicians' ability to provide high-quality patient care
■ Support team-based care
■ Promote care coordination

---

* The QI literature is rife with discussions on the desirability of reducing process variability, a laudable goal for some issues. But trying to standardize too much of medical practice makes no more sense than attempting to make all classroom teaching look alike, no matter the region, student socioeconomic status, teacher talents, local issues, native languages, etc. Understanding where it does make sense to consistently measure certain outcomes and to develop standardized ways to address these goals in pursuit of reducing process variability, lies at the heart of managing both education and healthcare well. Values and understanding, not technology, are the crux issues. In my opinion, we have way overshot the mark in our efforts to standardize both education and healthcare, thereby alienating a large segment of students, parents, teachers, patients and health care professionals. In education, high stakes testing has led us away from the art of teaching. In healthcare, the EHR has disempowered frontline professionals. Fortunately, both fields are fixable with a salutary change of attitude and understanding.

† As of July 2014, the contract with Cerner for using the web portal of their EMR contained this amazing language. "[Users are not to submit unsolicited ideas] including ideas for new advertising campaigns, new promotions, new or improved solutions, products or technologies, solution or product enhancements, processes, marketing plans or new solution or product names. Please do not submit any unsolicited ideas, samples, demos or other works." The contract goes on to say that if you foolishly ignore this warning and dare to make a suggestion to the company anyway, "Then regardless of what message accompanies the submission, the following terms shall apply to your submissions. You agree that: (1) your submissions and their contents will automatically become both the legal and the equitable property of Cerner, without any compensation to you; (2) Cerner may use or redistribute submissions and their contents for any purpose and in any way without limitation; (3) there is no obligation for Cerner to review the submission; (4) there is no obligation to keep any submissions confidential; and (5) you hereby agree to waive absolutely any and all moral rights arising from your submissions and their contents so far as is lawfully possible and any broadly equivalent rights you may have in respect of your submission and their contents in any territory of the world." I have two questions: (1) Does this sound like a partnership? (2) What the hell are *moral rights*? (Hirsch, MD. 5 unique EHR contract stipulations. FierceEHR [online]. July 17, 2014.)

- Offer product modularity and configurability
- Reduce cognitive workload
- Promote data liquidity [connectivity]
- Facilitate digital and mobile patient engagement
- Expedite user input into product design and post-implementation feedback

This is a good place to start organizing your thoughts when choosing an EHR.

There is not a global answer about what to do about usability. Less usable EHRs will lose market share and change or die. My suggestions are organized below under the rubrics selecting a system, contracting, installing and ongoing management. Notice that involving the staff is central to every one of these categories.

Selecting a System

- Involve clinical and business staff in the selection process from the outset.
- Find or develop a clinical champion, hopefully a leader. Everybody knows who the leaders are. They are not necessarily the people with professional credentials or titles.
- At a minimum, a few critical clinical data elements—problem list, medication list, encounters, allergies, immunizations and other health maintenance information etc.—must be easy to access and to keep up-to-date.
- Assure that the system you choose "talks" to the medical information systems of your main collaborators: medical practices, hospitals, etc. Better yet, see that the developers are actively growing their system to embrace the CommonWell Health Alliance standards for medical data exchange (or whatever set of standards is at the forefront at the time). (See Chapter 3, "Technology.")
- Data from clinical laboratories should automatically populate the appropriate places in the record. This may revolve around choice of clinical laboratory as much as choice of EHR. The greater the range of different types of reports that go automatically into the right electronic buckets, the better.
- See how the record connects up with a patient portal. These messages are a crucial part of a comprehensive medical record and an important pathway to patient engagement. (See Chapter 14, "The Connected World of Patients.")
- Do not choose a record that makes room for sponsored ads, curated drop-down menus or electronic coupons. Period.

Contracting with Vendors

- Be skeptical of vendor promises.
- Check bona fides. Interview references in depth, including managers, staff and providers. Arrange to visit sites that have experience with the system. Bring along clinical staff, clinicians and business staff. Don't invite the vendor.
- If you are seriously considering a system, get as much hands-on experience as you can with the demo, for as many prospective users as you can before you pull the trigger.
- If your organization does not have the expertise in-house, pay whatever you need to for the help of a really good consultant. Likewise, for a specialist attorney to review the contract.
- Assure that the product has all the standard certifications that the government currently requires of EHRs, as well as plans for meeting those regulations that you (or your consultant) know will be coming down the pike.
- The contract must explicitly detail the level of training support for installation and all updates to the system. Make it as generous as you can.
- Take a hard look at maintenance costs when calculating overall cost of the system.
- Be very clear, in the negotiations and in the contract, about the process for modifying the system. The ability to customize—such as choosing, authoring and setting sensitivity for reminders—is especially important. Based on their ability to generate prompts, the most consistent practice improvements attributable to computerizing the medical record lie in the realm of preventive health.

Installing a System

- The practice should document information and patient flows before EHR installation and then lead the practice through re-designing these processes in order to take advantage of the efficiencies that automation can afford. Sometimes the vendor can facilitate the practice analysis. If not, pay another expert to do it. It is well worth the investment.
- Begin as soon as possible transferring data from the old record to the new one. If this is your first EHR, brace yourself for scanning a whole lot of paper. Use people who know enough to label and file scanned documents in the appropriate places. Irretrievable data are useless.
- Delay the bulk of clinician training until just before go-live. Unless reinforced continuously, lessons learned too far in advance of being put into practice are quickly forgotten.
- Pay very close attention to support. Never underestimate how much support a new installation will take. For the first month at a minimum, there should

be enough trainers on-site to help everybody who needs it within five minutes or less.

■ Halve the rate at which patients are scheduled for at least a month after go-live. Gradually increase that rate as clinicians' comfort with the system grows.

Managing a System

■ For a while after go-live, hold frequent, convenient meetings with clinicians and staff. Manage griping by responding to concerns, expressing empathy, setting ground rules and employing every strategy you can think of to keep meetings constructive.

■ Figure out who your super-users are and get them together regularly to solve problems and formulate requests of the vendor. This group should include clinicians, clinical and business staff. Use them as two-way conduits to the rest of the staff, both collecting and disseminating information about the system. Figure out a way to recognize and reward super users.

■ Stay in close touch with the vendor. Nurture that relationship.

Using the System with Patients

Let's say your practice has an EHR that all of the clinicians are using fairly efficiently. Even the biggest naysayers will admit that being able to access a large chunk of their patients' data from wherever they are—office, hospital, nursing home, their own home and (hopefully not too much) on vacation—is a benefit. For many clinicians, that is where the perceived benefit of an EHR ends. The rest may be seen as: too many screens to navigate; clicks to click; pop-up reminders to address or not; and just too much busywork.*

Inroads into usability, as well as the gradual ascendency of digital natives in the healthcare workforce, will eventually make using most electronic health records just a routine, efficient part of taking care of patients.† I would be a fool to hazard a guess when this will happen. In the absence of some unforeseen killer app, I expect widespread comfort with using EHRs will just creep up on us.

Proceeding one step up the ladder of health informatics, from managing the acute pain that comes with radical change to actually doing a better job of caring

---

* In an article published in 2011, I found reference to clinicians who would misspell diagnoses, such as "diabeetes" on medical problem lists, so as to keep their system from picking up that fact and bombarding them with unwanted reminders about caring for a patient with diabetes. (Wright, A, Maloney, FL, Feblowitz, JC. Clinician attitudes toward and use of electronic problem lists: A thematic analysis. *BMC*, 2011:11(36), 1–10.)

† The great quantum physicist, Max Planck, said, "Science advances one funeral at a time." I would hope we could do better than that with advancing the EHR.

for patients, the first issue that pops up is: How does having a computer in the room affect the patient-provider relationship? By now, virtually everybody has had the unpleasant experience of being with a clinician who appears to pay more attention to the computer monitor than to you, not unlike conversing with a person who glances at her cellphone every time it's your turn to talk.

Before I go much further into how to manage the barrier that a computer may interpose between doctor and patient, let me say something that, unfortunately, too many of you already know from experience. Doctors generally are not good listeners. (I limit this discussion to doctors because, thanks to the damage done by our abusive training, paired with our elevated social status, when it comes to listening, physicians are more challenged than almost everybody else in healthcare. In fact, we are more challenged than almost everybody else, period, except maybe for rock stars, many of whom have the added impediment to communication of hearing loss.)

In a famous study that appeared in the *Annals of Internal Medicine* in 1984, in which the researchers reviewed video recordings of 73 office visits to a general internal medicine practice, the patient was able to complete her opening statement of concerns only 23% of the time before being interrupted by the doctor. The complete answer from 41% of that 23% took a little under 5 seconds because it was to state that there were no concerns.[40] Since those data were collected in 1984, the corporatization of healthcare has led to doctors feeling increased pressure and distraction, causing strain on the doctor-patient dyad. I doubt that, were that study to be repeated today, the average patient would get many more seconds before being interrupted by the doctor.

In a study reported in *JAMA Internal Medicine* in 2016, researchers asked patients to rate the care they had just received at an office visit. Forty-eight percent of doctors who were observed to devote a lot of their attention to the computer were judged to have delivered excellent care, compared to the eighty-three percent excellent ratings awarded to doctors who had paid less attention to the computer and more to the patient.[41]

Communication experts will tell you that a person's attention is generally where her eyes are. Looking into another's eyes is a sign of listening deeply. Deep listening is one of the simplest, most powerful and subtle healing skills. Needless to say, the distraction of a desktop computer, tablet or phone screen makes deep listening that much more challenging.*

---

* Speaking of distraction, here's an interesting little tidbit from the medical literature. A research team at the University of Florida analyzed for 15 days the anonymous network utilization records of 68 workstations located in the emergency department of a large academic medical center. They found that all together 72.5 staff hours had been spent making 9369 visits to Facebook. The higher the patient volume and the sicker the patients in the ED, the more time spent on Facebook. Go figure! (Black, E et al. Online social network use by health care providers in a high traffic patient care environment. *Journal of Medical Internet Research*, 2013:15(5), 1–9.)

Eye contact is not absolutely crucial to good verbal communication, however. Watch a couple of male buddies sitting on the front porch and talking about work, cars, sports, women, marriage, children, most anything. Chances are, they are perched next to each other, both looking out onto the front yard and the street, not gazing into each other's eyes. Parallel gaze can work, even for intimate conversation.

Now imagine that, instead of sitting on the porch, you are in an exam room. Place between clinician and patient a large enough monitor for both to see without straining as they converse. Make what is on the screen a topic for discussion too. Above all, have the participants pay attention to each other. Presto. You have a dialog with visuals.

One of the first times I saw an EHR used this way I was shadowing a pediatrician who used a system that our organization was considering buying. The patient was a small boy with a worried mother. Mom was concerned that her son wasn't eating well. There were no other symptoms. The history suggested no reason to be concerned about underlying illness. The physical examination was wholly normal. With a few clicks of the button, the doctor brought up a display of the boy's growth chart. The child's height and weight trajectories had tracked near the 90th percentile, from birth to present. The doctor said to the mom, "Sheldon [name changed to protect the innocent] wouldn't be growing so well if he were undernourished. In general, children know better than their parents what they need to eat. Their bodies tell them. Here's the proof."

I believe the mother left the doctor's office that day, with a printed copy of her son's growth chart in hand, more convinced than words alone could have accomplished, that her boy was eating just fine. At each office visit, every one of those lengths and weights had been added automatically to the growth chart for a Caucasian boy the moment the medical assistant had recorded them. In all of my practices, medical assistants were expected to enter these data. However, if keeping up growth charts was a manual process, they were often not up-to-date, no matter how many times I reminded the staff.*

A computer in the room adds potential modes of audio and visual communication between clinician and patient. It can be as simple as that child's growth curve. As electronic media push us away from the written word and toward other modes of communication, the multimedia capabilities inherent in the EHR will become ever more powerful. Just reviewing a radiology image with a patient can add understanding and engagement to her care. Digital natives will have a lot to teach us non-natives about how to use these tools to beef up our communication.

---

* One thing that did work was to keep track of growth chart completeness on every child I saw and feed the numbers back to the medical assistant monthly. There was no need to institute any sort of penalty or reward for doing her job. All she needed to notably improve her performance was to see, concretely, how she was doing.

Principle number one of using an EHR with a patient present is to position the monitor where both patient and provider can see it. This may take some rearranging of the office, maybe even tearing out built-in cabinets to make enough room. It is worth it, including for the provider. Many clinicians I have known have suffered neck, back and shoulder problems from constantly torquing their head, trying to do justice to seeing both the patient and the computer screen. Placing patient and provider next to each other, with the monitor in front of both of them, solves that problem.

The University of Chicago and Kaiser Permanente have codified their staff training on how to use an EHR in the presence of a patient. I cannot do better than to present the chart itself.

HUMAN LEVEL mnemonic: Ten tips to enhance patient-centered electronic health record (EHR) use.		
H	Honor the 'Golden Minute'	Make the start of the visit completely technology free. Greet the patient, start with their concerns, and establish an agenda for the visit before engaging technology.
U	Use the 'Triangle of Trust'	Create a triangle configuration that puts you, the patient, and the computer screen at each of the three corners. This allows you to look at both the patient and screen without shifting your body.
M	Maximize patient interaction	Encourage patient interaction with EHR. Pause for questions and clarification. Allow time for questions and to verify understanding.
A	Acquaint yourself with the chart	Review the chart before you enter the room to inform and contextualize your visit.
N	Nix the screen	When discussing sensitive information, completely disengage from the EHR (look at the patient, turn away from screen, take hands off keyboard, etc.)
L	Let the patient look on	Share things on the screen with your patients.
E	Eye contact	Maintain eye contact with patients as much as possible. Treat patient encounters as you would a conversation with friends or family members.
V	Value the computer	Praise the benefits of the EHR and take advantage of opportunities to use technology as a tool to engage patients (pull up lab result to review together, utilize graphics, etc.).

(Continued)

HUMAN LEVEL mnemonic: Ten tips to enhance patient-centered electronic health record (EHR) use. (*Continued*)		
E	Explain what you're doing	Be transparent about everything you do. Avoid long silences and aim for conversational EHR use by explaining what you are doing as you are doing it.
L	Log off	At the end of the visit, log off of the patient's chart while they are still in the exam room. This assures patients that their medical information is secure.
Source: Alkureishi, MD and Lewis, D. Incorporating the human touch: Piloting a curriculum for patient-centered electronic health record use. Medical Education Online. November 5, 2017. Used with permission of Elsevier Publishing, Amsterdam.		

The crucial skill to acquire for a clinician who strives to be effective in a room with both a computer and a patient is to know when to adopt a data-seeking and recording mode on the one hand, when to operate in an interpersonal mode on the other, and how to transition smoothly between the two modes.

Some fast-paced practices, particularly in emergency rooms, employ scribes, people who follow clinicians into patient encounters and fill in templates as the patient answers the provider's questions, as well as transcribing what the clinician calls out about she is seeing, hearing, thinking and ordering. In December 2015, it was reported that nearly one in five physicians used a medical scribe. There were about 15,000 scribes working in the US at that time. It was estimated that their numbers would swell to 100,000 by 2020. (Given the rapid progress of AI-driven voice transcription [see Chapter 3, "Technology"], the latter number may turn out to be way too big.)

In some places, the minimum education for a scribe is a high school diploma or GED plus some on-the-job training. Scribes are not very expensive. "Virtual scribes," who do the documentation after the fact, based on an audio recording of the encounter, are even cheaper. There are a few studies that show physicians' job satisfaction is generally improved when they take on a scribe. On the other hand, there is barely any literature that assesses the accuracy and comprehensiveness of documentation performed by scribes, in-the-flesh or virtual. Lack of licensing and standards could be a problem.[42] So could adding another dimension of malpractice exposure for the physician who entrusts patient care documentation to a non-professional. Sometime before signing off the record of an encounter documented by a scribe, the clinician must review the information, edit it and add her own comments.

Scribes can save clinicians a lot of valuable time; some claim an hour or two a day. On the downside, in-person scribes inject another person into the intimate patient-provider relationship, which can present a barrier to airing uncomfortable or embarrassing aspects of a patient's story.

Another solution to the problem of divided attention is to not use the computer while with the patient. In my own pre-computer practice, while with a patient I might jot a few notes on a piece of paper to jog my memory when I did my dictation, either right after the visit or at the end of the day.

There are several drawbacks to not doing documentation in real time. Short-term memory decays rapidly. The longer the delay between obtaining and recording information, the more room for error. One of the few things that even some anti-EHR clinicians say they like about their systems is that, if they create a record simultaneously with encounters, they do not have that hanging over them after a day in clinic. It was not unusual for me to spend an hour or more dictating notes at the end of a busy day in the office.

Along with the usual behaviors that actors playing patients help teach to healthcare students—things like the greeting, comfort level, listening, eye contact, respectfulness—is to reflect how the student uses the information device in the course of an interview and exam. Was there adequate eye contact? Did the patient still feel like the center of attention?[43]

In the name of engaging patients in their own care, providers are encouraged to share records with them, even to consider the record as belonging to the patient, not the healthcare institution. (See Chapter 14, "The Connected World of Patients," for a full discussion of open medical records.) One step in this direction is to write visit notes in patients' presence and review with them what you have written.

Changing Roles

Having up-to-date, reliable patient information at the fingertips of everybody who needs it paves the way for a big cultural shift in how things get done. If allowed, and better still, encouraged, collaboration can replace some of the isolation, stress and burnout that come from the individualistic model of medical practice we have lived with for centuries. Pyramids get flattened as people on the fatter parts nearer the base gain access to the same data and information that people have nearer the apex.

With immunization records and protocols embedded in the electronic health record, a medical assistant (MA) can assure that every patient who needs one gets a pneumonia shot, so can the well-prompted patient herself. Care managers can refer diabetics to an eye doctor for their annual retinal exam without having to go through one of the practice's doctors. (Even better, if the practice has a retinal camera and the appropriate contract with a consulting ophthalmology outfit, the MA can take pictures of the patient's retinas, forward them to the eye doctor, get a report back, record it, inform the patient if she needs further follow-up with an eye specialist, and make an appointment without the provider ever being involved. [See Chapter 10, "Telehealth."])

Putting more information in workers' hands has the potential, if their work is designed and managed well, to: empower them to do a much more effective and efficient job that is commensurate with their abilities; please patients; free those "higher" on the pyramid to do what they do best; and make for an altogether happier workforce. It takes humans, of course, to engage and manage employees toward these goals. Information may be necessary, but it is far from sufficient for good patient care.

Quality of Care

Electronic health records are meant (as, theoretically, every advancement in medical technology is meant) to improve patient care and, ultimately, patients' health. It is no surprise that early adopters of EHRs among medical practices have also been early adopters of patient centered medical homes and of alternative payment models, like accountable care organizations.[44]

It does not require a sophisticated quality improvement (QI) program to take advantage of the power to search data that have been recorded electronically. For example, if a certain drug has been recalled, an electronic medical record system ought to be able automatically to spit out a list of everybody in the practice on whose medical record the drug appears; send them a message by email and/or snail mail; and provide a checklist, with emails and phone numbers, for contacting patients from whom you have not heard back.

A first step a medical practice needs to take if it wants to develop a quality improvement program for its patients with chronic obstructive pulmonary disease (emphysema and others), for example, is to make a registry of all patients with one of these diagnoses. This low-hanging fruit should be found dangling from just about any EHR, and even from any billing system, which will have recorded diagnosis codes for every patient encounter.

Sometimes QI efforts based on EHR data do make things better. And sometimes they don't. Even if a QI project does not pan out, it may turn out to have been worth doing anyway, if for no other reason than to cultivate the attitudes and learn the skills—problem selection and formulation; teamwork; data acquisition and analysis; process re-engineering; outcome analysis, etc.—that can be applied to future efforts that really do make a difference.

Above and beyond individual skills, quality assurance is a culture that makes it every employee's job to observe critically, think creatively and act collaboratively in pursuit of better outcomes for an organization and its clients. Poorly conceived QI efforts, or good ones that lack the information infrastructure to make them doable, can move an organizational culture in the opposite direction by creating doubt about the value of the whole process. Just because you have a cool electronic health record, scads of data and the money people whispering to you about MACRA incentives (see "Medicare Access & CHIP Reauthorization Act" in the Glossary), do not embark on a QI program unless you have the vision and commitment to really go after it.

Several factors appear to go into whether a quality improvement effort helps to move the dial on a particular health problem:

- Choosing a well-defined, easily-measured outcome to address, like glycohemoglobin or blood pressure.
- Getting buy-in from the whole staff, not just the providers (and patients if you can), on the importance of the problem and input from everybody on how to address it.
- Developing the patient data recording; patient, staff and provider prompts; work flows; and most importantly, follow-up routines that will make the program work. Duties need to be reassigned in a way that makes sense. For example, a non-clinical person could make some follow-up reminder calls. A patient portal might be leveraged to keep patients engaged. Nurses and medical assistants can be trained to do most of the patient education. Get everybody involved and working near the top of their range of capabilities.
- Have a skilled leader for the project. You always need a champion who can provide ongoing clinical insight into why the endeavor is important, whether or not that person is the project leader. Like it or not, doctors and other clinicians are looked to as leaders. Just try not to give us too much to do.
- Depend on clinicians as little as you can. We tend to be (or feel ourselves to be) too full to digest one other item, no matter how nutritious, that has been put on our clinical plate.*
- Frequently reassess how things are going using something like the plan-do-study-act (PDSA) cycle.

(If you have ever trained as a manager, you have probably noticed that I have just presented the standard prescription that everyone is taught in Quality Improvement 101.)

As always, when it comes to using data to improve patient care, how you get the buy-in and follow-through of the people involved is the most important determinant of whether a program reaches its goals. A paper-based information system, though less efficient when it comes to extracting data, may be all that you need. If you do go with electronic data, be sure that those who need them can easily get reminders, data and reports. If you are fortunate enough to have the support of a capable IT department or a responsive vendor, involve them in the process from the start.

I have been talking so far about a methodology for making bounded, practice-specific improvements in patient care, a process that can be greatly facilitated by

---

* I am aware that this point appears to contradict the one just above it. Nobody said this would be easy.

smart exploitation of the capabilities of an electronic patient record. I will discuss learning bigger lessons in Research (with a capital "R") in Chapter 11.

The following list of ten fallacies about health information technology, from an article entitled, "Health information technology: fallacies and sober realities," that appeared in 2010 in the *Journal of the American Medical Informatics Association*, is particularly pertinent to EHRs. It really boils down to the central theme of this book: **HIT is much more about people than it is about machines**. If you remember only that, my goal in writing this tome will have been accomplished.

- The "risk-free HIT" fallacy—There are always complications and downsides.
- The "HIT is not a device" fallacy—Just because it resides only in cyberspace and never moves atoms, software is just as real and has just as much potential to do good or harm as any device made of steel, Teflon, titanium or kryptonite.
- The "bad apple" fallacy—Very few of the harmful mistakes that occur in patient care are the result of a single clinician, staff person or manager not being on the ball. They are due to problems embedded in the system.
- The "use equals success" fallacy—Just getting people to use an HIT system is an important but limited goal. When all is said and done, outcomes that make a difference in patients' health are what must be measured.
- The "messy desk" fallacy—Clinical work is messy. Over-rationalizing it with templates and checklists may make it worse, not better.
- The "father knows best" fallacy—Clinicians and other staff closest to the patient should have the majority of the say in design, choice and implementation of clinical systems, not administrators or techies, no matter how high-ranking, well-meaning and enlightened.
- The "field of dreams" fallacy and the "sit-stay" fallacy—Build it (an HIT system) and they will come? Maybe. Bribe and coerce them and they may stay. Whether care will be better or worse as a result is an open question.
- The "one size fits all" fallacy—A hospice bedside nurse and a retinal surgeon have very different informational needs.
- The "we computerized the paper, so we can go paperless" fallacy—HIT provides wonderful opportunities to re-engineer processes. If you computerize the paper mess you've got, you'll come out with a computerized mess.
- The "no one else understands healthcare" fallacy—Healthcare is way behind other industries in how it employs IT. There is so much to learn from banking, aviation, Amazon, Facebook, Google and Walmart, especially when it comes to human-machine interface design, processes re-design and use of big data.[45]

Chapter 9

Patient Care

ITPS: It's The Process, Stupid

**—David Alschuler, a personal friend who spent decades
as a consultant in the computer industry**

If doctors were in charge of airports, they never would have installed radar. They just would have put intensive care units all around them.

—Larry Weed

This chapter, about how information technology impacts (and could impact) our efforts to do what is best for patients, is where the rubber meets the road, at least for health professionals.

It should be clear from reading previous chapters that information technologies do not, in themselves, make things better. Sometimes they make things worse. Which of these powerful tools we choose and how we use them determines whether they will help or hinder the care process and, ultimately, patient and professional wellbeing.

Evidence Based Medicine and Best Practices

As discussed in Chapter 1, Western medicine has been on a millennia-long trajectory that is ever more tightly focused on science. A relatively recent step in this direction for medical science is the evidence based medicine (EBM) movement that was named in the early 1990s by doctors at McMaster University in Hamilton, Ontario. Sackett and colleagues defined EBM as "the conscientious and judicious use of current best evidence from clinical care research in the management of individual patients."[1]

When I first encountered the EBM literature, I asked myself, "Isn't that how I was taught in medical school and how I've striven to practice ever since?" The answer is "yes and yes." EBM employs an array of long-established methods to weigh evidence from the medical literature, then develops protocols for best practices based on the duly-considered information. The difference is that EBM-ers tell you, explicitly, that's what they are doing.

A crucial and innovative feature of EBM is a formal classification of levels of evidence. Levels of evidence revolve around the types of studies performed to yield information, ranging from the gold standard of well-designed and well-executed double blind controlled studies on large populations to haphazard descriptions of what seems to be out there. Level of evidence figures strongly into determining best practice recommendations. The higher the quality of the evidence, the stronger the recommendation.

Now, let's consider just how well what a clinician does is backed up by science. The last such summary I could find is dated 2004. The numbers probably have not changed that much in the intervening years. *Clinical Evidence*, put out by BMJ, a very highly regarded organization (the initials come from its origins as the *British Medical Journal*), estimated that 15% of the 2148 medical treatments that they reviewed were definitely beneficial and 21% were likely to be beneficial. The other 58% were relegated to unlikely to be beneficial, likely to be harmful and unknown, with 6% left for tradeoffs between benefit and harm.[2] In 2009, nearly half of the clinical practice recommendations issued by the authoritative American College of Cardiology and by the august American Heart Association were based on expert opinion, case reports and common standards of care, not on solid scientific studies.[3]

A large share of these recommendations, even those deemed to be grounded in solid science, change every year. As an example, in a research project that studied what influences pediatricians to keep up with changing practice standards, published in 1990, two of the three standards chosen (intermittent phenobarbital for preventing febrile seizures and long-acting theophylline for asthma) were themselves passé by the time I encountered the report in 1994.[4]

As a generalist clinician, I have had little reason to and, consequently, little expertise to assess levels of evidence on my own.* Experts have estimated the

---

* I am in good company. When 437 pediatric residents were quizzed on two fundamental concepts of statistics, correlation and probability values for statistical significance, only 20% answered the first question right and less than half the second one. Doctors who were further along in their training program did no better than beginners. (Friedman, SB, Phillips, S. What's the difference? Pediatric residents and their inaccurate concepts regarding statistics. *Pediatrics*, 1981:68(5), 644–646.) Ninety-seven Danish doctors did not shine when they took a nine-question test of statistical knowledge. They answered between 2.5 and 4 of the test items correctly. (Wulff, HR, Andersen, B, Brandenhoff, P et al. What do doctors know about statistics? *Statistics in Medicine*, 1987:6, 3–10.) Here's one more study about physicians' skills at critical appraisal of the medical literature that I mention just for its perversity. An exhaustive search of the medical literature on the effectiveness of teaching critical appraisal skills to clinicians concluded that the 10 studies that did turn up were so poorly designed that the authors of the review could come to no conclusion at all about whether training doctors in how to review studies was worth the effort. (Taylor, R, Reeves, B, Ewings, P et al. A systematic review of the effectiveness of critical appraisal skills training for clinicians. *Medical Education*, 2000:34, 120–125.)

majority, or even the vast majority, of medical research findings eventually turn out to be false.[5] If I want to learn about a subject, I look for a good review article written recently by experts in the field; or I seek a meta-analysis, a study of studies that strives to increase validity by using sophisticated statistical techniques to combine data from multiple reports, thereby increasing the total number of subjects.

Because of the disparate sources and types of data that it must consider, a meta-analysis runs the risk of comparing apples and oranges. Nevertheless, meta-analyses are overall more heavily cited in the medical literature than single randomized controlled trials, which are considered the gold standard for revealing reliable clinical truths. (See Chapter 12, "Research.")[6]

When looking over a research report, I might consider: the setting of the study (Was it done in a large university referral practice or in small community practices?); study population (How do participant race, age, sex, class, occupation, etc. compare to my practice?); and methods (Is the studied intervention practical for the population I care for?). I hardly ever get into the nitty-gritty of subject selection, statistical analysis, etc. I leave those matters to the experts.

Translating level of evidence into a strength of practice recommendation is, to my eye, the most important product of the EBM movement. Well-founded practice recommendations can actually tell us clinicians what to do, some of the time. My home team professional organization, the American Academy of Family Physicians (AAFP), came up with a widely-used classification called SORT, Strength of Recommendation Taxonomy, which has just three large categories: Level 1—good quality patient-oriented evidence; Level 2—limited quality patient-oriented evidence; and Level 3—other evidence, such as consensus guidelines, extrapolations from bench research, usual practice, opinion, or uncontrolled case series. I think SORT is great.

A more universally accepted system for valuing expert clinical guidance is Grading of Recommendations Assessment, Development and Evaluation (GRADE), a collaboration of professionals that began in 2000 to develop "…a common, sensible and transparent approach to grading quality (or certainty) of evidence and strength of recommendations [in healthcare]." GRADE scores run from zero to four, with four being the best, reserved for clinical recommendations that are supported by well-done randomized, blinded, prospective studies.

There are gazillions of overlapping practice recommendations and guidelines, published by every professional organization and medical institution you can imagine. Whose guidelines to trust is a fundamentally important decision. I choose a guideline largely in the same way I purchase a bottle of wine, by the label. Who made it? Do they have a good reputation? Have they gotten good reviews? How similar are the organization's doctors to me and its patients like mine? Is there a lurking financial interest? The final judgment of the suitability of a guideline is not made until I have actually pulled the cork and drunk it (to stretch the metaphor), that is, until I have tried out how the guideline actually works in my particular practice with my particular patients.*

I nearly always have to modify the guidelines I do choose so they fit my practice's panel of patients. I do so in close consultation with colleagues. An early step toward reducing variability and improving quality in a group practice is to generate and adopt solid guidelines that every practitioner can get behind.

As a generalist, I tend to start with guidelines promulgated by the American Academy of Family Physicians, the National Institutes of Health, the Cochrane Review, the American Public Health Association and such. To my family doctor sensibilities, these groups favor a more practical, population-based view of medical practice, consonant with my own beliefs about what patients really need. Specialty organizations, grounded in the more narrowly focused experience of their members, sometimes recommend more frequent screening and more aggressive intervention than what I believe is overall best for my patients.†

"Best practice" means different things in different places. How you diagnose and treat pulmonary embolism in the 18-bed critical access Star Valley Medical Center in Afton, Wyoming is likely different from how you do it 437 miles away in the 218-bed Cheyenne Regional Medical Center, with its panoply of specialists and diagnostic services. As one study showed, either hospital could be twice as efficient and just as safe in ruling out blood clots in the lungs by using the simple, explicit Wells Rule checklist for predicting pulmonary embolism in patients with suspicious symptoms. As long as it is easily accessible, that checklist does not even have to be in an electronic format.[7]

Here is one little example, selected from an endless supply, that illustrates what may happen when one doesn't/can't take practice setting into account. For several years, I served as medical director of a hospice. We leased our inpatient unit from the local hospital. The hospital regularly sent us patients from their intensive care

---

* The Institute of Medicine gives these more objective criteria for a good practice guideline: scientific validity, reliability and reproducibility of the underlying studies, applicability to actual practice, flexibility and clarity. A guideline ought to be developed by people from all disciplines that are involved in caring for this type of patient. The information that underlies a guideline should be well documented. There should be a scheduled date for review and revision (Marilyn J. Field, Kathleen N. Lohr, eds. *Clinical Practice Guidelines—Directions for a New Program*. National Academies Press. Washington DC, 1990, p. vi). Patients have been added to some guideline development groups of late. This perfectly sensible concept of incorporating into a disease management guideline those things that are understood only by people who suffer with that disease is still considered, in many professional circles, to be a far-out idea. In recent years, there has been a lot of talk about the need to engage patients and communities in research and practice, with a small but perceptible shift of the culture of healthcare in that direction.

† For example, if you see the world through a cystoscope, as a urologist does, you're liable to put a higher value on diagnosing and treating prostate problems than I do as a generalist. An aphorism, sometimes attributed to Mark Twain, says it best. "To a small boy with a hammer, everything looks like a nail."

unit who were on the verge of dying. These patients were sometimes so sick that every now and then one of them died in the elevator, on her way from the ICU to the hospice unit.

Transferring such patients to our ward was a win-win-win situation: for the patients and their families because the hospice staff was so good at providing care at the end of life; for the hospice organization, because it increased our business; and for the hospital, because its acute care mortality statistics looked better.

Upon arrival at the hospice unit, after seeing to it that the patient had enough comfort medications, my next task was to look over the medication orders that the patient had arrived with and discontinue all those that did not contribute to symptom relief. I found that every patient with a cardiac diagnosis came to us with a prescription for a statin, a cholesterol lowering drug. These medications, which reduce risk of coronary and other arterial disease over the course of years, had been prescribed for patients who had but hours or days to live, by heart specialists who knew better.

I asked a cardiologist buddy why he and his colleagues would prescribe a statin under such circumstances. He explained that they had to follow Center for Medicare and Medicaid Services (CMS) guidelines that mandate a statin prescription for every cardiac patient discharged from the hospital. Doctors and hospitals are dinged for any coronary artery disease patient who does not have a statin prescription documented on her hospital discharge orders.

Physicians and other clinicians are subject to mandates issued by multiple regulatory bodies that often do not allow us the leeway to choose when the standards we will be expected to adhere to make sense and when they don't. If a physician is employed, which more and more of us are, the larger the organization we work for, the less voice we are liable to have in how we practice.

The first, most important principle for administrators to keep in mind about practice guidelines is, as deeply and widely as possible, to involve the staff who will use the guidelines in the process of choosing, developing, implementing and monitoring them. The best decision tree in the world is of no use if clinicians refuse to hang their hats on it. As always, cultivating respected opinion leaders from among the staff to head-up the project is a crucial step. Pay close attention to clarity and frequency of communication with the people who will be using the new guidelines. The greater the sense of ownership a staff has of the standards they are expected to practice under, the better it goes for everybody.

No scientifically-trained practitioner would deny that she ought to use the best available evidence in her medical practice. The problem with evidence based medicine is that, in spite of our best scientific efforts, we still do not know all that much about most medical problems. (This fact terrifies my lay friends.) And what we do know has to be applied to the infinitely diverse trajectories that infinitely diverse people traverse through health and illness. It is more the exception than the rule when a patient fits neatly and completely into the flow of particular protocol. Too often the rules turn out to be a procrustean bed.* The rules themselves are usually not to blame. Rather it is our attempt to make individual cases conform to them.

A few guidelines really do map out straight and narrow paths that every clinician should follow on nearly every patient. Immunization protocols are a good example.

The essence of the art of western medicine lies in how to apply what is known scientifically to a particular patient in a particular context at a particular time. Guidelines should incorporate more or less wiggle room, based on how good the evidence is that underpins them and how applicable they are to the patient at hand. The higher the SORT number and the looser the fit to the population, the greater the clinician's decision-making latitude ought to be.

Then there is the issue of multi-morbidity, the medical way of saying more than one significant medical problem. For example, coronary artery disease is the sole condition in less than one out of five of patients with that diagnosis. Almost 3 of 4 individuals over 65 have more than one chronic condition, as do 1 in 4 younger adults.[8]

The authors of a study published in the journal *Age and Ageing* in 2013 attempted to apply well-vetted guidelines for caring for two hypothetical patients: Mrs. A., who suffered with mild-to-moderate severity diabetes, osteoarthritis, chronic lung disease, depression and who had previously had a heart attack; and Mr. B., a 75-year-old man with mild-to-moderate diabetes and chronic lung disease. Both scenarios are plausible and common. If they were to follow all of the individual guidelines for Mrs. A., the doctors learned that they should prescribe a minimum of 11 drugs, with another 10 drugs recommended, depending on symptoms and progression of disease. Mr. B. would get only five drugs, with another eight possible. And this is just medications. There are all sorts of tests, lifestyle alterations and follow-up appointments mandated by the guidelines. This study alone should make it clear why we still need human doctors.[9]

No doubt, with the help of artificial intelligence, many more righteously narrow paths through the thicket of patient care decisions will emerge.† But for the foreseeable future, human beings will be making the final judgments about how to apply scientific knowledge to individual patients. Evidence based medicine is not the answer in itself. It is just another tool to be employed by human beings as we care for each other.

---

* Procrustes is a Greek mythological figure, a smith and bandit who cut his victims' legs off in order to fit them into the iron bed he had fashioned for prisoners.

† The Food and Drug Administration has so far failed to apply different vetting standards for clinical decision systems that make recommendations regarding diagnosing and treating potentially high-risk symptoms and diseases, like cancer, versus lower-risk situations, like earache. Developers and vendors of medical AI systems complain that its current level of regulation is stifling their ability to innovate. (Sweeney, E. After a 6-year wait, FDA's clinical decision support guidelines get a mixed reaction. *Fierce Healthcare* [online]. December 7, 2017.)

Alerts and Embedded "Intelligence"

In the course of my career as an educator, I have learned that an absolutely fundamental principle for improving patient outcomes is to leave doctors out of the equation whenever you can. The simple paper-based prenatal record that I used for much of my career, which prompts the nurse or medical assistant to perform a blood count to check mothers for anemia around the 28th week of pregnancy, worked much better than expecting me to remember to order the test. The smaller the number of things that depend on memory, especially the busy doctor's memory, the more reliable the system.

Simple alerts built into an EHR that help physicians decide when a hospitalized patient needs a urinary catheter, and then send timely reminders to consider removing it, have been enough to reduce the incidence of urinary tract infection by 17% in patients admitted to University of Pennsylvania Health System hospitals. This is a big deal. According to the Centers for Disease Control and Prevention, if we could duplicate these results throughout the country, US inpatients would contract 76,000 fewer urinary tract infections, avoiding 1,000 excess deaths, not to mention a whole lot of suffering and cost. That's just a start. The CDC has stated that, with the best management, inpatient UTIs could be reduced by 70%.[10]

A system that has worked very well to reduce infections acquired in-house tracks staff behavior, not patient status. Combined with constant feedback to staff, a real-time location system that recorded compliance with handwashing standards showed not only an increased rate of handwashing before and after each patient encounter, but a significantly lower incidence of methicillin-resistant *Staphylococcus aureus* infections. MRSA is a nasty bug that is rife in most healthcare institutions because it is carried from patient to patient by inadequate hygiene. The data gathering system employed a position monitor in hospital rooms, linked to staff badges, which reported closely approaching patients and using the sink. Simple though it may seem, getting staff (particularly doctors) to perform routine handwashing in the course of seeing patients remains a huge challenge.[11]

Electronic systems provide infinitely more opportunities to build in automatic prompts and subroutines, including: simple lists of patients to call for follow-up; reminders to administer papillomavirus vaccine that pop up on the EHR screen of 14 year-olds; and automatically ordering tests like serum potassium levels for patients taking diuretics, scheduling them, calling, mailing, emailing or texting patients to remind them of the test, reporting and tracking results.

A reminder system need not be sophisticated to generate outcomes that are vastly better than what you get with unaided memory and good intentions. One thousand and eleven patients with HIV who were cared for in Boston by thirty-three doctors had significantly improved blood cell counts, as well as timelier follow-up for complications, thanks to a simple automated reminder system that notified doctors of dropping counts and adverse events, with a link on the reminders that allowed for immediate scheduling of follow-up appointments and laboratory tests. Most telling, 90% of the doctors who used the system supported rolling it out institution-wide. Keep in mind, though, that these were infrequent reminders sent to doctors whose practices mostly focused on a narrow range of diseases.[12]

The most critical factors to realizing benefits from reminder systems are: organizing the team around good information flow; clearly specifying roles and expectations; and, as always, cooperating. Electronic reminders do not, in themselves, lower the rate of missed test results. A review of published studies that came out in 2011 reported rates that ranged from 20% to 62% of tests performed on inpatients and of 1% to 75%(!) of tests completed on ER patients that were not followed up. There was not a correlation between whether the system was paper-based, electronic or a hybrid of the two, and success at follow-up.[13]

The medical workplace is rife with workarounds. Forty-three percent of respondents to a survey of primary care practitioners at the Veterans Health Administration (VHA) admitted to supplementing or replacing an electronic medical test result communication system with notes written on paper to remind them about results to follow-up.[14]

Clinician reminders, electronic or not, are far from infallible. A VHA study that was conducted in 2011 and 2012 found in cases in which there had been a delay in acting on a critical diagnostic value that might be indicative of lung, colon or prostate cancer, an email reminder to the clinician provoked appropriate medical follow-up within a week only 11% of the time. Three attempts to reach the provider or her nurse by phone, followed by contacting the clinic director if necessary, still led to follow-up in only five of the eleven remaining cases.[15]

Organizing patient tracking and call-backs is a good place for a practice to begin exploiting the intelligence embedded in an electronic medical record. Notice, in this case, how low I have set the bar in my definition of "intelligence." For this purpose, "intelligence" means merely turning patient data into actionable items in the course of delivering care, which just scratches the surface of what systems can do now and will be able to do in the future.

Based on subtle patterns of parameters like vital signs, fluid input and output, alertness, etc., today's intelligent intensive care monitoring systems give ever earlier warning that a patient is about to deteriorate, allowing for faster intervention and better outcome. Multiple studies have demonstrated the effectiveness of informationally enhanced intensive care in reducing morbidity and mortality. One paper, published in 2014, reported that for 450 remotely monitored ICU beds in 5 different states, malpractice claims decreased from 70 to 30 per year and payouts from $6 million to $0.5 million.[16]

Since the data are in electronic format, it does not matter if they are being sifted and interpreted by computers and people located in the next room or in the next state. Electronic Intensive Care Units (eICU) have been one of the most successful and widely-applied telehealth technologies to date. They are a boon, especially to small hospitals in underserved areas that cannot afford to employ the intensivist physician and nursing staff it takes to keep a moment-to-moment eye on their sickest patients.

A retrospective study processed, using a simple artificial intelligence program called InSight, data from 52,000 ICU admissions to Beth Israel Deaconess Medical Center in Boston between 2001 and 2012, to see how early the system could learn to predict sepsis (bacterial infection of the blood). The earlier sepsis is suspected, the earlier antibiotics can be started and the better the outcome in treating this deadly disease. Eleven percent of the ICU patients had been septic. Using just vital signs, age and the Glasgow Coma Score (a measure of alertness), the system was able to predict sepsis up to four hours earlier than other scoring systems, which could have had quite a positive impact on clinical outcomes for the nearly six thousand Beth Israel Deaconess ICU patients who were diagnosed with sepsis during the period of the study.[17]

Simply by notifying physicians, via their smartphones, of the results of a single blood level of troponin (an enzyme released from a damaged heart in the course of a heart attack), and labeling that result as "critical," "high" or "normal," chest pain patients were discharged from the emergency department 28 minutes sooner, a big deal for many medical as well as financial reasons.[18]

Getting prior authorization for expensive tests or medications from a payer, whose primary goal is to save money, is the bane of many clinicians' existence (and even more so for their staff who do most of the paperwork and spend the lion's share of the time on the phone stuck on hold with insurance companies). In an innovative program in Minnesota, a large payer collaborative was able to improve appropriateness of orders for CT and MRI scans from 79% to 89% by getting physicians to use a decision-support system tied to the radiologic order part of their EHRs. In exchange, the insurers agreed not to subject the doctors to prior authorization hoops and hurdles.[19] A similar decision support system, based on American College of Cardiology criteria, reported by scientists at Weill Cornell Medical College in New York, was able to reduce inappropriate heart imaging scans from 22% to 8%.[20]

Systems that automatically look at drug-drug interactions and alert the prescriber and dispenser are commonplace, and badly needed. A study of 950 physicians who answered a mail questionnaire in which they were asked to classify 14 pairs of drugs into 1 of 3 categories—contraindicated to use together, may be used together with monitoring, and no interaction—selected the right answer only 43% of the time.[21]

Another place where clinicians should not be asked to rely on unaided memory is in ordering the laboratory monitoring that needs to go with certain prescriptions, tests like measuring potassium for people taking diuretics and kidney and thyroid function for those on lithium. After achieving consensus guidelines for the need to do 61 different laboratory tests to monitor patients taking 35 different drugs or drug classes, researchers found a compliance rate for test ordering that ran from under 20% to 90%, with many at less than 50%.[22]

Due to alarm fatigue, many physicians choose to turn off reminders and warnings, either within the EHR system if they are able, or mentally, by ignoring them. (My wife once solved a stubborn "Check Engine" light problem on our vehicle's dashboard by putting a Band-Aid over it.) Studies have reported alarm override rates of up to 90%. In an analysis of 614 reasons given for prescription overrides performed over the course of 6 months in a 39-physician practice, experts disagreed with 19 overrides, just 3%.[23] (Doctors chose not to give a reason for their override choices in another 36 cases.) This study was done in 2010. By now, I expect those docs are not bothering to supply a reason for their overrides a large share of the time. Most every clinician I know pays less attention to pharmacy alerts than she used to, whether by conscious choice or not.

Think of the commercials for prescription drugs that you see on television. I estimate that a third to a half of the narrative of the average ad is devoted to the mandated recitation of possible side effects. How much of those lists, which are not even the full ones, do you actually hear? If you get down to the case report level, literally most any drug can produce most any side effect. And each preparation interacts with dozens to hundreds of other drugs.

There is no way for a human being to remember all of this stuff. Clinicians do our best to keep in mind important drug contraindications and interactions. Having a computer to aid our most imperfect memories is a great boon. But if, for each prescription we write using an electronic system, we get alerts that deliver multiple screens of contraindications, interactions and side effects, we have the choice of either constantly wading through a whole lot of mostly useless information, thereby degrading the efficiency and quality of the service we provide to patients, or else we gradually learn to take most of it with a grain of salt, if not to ignore it altogether. A study, reported in 2015, found that 96% of alerts about opiate prescriptions generated by the Epic EHR were overridden and that for every one adverse drug event prevented, the system would have sent 123 unnecessary warnings.[24]

A panel of high-powered experts in pharmacology and clinical medicine was able to trim a system's interruptive notifications of potentially harmful drug-drug interactions by over a third. They started with a list of messages that had been overridden at least 90% of the time, then arrived at consensus about which of these alerts the system didn't need to bother with putting right under the physicians' noses. Doctors were sent email messages about these low-priority classes of interactions, to be opened at their leisure. I imagine that most of these messages were ignored too.[25]

A working group of the American Medical Informatics Society drafted a number of sound suggestions for making drug-drug interaction (DDI) alerts more effective. They insisted that any project to be developed along these lines ought to be led, or co-led by a pharmacist.

- Strive for uniformity among systems in terms of format, color, location on screen of drug alerts. (At this time, with EHR companies constantly battling each other for market share, such a level of cooperation is a pipedream. (See Chapter 6, "Economics.")
- Alerts should include a level of seriousness of possible ill-effects, employing a consistent, well-understood terminology and a description of those conceivable outcomes.
- Mechanism of interaction should be tersely summarized, both so the clinician can know whether to choose a different class of drug and to lend credibility and depth to the warning.
- Alerts should come as early as possible in the process of ordering a medication so that the clinician has not invested too much time and too many clicks before making a change.
- Drug-drug interaction alerts should recommend alternative actions, including modified dosages, choice of a different drug, lab monitoring, etc., and provide check boxes and paths to these alternatives.
- When the clinician chooses to override an alert, there should be a box where she can indicate the reason why. These reasons should be saved in the system and reviewed frequently to monitor the need to change the system's routines or to indicate the need for individual or group education.[26]

The Lucile Packard Children's Hospital at Stanford University in Palo Alto, California chose to derive its standards for triggering alarms for abnormal heart and respiratory rate locally, directly from 7207 patients who had been hospitalized there. These kids were sick to start with, as opposed the healthy children who had contributed the data used to generate the normal ranges, established by the National Institutes of Health 2004, that the hospital had adopted previously to set its alarm triggers.

By stipulating instead critical values generated by their homegrown 5th and 95th percentile measurements for each age range, the hospital staff received 55.6% fewer vital-sign based alerts. There was no adverse effect on clinical outcomes. Vital signs that were out of the old normal range but within the new one did not, in themselves, appear to identify children in medical trouble. There were always other clinical indications calling nurses' attention to acute problems in sicker kids. These results will have to be validated. I expect that, if anything, children monitored using the newer criteria will have better outcomes because the staff caring for them will be less alarm fatigued.[27]

A study that looked at nurses' response time to physiologic monitor alarms in another children's hospital appears to indicate that, in the short-term, plain old fatigue plays a larger role than alarm fatigue in influencing how long it took to arrive at the bedside. Each additional hour worked added 15% to the response time. The presence of a patient's family members shortened response time, as did (as expected, thank God) the gravity of a detected heart rhythm disturbance. Non-actionable alarms occurring in the two hours prior to a fresh alarm did appear to slow down nurses' trips to the bedside.[28]

System responses to problematic orders can be tuned to the potential consequences of an error. For example, a drug order entry system should simply make it impossible to order 1000 times the usual dose of thyroid hormone. On the other hand, a simple dialog box on the computer screen would suffice to remind a clinician prescribing an antibiotic for a patient taking an oral contraceptive that the new prescription might reduce the effectiveness of her birth control pill.[29]

A student or novice practitioner, lacking a feel for what she does or does not need to worry about, might choose to dial-up the system sensitivity, willingly trading the extra alerts for the assurance that she is not missing something. An experienced user, on the other hand, might elect to have the system report only frequent and significant drug side effects and interactions.

Even the best expert who chooses a lower alert sensitivity takes on some risk of overlooking a datum that, if ignored, could lead to a seriously bad outcome. No matter how intrusive and unreasonable an alert system may be, and how competent the expert clinician who ignores it, if a malpractice claim related to a prescription drug is filed against her, she can count on the plaintiff's attorney asking, "What sort of warnings are built into the electronic prescription system?" and "Why did you ignore this one, *doctor*?" Still, no patient wants a doctor who takes an hour to write every prescription for fear that something bad could happen. And no doctor I know wants to practice that way.

During an 18-month period after installing a computerized physician order entry (CPOE) system, Children's Hospital of Pittsburgh found that mortalities *increased* from 2.8% to 6.7%, attributed in part to the slowdown in delivery of care. These results raised a storm of controversy when they were published in 2006. The final word on the matter calls into question the cause-effect relationship between CPOE and mortality, blandly concluding that there were "significant problems" with how CPOE was implemented at that institution. This example should still serve as a warning to be very deliberate any time you install new a clinical information system. You cannot simply assume that the latest thing will make things better.[30]

An electronic prescription system is no guarantee of a reduced error rate. A pharmacy chain reported in 2011 that the error rate in 3850 prescriptions submitted electronically—about 1 in 10 prescriptions, 35% of those potentially harmful— was no lower than it had been prior to implementation of the electronic system. They attributed the lack of improvement to poor training of the new users and lack of understanding of the work process by the system's installers.[31] Not surprisingly, no matter how well planned and executed, things are almost always at least a little dicey during transition between systems.[32]

A number of studies have been done that do show positive changes in prescribing behavior based on specific alerts built into order entry systems. A literature review of the subject published in 2013 found that computerized physician order entry reduces the likelihood of a drug error by half.[33] But it stops there. Nobody yet has demonstrated, by sound science, how to design a system that consistently does much more over the long term than to avoid gross errors, a worthwhile goal in itself, but way short of the promise of "smart" EHRs.[34]

Another simple measure, front-loading electronic prescription pick-lists with generic drugs, could save untold millions in pharmaceutical costs. A 2009 study found that Medicaid could have saved $329 million that year if prescribers had chosen generic products in place of just 20 common name brand drugs.[35]

One very simple system called MedEye promises to significantly reduce the errors that occur in drug administration. Before a dose is given, a bar code reader scans the patient's ID bracelet while a computer vision scanner directly identifies the pills in the medicine cup, based on their shape, color and markings.[36] It amounts to adopting a simple inventory system to a medical setting. The only fancy bit is the ability of MedEye to identify pills by AI-driven pattern recognition.

Tying expert pharmacists into the prescription system and using them wisely in designing and filtering alerts (in other words, putting people back into the loop) can resolve a good share of the chaos and inefficiency introduced by rigid rules that have been built into software.

Education in United States pharmacy schools has evolved from training graduates to work in retail pharmacies to preparing them for clinical jobs in hospitals and clinics. Beginning in the 1970s, a big chunk of the time spent in classroom and laboratory, learning chemistry, physiology, pharmacology and about how to prepare and dispense medications, has been shifted to rotations in hospital and clinic, where pharmacy students learn how to manage diseases in collaboration with clinicians. Today pharmacists adjust on their own finicky anticoagulant doses, as well as provide the extensive patient education that goes with it. They help to manage hypertension, heart failure, diabetes and a host of other chronic diseases.[37] In some states, pharmacists dispense vaccines and oral contraceptives without a doctor's order.

In every burg where I have practiced, I have cultivated the most knowledge-able pharmacist in town, by calling her with the "Difficult Question of the Day" (of which sometimes there were several more than one a day). These professionals had spent almost as much time training for their profession as I had for mine, with virtually all of their education devoted to drugs, making them much more expert in pharmacology than I. They loved being asked hard questions, which helped to stretch their minds, not to mention taking them away from counting pills.

Thanks to electronic information systems, in-house pharmacists can access all the same patient data as clinicians, making their advice that much more potent. Many organizations expect every prescription to be reviewed by a pharmacist. The tools that today's pharmacist can apply to clinical care are formidable.

By dint of shared information and information systems, pharmacists and clinicians get dragged into collaborating, even without a Difficult Drug Question of the Day. Collaboration is always better, of course, when there is a relationship between clinician and pharmacist that is trusting enough for us to feel comfortable asking and answering questions of each other, and even being able to say once in a while, "I don't know. But I'll find out and get back to you."

The principle of fostering teamwork through information and relationship requires a human touch to make it work. You have to start out with at least one person who has the requisite vision and people skills. Those sorts of leaders, equipped with good enough information systems, will find all sorts of opportunities for collaboration among all sorts of different workers with all sorts of different competencies.

As EHRs get more sophisticated, they incorporate more domains. Here is a simple example of embedded intelligence that was rolled out eons ago. (In the information technology, an eon is a decade.)

Digoxin is a heart drug that is mostly passé today, in part because it has what is called a "narrow therapeutic window," which means that there is not much real estate between too small and too large a dose. Give too little and the heart disease is undertreated; too much and the patient may die from a malignant cardiac rhythm. Too much digoxin is especially dangerous if the blood potassium level is low.

As far back as 1998, Samaritan Health System in Arizona set up the pharmacy, order entry and laboratory subsystems of its primitive electronic medical record to send a four-alarm warning to the attending doctor if a patient who was receiving digoxin had a low potassium level, 1 of 37 different warnings of possible adverse drug events the system was rigged to trigger. The program issued, in a six-month period, 265 true positive alerts of patients with low potassium levels who were receiving digoxin.

Not surprisingly, the scheme was too small to significantly move the needle on the dials that measure the outcome parameters that finally make a difference to patients, like patient complications, length of hospital stay, cost or mortality.[38] It takes a whole lot more than 37 different isolated drug alert protocols before a hospital can show that its patients have tangibly benefited because its pharmacy information system turned data into actionable information by collaborating with the laboratory information and physician order entry systems.

One way to increase the number, acceptability and power of data-driven clinical reminders, and hopefully make a dent in the quality of patient care, is to get the whole clinical staff involved in designing the alerts. The Regenstrief Institute in Indiana has addressed the issue by creating a sort of Wiki system that empowers clinicians, including physicians, nurses and pharmacists, at Eskenazi Health, a large safety net hospital in Indianapolis, to write their own decision support rules using an intuitive software rule-authoring tool. A new rule will apply at first only to the professional who wrote it. Once it has been evaluated and tested, the subroutine may be rolled out, perhaps after some tweaking, to other system users to whom it could be useful. It will be worth keeping an eye on this system to see if it can more directly harness the creativity of users, turning the IT hierarchy on its head.[39]

Integrating Different Types of Data

If you haven't lived in a rural place, you may not know a feed mill when you see one. It's one of those clusters of various-sized silos, connected at the top by tubes that run between pipes sticking up from the top of each silo. A larger vertical pipe, connected to all the others by horizontal pipes, carries product for delivery at its lower end. Each tube attached to a silo houses an augur that moves grain up from its bin on its way to the main tube. Different silos contain different products—corn, sorghum, soy meal, oats, etc. By controlling how much of each grain she delivers into a waiting dump truck or bagger waiting under the big vertical delivery tube, the operator of a feed mill can customize the mixture of nutrients she sends out to feed a herd or a flock.

Much of medical information—dictated reports; scanned paper documents; data from electronically filled templates; physical measurements like blood pressure, eyeball pressure and temperature; number values of laboratory tests; radiology images; demographic data; billing information; electrocardiograms; fetal monitor records; etc.—resides in electronic silos called databases. Turning all of these data into a palatable final product is a lot more daunting than portioning out maybe a dozen different nutrient products to manufacture the ideal feed for a particular cattle herd on a particular day.

Fortunately, in the case of medical information stored in electronic form, we are talking about moving around nearly massless electrons, not the bulk quantities of the grain and things that go into fattening livestock. Unfortunately, we are talking about silos, the contents of which are much more different from each other than corn is from soybeans.

This is where the appeal of big integrated medical record systems, like Epic and Cerner, comes in. Their EHRs start out with (electronic) augurs and conveyor belts that already connect most of the silos to each other. On the downside, integrated systems are expensive, usually hospital-centric and don't communicate well with other systems (see "Interoperability and standards" in Chapter 3).

Care Management

As I write this, chaos swirls around the future of the tatters that remain of the Affordable Care Act. I am far from optimistic that, by the time you read these words, our politicians will have settled on any sort of mechanism that provides more people with better healthcare at a reasonable price. My pessimism stems not just from the politics, but from the underlying structure of healthcare itself in this nation.

Once it became law in 2010, the Affordable Care Act (ACA, dubbed "Obamacare") brought health insurance, by understated estimates (I almost said "by conservative estimates"), to 20 million previously uninsured people.[40] From 2010 to 2015, national healthcare expenditures grew from $2.6 to $3.2 trillion, in part because of the large increase of insured patients, and in part due to escalating costs per patient. A goodly share of those rising costs is attributable to piecemeal, uncoordinated care. (See Chapter 6, "Economics.")*

The ACA, plus a heap of federal regulations, mostly promulgated through the Centers for Medicare and Medicaid Services (CMS), have attempted to address this incoordination by providing incentives that reward those who manage care well and penalize those who do not. Measures, such as more frequent hospital readmissions shortly after discharge and higher infection rates, provide reasons for financial whuppins. At the same time, monetary incentives to create accountable care organizations, alternative advanced care models, merit-based incentive payment, quality payment, etc. are dangled before the noses of providers and the organizations they work for.

Under the onus of stiff CMS penalties for a high early readmission rate, hospitals are rifer than ever with discharge planners and care coordinators. These folks, usually RNs, see to it that patients have the follow-up appointments they need and an up-to-date list of the medications they really ought to be taking when they leave the institution. Just getting the medication list right is a huge challenge, especially when there have been multiple prescribers, both in and outside the hospital, and multiple care providers at home. Which medications should the patient take? Which prescriptions were discontinued (or should be)? Which ones is she willing to take? Which can she afford? Is the patient able to administer her own medications? Does she need reminders? If she cannot mind her own drug regimen, who will? How will all of the patient's prescribers and pharmacies and care providers be updated? And so on. (See Chapter 6, "Economics," for a discussion about a telehomecare project for high utilizers of emergency room and inpatient hospital services that failed to get off the ground.)

Discharge coordinators' jobs do not usually stop at the hospital threshold. They may make phone queries or home visits to assure that the regimen recommended at discharge is actually being followed. Interactive video and other higher-tech tools can make an impact in this setting.

Even when there is a person who is a designated case manager, doing an effective job still requires that the whole team contribute its ideas and energy to achieving them. Collaboration is always a crucial part of the solution.

Most all of these sticks and carrots are data-driven, which means they depend on information technology. There are incentives for the technology itself, starting with the Meaningful Use (MU) provisions discussed in Chapter 6, "Economics." The government keeps raising the bar that EHRs and the organizations that purchase them must clear in order to qualify for the ample rewards doled out under MU and other programs. Stage One Meaningful Use requirements for hospitals included objectives like computerized provider order entry, e-prescribing capability,

---

* For a great exposition of the cost of uncoordinated medical care, see Gawande, Atul. The cost conundrum. *New Yorker Magazine.* June 1, 2009.

automated drug-to-drug and drug-to-allergy interaction checks and electronic recording of patient demographics. Under 2016 rules, to qualify for Stage Three Meaningful Use payments, systems must, by 2018: provide patient access through a functional electronic portal; have some embedded clinical decision support; exchange records electronically with other systems; report electronically to public health and other clinical registries; and other stuff. At the time of this writing, the feds appear, at the urging of just about every healthcare organization there is, to have relaxed the MU guidelines some.

It was estimated that, in 2016, practices spent $40,000 per provider reporting quality measures, one point on an upsloping curve. All too often, a better report card does not correlate with real improvements in quality or cost. In the process of practicing to the report card (similar to teaching to high-stakes standardized tests in our schools), harried clinicians are regularly alienated by being pushed to pay attention to yet another set of data points, perceived as yet another distraction from what they ought to be doing, which is listening to their patients.

Care management can be made less daunting when it addresses one disease at a time. Five chronic diseases—heart disease, diabetes, mood disorders, asthma and hypertension—account for nearly half of US healthcare spending. Kaiser Permanente reported in 2009 that, leveraging their EHR to coordinate teams of pharmacists, nurses, primary care physicians and cardiologists, they were able to reduce deaths of coronary artery disease patients by 73%.* The program leaders made it quite clear in their report that it was the coordination of care, not any new test or treatment, that allowed them to achieve such astounding results.[41]

Intense statistical scrutiny of hospital care, under the shadow of a big CMS sledgehammer, has, of late, driven significant reductions in hospital re-admissions, as well of as of avoidable infections, adverse drug events, pressure ulcers and falls.[42] Perversely, epidemiologists have noted that morbidity and mortality attributable to some chronic diseases, like heart failure and diabetes, may have actually increased in the last few years. One study published in *JAMA Cardiology* in 2017 even suggests that reduction of hospital readmissions for heart failure has actually increased the risk of 30-day and 1-year mortality for patients with these conditions.[43] Some speculate that, thanks to Obamacare, patients in general are getting more care that is less well coordinated, resulting in more medications, more interventions, more complications, more cost and worse outcomes.[44]

The answer is not "get bigger computers." And it certainly is not "enforce more regulations." Where does that leave us, then? Back to basic principles. Engage staff and patients. Assess needs. Think creatively about how to meet them. Design processes. Decide what roles people will have. Then choose the simplest, most reliable technology to support them. Piggyback on other systems if you can. Assess. Install. Run. Assess. Adjust. Run.... It all boils down to the standard Deming

---

* This is a pretty audacious claim. I think we need to wait for confirmation before we accept this number at face value.

quality improvement cycle of plan-do-check-adjust (PDCA) that lies at the heart of today's various QI systems whose names, like "Lean Manufacturing," "Six Sigma" and the "Toyota Production System," have achieved buzzword status.

Remember that none of these quality programs occurs in a vacuum. It takes a corporate culture (even a one-provider office with a nurse, receptionist and biller has its own corporate culture) that flattens the hierarchy, empowers workers, and promotes collaboration, still a far cry from the old way of doing things, where doctors are doctors and everybody knows her place.* Now doctors have largely been replaced at the summit of the pyramid by administrators, which is hardly an improvement.[45]

A random sampling done in 2013 of 857 patient safety incident reports from general practices in England and Wales found that an individual person was blamed in 45% of the cases, an unfortunate deviation from a core principle of quality improvement, which is to take the focus off of individuals and put it on the system.[46] Were the same sort of study done in this country, I expect we would find the same blaming culture as the Brits did.

A Hypothetical QI Project

If, for example, a group wishes to pursue better outcomes for the diabetic patients in their practice,† the first thing they ought to do is to meet, a lot if necessary, until they can agree on specific outcomes to target. Bringing some of their patients with diabetes into the conversation to discuss what really matters to them would be even better. An ideal outcome to target is something that has a significant impact on patient well-being, as well as being both relatively easy to measure and to address. If a group is just starting out doing QI, and they have to choose between ease and importance, they ought to go for the easier project so they can generate some success, which is a key part of learning.

Suppose (for the sake of discussion, this is way too ambitious a project for novices) the group decided to focus on: increasing the percentage of patients with diabetes whose glycohemoglobin (a standard measure of average blood sugar levels) falls within the target range; increasing their rates of influenza vaccination; increasing the percentage who get annual retinal checks (to head off vision complications as severe as total blindness); assuring that patients get a foot examination at each office

---

* A survey of personnel from 60 US operating rooms found in 2006 that surgeons rated their colleagues' collaboration and cooperation in the OR "high" or "very high" 85% of the time, whereas the nurses they worked with awarded those high ratings only 48% of the time. (Makary, MA, Sexton, JB, Freischlag, JA et al. Operating room teamwork among physicians and nurses: Teamwork in the eye of the beholder. *Journal of the American College of Surgeons*, 2006:202(5), 746–752.)

† A logical choice. In 2015, 70% of practitioners involved in mobile health, rated diabetes the disease with the highest market potential for mHealth solutions in the next 5 years. This was the fifth year in a row that disease had topped this particular chart. (http://research2guidance. com/2016/01/19/diabetes-management-solutions)

visit (to prevent and diagnose skin ulcers that can eventually lead to amputations); and increasing the number who are taking a cholesterol-lowering statin drug. Each of these outcomes is easy to measure and important to diabetics' health. Hopefully, once they get these first five measures (best addressed one at a time) under their belt, the practice will get around to tackling more outcomes.

From here on out they need to involve the staff—including receptionists, administrators, medical assistants, nurses, laboratory workers and IT people— maximally at every step. The less you depend on providers to remember to do what needs to be done, the better. It is the staff who will make the system succeed or fail. They know how things really work around the office.

Look at where the data reside that are needed to make the QI effort work. How can they be brought together in a single report, if not electronically, then manually? How can this be accomplished without causing significant disturbance to staff workflow?

As a first step, identify and find a way to track all of the practice's diabetics. Establishing a registry, which is just an index, should be easy. A registry provides a platform for the data that the diabetes QI effort will run on.

Where might information technology fit into the process? The right EHR could, in a heartbeat, create a registry of diabetic patients by sorting the diagnosis codes that are tied to every patient encounter. If the practice is lucky, it will be easy to design a query that pulls, from the records of patients in the registry, the information they are interested in tracking on every diabetic. Even better, the EHR might be capable of collating these data to generate reports, at regular intervals, that reveal how its diabetics are doing and how the practice is doing at caring for them.

Notwithstanding what vendors say, getting custom reports out of most EHR systems is still a headache. A 2015 report on three ahead-of-the-curve family medicine patient-centered medical homes found that all of them had chosen to use homegrown systems to do at least some of the patient and population monitoring that their mission required.[47]

Ease of generating the sorts of information a practice can use to improve patient care is a feature to consider when choosing an EHR. But be sure to cover first the more basic things like ease-of-use, vendor responsiveness and ability to communicate with outside systems.

If it needs to, a practice can choose less automated ways to organize and use patient data, even if it means keeping a standard paper flow sheet in each diabetic patient's chart, updated by hand at every office visit and photocopied. This latest copy replaces the previous one in a folder marked "diabetic registry," which holds duplicates of everybody's flow sheets, to be used for data extraction.

The practice should, if it is an available feature in their EHR, set electronic reminders for the staff who are assigned to assure that patients are getting their glycohemoglobin levels and retinal exams at agreed-upon intervals. Otherwise, they can devise a card file tickler system.

The practice ought to check and see if it makes sense to do glycohemoglobin tests in the office or, if done by a contract laboratory, if it is possible to populate the electronic diabetic flow sheet automatically with the results. Doing such clerical tasks automatically is of much lesser importance than seeing to it that data, in whatever format, are collected when they should be, consistently recorded, and reliably followed-up. The group needs to know how a process is actually functioning before it can know if that process is making a difference in outcomes. An effective quality improvement program braids together assessments of process and of outcomes.

If a practice prescribes electronically, it might have a leg-up on keeping track of which diabetics are receiving statins. For patients who do not take a statin, the practice must decide how exactly the provider will be notified. If there is a contraindication to that class of drugs, where will that be recorded? How will it be counted when it comes time to evaluate how patients, providers, and practice are doing?

Seemingly trivial issues, like specifying who in the office will ask patients to remove their shoes and socks and when will they do it, can make a significant difference in the time spent on caring for these complex patients, while increasing the overall rate of foot exams and providing opportunities to teach self-care of the feet.

For retinal exams, the group might consider contracting for a system that lets them take pictures of retinas in the office and send them electronically to a consulting ophthalmologist. It is a great use of store-and-forward telehealth technology. Tyson Kim, MD, PhD, an ophthalmology trainee at the University of Michigan, is working on developing an iPhone-based retinal camera.[48] Google has already tested a neural network driven system that identifies signs of diabetic retinopathy, trained on 128,175 annotated images from the EyePAC database.[49]

The practice needs to figure out how to be sure every diabetic patient gets a flu shot annually. There might be an easy way to tie into the local immunization registry. What are the alternatives? Who and how are patients reminded of needed immunizations?

Every organization will answer the sorts of questions posed by this hypothetical QI project differently. The important thing is that each practice design (or adapt) something that works for them and then keep on evaluating and fiddling with their process, with an eye toward improving the target outcomes.

Personalized Medicine

When President Kennedy announced in 1961 that Americans would set foot on the moon before the end of the decade, he lent a whole new meaning to the word "moonshot," (said to have been coined a couple of years earlier by the baseball announcer, Vin Scully, to describe towering home runs hit by outfielder Wally Moon over the enhanced left field wall of the old Los Angeles Coliseum). Tragically, Jack Kennedy did not live to see the resounding success of his moonshot when, on July 21, 1969, Neil Armstrong became the first human being to set foot on the lunar surface.

The mission was accomplished using way less computing power than resides in the smartphones you and I carry around in our pockets.

It is not hard to argue that this man-on-the-moon mission did not yield nearly the amount of scientific information as could have been gotten at far less expense and risk of human life from data gathered by a myriad of un(wo)manned satellites. Another "moonshot," the Hubble space telescope, was launched into low earth orbit in 1990 at an initial cost of $1.5 billion. There have been ongoing costs for the Hubble too, including for periodically transporting astronauts to service the satellite.

As of 2016, Hubble's instruments had collected an estimated 125 terabytes of data. These data are open to mining by anybody who takes the trouble to register and learn how to access them online. It seems that every week astronomers and their mathematician sidekicks, with the help of big data analytic techniques, wring out of this enormous database new insights into how the universe works.

Was the huge expense of the hyper-ambitious Hubble Program worth it? Yes, if you think understanding what makes our solar system, galaxy and the whole universe tick is worth it. Maybe not if you are looking for results that make life tangibly better for earthbound humans. The same is true for the moonshot that came a decade or so after Wally Moon's crushing homers. Nevertheless, Neil Armstrong's famous words, "…one giant leap for mankind," broadcast worldwide as he made the first human footprint on the moon, continue to echo, at least in the American psyche.

Another scientific moonshot, the Human Genome Project, set out in 1990 to write down every one of the more than three billion letters (DNA base pairs) that serve as a blueprint for producing, growing and maintaining a human being. It was a huge effort, funded to the tune of $3 billion, by the governments of six wealthy countries, plus China (which, at the time wasn't considered wealthy). The work was done at 20 research centers in these 7 nations. It was estimated that it would take 15 years to fully delineate the human genome. It took ten. Starting with the seed money that was distributed to scientific laboratories, engineering departments and computer centers, the cost of fully delineating an individual human's genome has declined from $100 million to $1000–$2000![50]

There can be no doubt of the utility to human life of being able to rapidly and inexpensively elaborate every last bit of a person's DNA blueprint. Today you can spit a few milliliters of saliva into a collecting tube, mail it to 23andMe (named for the 23 human chromosomes), along with $99. In six to eight weeks, you will receive a report that says where your ancestors came from, based on a comparison of the DNA in the cells suspended in your saliva with a database of the DNA obtained from populations worldwide, including Neanderthal remains. For another $100, they will send a report that covers 19 traits that range from asparagus odor detection (some people can't smell it) to widow's peak; as well as presence of 35 recessive traits, from Autosomal Recessive Spastic Ataxia of Charlevoix-Saguenay (an inherited progressive neurological disease found in French Canadians) to

Zellweger Syndrome (a rare congenital disease that affects brain, liver and kidneys), with cystic fibrosis and sickle cell anemia in between.

It is interesting to note that BRCA, a well-studied family of genes responsible for increased breast and ovarian cancer risk, is not on this list. I imagine that is because these malignancies are so publicized and feared that the folks at 23andMe do not want to step into those roiling waters, which underlines the human side of using these gigantic genetic databases. It is crucial that individual and societal contexts be taken into account when considering when to collect and how to report and use the data.

Thanks in large part to technology that got its start with the Human Genome Project, today's scientific literature is continuously barraged with reports that tie particular genetic sequences to particular physical traits, diseases, tendencies to diseases and therapeutic responses.* The emotional, social, scientific and ethical issues raised by the potential to know too much about yourself or about somebody else are countless.

Some attempts have been made to establish, based on their genes, the way certain patients metabolize certain drugs, then to use this information to choose drugs and dosages that will be best for the particular patient with the particular disease. This is an example of personalized medicine. The overall idea is to know exactly what makes a person tick. "Personalized medicine," one of this decade's biggest medical buzzwords, holds great promise.

DNA is only one way to look at a person's makeup. It tells you what the blueprint is but not how the building works. For that you need to understand a body's other constituents, especially the proteins that are assembled on DNA and RNA templates. Casting a wide net for proteins, cataloging and quantifying them is called proteomics, similar to what genomics does with the nucleic acids that carry genetic information. Broad assays of small molecules, such as sugars, amino acids, nucleic acids and vitamins, are also helping to sharpen the picture of how the body works. This is called metabolomics.

Finally, the whole bacterial load of the body, especially in the gut, is being measured and assessed, mostly by way of the microbes' DNA and RNA. This is called biomics, a field still in its infancy. Biomics is teaching us that we have heretofore vastly underestimated the effect that the myriad organisms that live on and within us have on our health.

-Omics (genomics, proteomics, metabolomics, biomics) all depend on the ability to analyze huge amounts of data in creative ways. These fields of study are driven as much by the information revolution as by the biologic one. Alone and separately, the -omics are considered gateways to personalized medicine. Experts

---

* In 2017, the scientific journal, *Nature*, published a report, authored by a cancer researcher and a computer scientist, of a computer program called Seek & Blastn that had uncovered flaws in the DNA sequencing of over 60 papers, most of them in the cancer literature. (Phillips, N. Tool spots DNA errors in papers. *Nature*, 2017:551, 422–423.)

keep predicting that one of these days your doctor will have these data at her fingertips to be consulted in the same way she would look at your blood pressure or blood sugar. And that she would know how to use the information to chart a course of therapy that fits you like a glove.

Once we understand enough about how the genome works, in concert with the structural and metabolic machinery, we can actually fix some things. At the end of 2017, the FDA gave its first approval for gene therapy, a product called voretigene neparvovec-rzyl (Luxturna) that corrects the flaw in the DNA of people with the rare congenital disease, biallelic RPE65 mutation-associated retinal dystrophy, which causes total blindness in some patients. The drug, injected directly into the eyeball by an experienced eye surgeon, inserts a normal copy of the RPE65 into the patient's flawed DNA, restoring at least some vision in most cases. (Don't worry if you hadn't heard of this affliction. I hadn't either. It's extremely rare.)

We are getting better at editing DNA. The means for doing so, primarily CRISPR gene-editing technology, are well established. The devil is in the details. Theoretically, we could even edit fertilized human eggs to cure some inherited diseases, not just in the newly forming being, but also in all of her progeny forevermore.

Let me come back to earth now, before going all Tom Swift* on you. We are many years away from knowing what to do with most of this stunning wealth of -omic data we have been collecting. There are now, and gradually there will be more, bits of medical practice that will be tailored to patients' individual heredity, structure and metabolism. A few rare genetic diseases are already being mitigated and even cured by gene therapy. But it will be a long time before most of my colleagues and I are practicing personalized medicine that is grounded in -omics. Translating those data into understandable and actionable information, as well as working through the ethical and social issues raised by these approaches, will take a lot longer than it took us to fulfill President Kennedy's promise of an American on the moon.

Patient Engagement

"Patient engagement" is another of the most fashionable of today's buzzwords (actually two words). The term appears somewhere in the standards for most every mandated practice improvement program, including the Patient-Centered Medical

---

* Tom Swift was an amazing fictional boy inventor, modeled after Henry Ford and Thomas Edison. There are over 103 books in the five Tom Swift series for children, published from 1910 to 1993. The non-lethal TASER is said to be named after one of Tom's inventions, Thomas A. Swift's electric rifle. *Tom Swift and his Photo Telephone*, published in 1912, might be of particular interest to this audience.

Home and Meaningful Use. The laudable concept behind these words is to make patients into partners with health care practitioners and institutions, to empower (another hot buzzword) patients to take charge of their own health. If they truly feel responsible for their wellbeing and have the right information before them, the reasoning goes, people will make healthier lifestyle choices, feel better, live longer and save the system from spending so much money on treating their diseases.

Empowering people as patients also means empowering them as customers. The better they understand the benefits and costs of their alternative choices, the better course they can choose as they navigate healthcare labyrinth. And the better healthcare providers understand their customers, the better job we can do in serving them.

Here is one small example of patient engagement on a community level. A group of academicians from Hofstra University in Great Neck, New York proposed implementing a program that placed telemedicine equipment in the homes of disadvantaged people of color who lived in their community and suffered with heart failure. As community-engaged researchers, still a rarity in healthcare academia, they chose to bring their proposal to a sample of the people in the community whom they sought to serve. Here are the sorts of lessons the researchers learned from the focus groups they had convened:

- They needed to use a larger font on the monitor screen to make it readable to patients with diminished vision.
- The Spanish translation of patient instructions had a lot of obvious problems.
- Medical jargon needed to be reduced and language simplified to be understandable to people who read at a third-grade level.
- Given the size of some people's living space, electronic scales brought to their homes for measuring body weight were too big.
- It was suggested that patients have at least one in-person visit with the tele-monitoring nurse near the beginning of the program.
- The nurse needed to frequently reiterate that program participants had continued, unreduced access to their regular medical care.
- Undocumented patients needed reassurance that participating in the program would in no way jeopardize their stay in this country.
- Everybody needed to acknowledge that using the equipment was initially daunting to some patients.*,[51]

---

* When researchers gave tasks to twenty-six diverse people with diabetes or depression or to their caretakers—checking blood sugar, recording mood, taking a depression questionnaire or entering a drug name and dose or an appointment—using commonly available health apps, they were able to complete only 79 of 185 tasks (43%) without assistance. (Sarkar, U, Gourley, GI, Lyles, CR et al. Usability of commercially available mobile applications for diverse patients. *Journal of General Internal Medicine*, 2016:31(12), 1417–1426.)

Doesn't this list sound to you like a number of things you would want to know before doing a study or launching a project? This book is not the place to expound on the value of community engagement in doing health research. But I urge you to look into it. (See, for example, the book by Minkler and Wallerstein listed in the "Suggested Reading" appendix.)

One reason why the medical marketplace does not promote the sort of efficient valuation that the markets in pork bellies and SUVs do, is the disconnect between purchasers (insurance plans) and consumers (patients). Most of the time, patients do not know (nor do they care much if the money is not coming out of their own pockets) what things cost. Furthermore, though a trader at the Chicago Board of Trade may not know what a pig farm smells like, she certainly knows everything about the pork belly future contracts she is trading. And a person in the market for an SUV, though not a mechanic, can learn online what the dealer is actually paying for a vehicle, as well as test drive one before plunking down a chunk of her own money to purchase it.

Not so for healthcare. There have been feeble efforts to make patients prospectively aware of the medical costs they incur. Unfortunately, today most consumers still come to grips with the high price of healthcare only when they experience sticker shock upon arrival of a medical bill, worse than ever these days, even for the insured, due to stratospheric co-pays and deductibles. Not getting needed care and, ultimately, higher expense to the individual and to the system, is the all-too-frequent result. So is bankruptcy. Presenting cost information in a way that informs good choices for healthcare consumers is still way more in the realm of theory than of practice.*

A secure portal that keeps patients informed seamlessly about their medical care can be invaluable for patient engagement. Test results, appointments, reminders and prescription refills can be handled simply and efficiently. A good portal has a combination of push functionality, by which messages are sent out to patients, and pull functionality, which allows patients to enter the system to look things up themselves.

Making financial and medical information understandable and of use is the hard part. A formal way of getting feedback about how the organization communicates, such as a diverse patient advisory panel, is strongly recommended. Every organization needs customers who can tell them when they are and are not getting through.

Today the healthcare literature is rife with reports of attempts to influence patient behavior, via email, text messages, tweets and carrier pigeon. (I'm kidding about the carrier pigeons.) Some of the studies involve one-way reminders. Some

---

* A friend who teaches healthcare administration brings copies of her own medical bills and insurance reports to class and hands them out. Invariably, these *masters level* students are unable to make sense of them. She and I have admitted to each other that we don't understand our medical bills either.

engage patients in dialog. Clinicians and researchers have sought to influence, via electronic channels, diet, exercise, drug use, health literacy, depression, diabetes management and most any other behavior or condition you can think of (see Chapter 14, "The Connected World of Patients.")

So far, success at engaging patients through portals has been uneven. Any health issue that is hard to address face-to-face is at least as hard to address from a distance, even for young people whose consciousness seems never to stray too far from their smartphones.

Reminders may help keep a person on the straight and narrow when it comes to food intake (Weight Watchers online programs do this vigorously) or resisting the next cigarette or taking a scheduled walk. Programs that ask depressed people to check in regularly with an estimate of their stressors and mood may be of some help between counseling sessions. Text messages or tweets may educate teens, a little at a time, about safe sex. Nobody yet has achieved huge success in affecting a health behavior via social media.

Disease management is another matter. Some well-designed programs, based on internet connection, have shown terrific improvement in patients with congestive heart failure (CHF). Partners HealthCare, a large Boston healthcare system, found in 2010, that for 3000 CHF, patients who had received in-home equipment to monitor and report daily weight, blood pressure, heart rate and blood oxygen level, and were followed by just four RNs who called patients when they needed attention, their hospital re-admissions were reduced by 44% at a cost savings of more than $10 million over six years.[52] An overview of 15 reviews that had been published between 2003 and 2013 about chronic heart failure patients estimated that telemonitoring in the community reduced all-cause (not just cardiac) mortality by 15–40% and heart failure related hospitalizations by 14–36%.[53]

The key to success of any chronic disease/care coordination telehealth program is a close relationship between the people with the disease and the ones monitoring their illness from afar. Personalized messages, combined with data such as blood sugar or daily weight, can have a profound influence on how well someone cares for her disease.

Chapter 10

Telehealth

> I'm not blaming AOL, but if I had a guy's aorta in one hand and a needle in the other, and a doctor in Sweden was telling me how to do a schtick, and all of a sudden I got "Your session has been interrupted," I would be pissed off.
>
> **—Danny DeVito, actor**

You may wonder why I chose to write a whole chapter on telehealth, rather than to make it a section in the "Technology" or the "Clinical Care" chapter. It is because telehealth is the area of information technology with the most potential to revolutionize healthcare delivery right now. Telehealth is just not that hard to do, at least not technologically speaking. It is coming on like gangbusters in some places. Parks Associates, a marketing intelligence firm, reported in 2017 that 60% of US households with broadband access said they were interested or very interested in remote healthcare via internet or telephone.[1]

The Federal Communication Commission's Rural Health Care Fund, created in 1997, provides subsidies to supply rural communities with broadband access for healthcare. It was hugely undersubscribed until 2015. Ever since, annual requests have exceeded the $400 million cap on funding.[2]

Based on a 2017 survey of c-suite healthcare executives, stroke, mental health services, primary care, urgent care, dermatology and emergency care are the clinical areas with the most telehealth activity.[3] (This is far from a ground level view. See Chapter 14, "The Connected World of Patients," for that perspective.)

Kaiser Permanente, the nation's largest integrated health system, stated that, in 2015, 52% of its patient transactions (59 million out of 110 million) were conducted online.[4] For capitated systems, online transactions make sound money-saving sense, especially when coupled with an EMR. Please take note that this astounding statistic comes from an integrated health system, where financial and patient care incentives really do align (See Chapter 6, "Economics.") and that they probably count emails between patients and medical assistants as online transactions.

Even in the plain vanilla, fee-for-service, productivity-driven world, simple telehealth interventions can result in big cost savings. In 2006, the Centers for Medicare and Medicaid Services began a several-year study of supplementing the care of Medicare patients at two clinics in the Northwest who had heart failure, chronic obstructive lung disease or diabetes. The practices employed a Health Buddy, a home telehealth unit linked by phone line to care managers. Patients checked in daily by answering a set of disease-specific questions about their symptoms, vital signs, health behaviors and knowledge of their disease. Care coordinators called patients whose uploaded data gave reason for concern. Compared with a Health Buddy-less control group, the intervention group had slightly lower mortality. Their care costs were, on average, $1248–$2168 less per year.[5]

The notably conservative American Medical Association has even come onboard.* In 2016, the AMA House of Delegates passed a revised code, entitled "Ethical Practice in Telemedicine," that essentially blesses patient diagnosis- and treatment-at-a-distance. The code includes physicians' obligation to disclose financial interest in a telemedicine service they provide; to protect patient data; to assure that the choice of technology is appropriate to the patient's medical needs; and, of course, to urge all telemedicine patients to establish a relationship with a primary, face-to-face physician. The AMA doctors also resolved to develop model state legislation that would require insurers to open their customers' telehealth options and pay on a par for these services. They even adopted a policy that encourages "appropriate use" of telemedicine in education medical trainees and practicing physicians.[6]

Telehealth to the Rescue

Somebody has to care for the growing and aging population. There will not be enough doctors to do it face-to-face, especially not if, one of these days, everybody finally gets medical coverage. Telehealth technology is one important way to make a physician's labor stretch farther, both literally and figuratively. A good deal of the slack is already being taken up by non-physicians, including nurse practitioners and physician assistants. Thanks to telehealth, they too will be able to extend their

---

* When Medicare was enacted in 1965, it was over the strong, loud, public objection of the AMA, which declared the program to be "socialized medicine." It didn't take too many years before the doctors' organization discovered the benefit of public payments to care for all of their older patients on a cost-plus basis.

reach, as will home health nurses, physical, occupational and speech therapists, and virtually every other health professional you can think of.

Compared to some of the electronic gadgetry out there, telehealth technology is mostly pretty simple. There are: interactive video; radiologic image sharing; image capture and transmission by electronically enabled otoscopes (ear looker-inners), ophthalmoscopes, dermatoscopes colonoscopes etc.; remote monitoring of blood pressure, pulse, pulse oximetry, respiratory airflow, newborn jaundice, weight, activity level, joint range-of-motion, and a host of other factors; automated off-site laboratory testing, such as blood sugar and INR (a blood clotting test); electronic symptom and functional-level questionnaires; and more. The outputs of all of these gizmos can be viewed from a device perched on the lap of a clinician in a hammock.*

There is huge potential, as yet mostly unrealized, in remote continuous monitoring, which is telehealth technology too. Based just on their activity levels, measured with the accelerometer and GPS built into Android smartphones, researchers were even able to distinguish between depressed and non-depressed people with an accuracy of 86%.[7]

In itself, an activity monitor can only help so much. One study of 471 moderately obese participants, aged 18 to 35, who were seeking to lose weight actually found that the people who, besides receiving counseling about diet and exercise, also wore an activity monitor, were no leaner after six months than the control group participants, who just got the counseling.[8] Another study, performed on 800 people in Singapore, concluded that, over the course of 6 months, cash incentives helped people lose weight but Fitbit (an activity monitor that is worn on the wrist) didn't. Six months later, after the incentives had stopped, previous success in weight loss was nullified across the board.[9]

A study of 90 patients with chronic obstructive lung disease published in 2017 found that people who did their 6-week pulmonary rehabilitation program at home, consisting merely of online education about the disease and prescribed exercise, had made just as much improvement in their objectively-measured exercise tolerance as those who attended a group exercise class in person. This is the sort of simple to perform non-inferiority study that is the basis of a lot of telehealth research.[10]

The Veterans Health Administration has been running an experimental telehealth program with stroke patients in rural Alabama and Georgia. The veteran plays a videogame by operating a device with the limbs that need rehabilitation. The computer records parameters like range of motion, strength and time spent playing. Therapists use the device to monitor the data and set programs and goals.

---

* Many years ago, a friend told me about his plan to use an analog activity monitor, his self-winding watch, on vacation. His goal was to wear the watch the whole time and still have it wind down.

Results, in terms of improved independence in daily living, have been very encouraging.[11] This is exactly the sort of outcome that healthcare researchers and planners are most eager to see. It wasn't just the range of motion or the strength that improved in these patients, but their actual quality of life.

One of my favorite gadgets, and one of the most valuable, is the automated medication dispenser that reminds a patient when it is time to take a dose, then either dispenses the drug and records it, or alerts the patient and/or care providers of a missed dose. A group of researchers, who apparently understand people as well as they do technology, incentivized patients to take their anti-coagulant medication by tying an electronic pill dispenser to a daily lottery. Patients were eligible for a payoff only if they had taken their medication the day before. Small payoffs came on the average of one in five days, with a rare $100 payoff. For an overall cost of $3 per day per patient, the rate of missed and incorrect doses decreased from 22% to 3% a day, and the rate that patients' level of blood thinning fell within the target range increased from 65% to 88%.[12]

A fancy new gizmo, called a "digital pill," contains a bit of electronics. When swallowed, it transmits a signal to a sensor worn by the patient, which relays the message to her own electronic device and/or a healthcare provider. Digital pill data can be correlated with other information, such as blood pressure or blood sugar, or used alone to track compliance with a medication regimen.*[13]

Otsuka, the company that makes aripiprazole (Abilify), a widely-used antipsychotic that has recently gone generic, has teamed with Proteus Digital Health to offer a formulation that contains a grain-of-sand-sized transmitter that sends a message to a Band Aid-sized skin patch, which relays the message to an internet-connected device that keeps tabs of adherence with the drug regimen. The FDA has given its blessing to both the drug and the sensor. The collaborating companies have been very careful about how they word their product announcements. "We're not managing. We're about empowerment and enablement," said Andrew Thompson, Proteus CEO.

Otsuka and Proteus have understandably been a little touchy since Steven Colbert ripped into them on his television show saying, "…nothing is more reassuring to a schizophrenic than a corporation inserting sensors into your body and beaming information to all those people watching your every move." No price has been announced yet for the first digital drug. You can be sure it will be a good deal more than the generic product.[14]

---

* Let's still not forget plain old human interaction as a strategy for accomplishing patient adherence to a drug regimen. A study reported in 1984, before we had any fancier modes of tracking adherence than counting pills and monitoring prescription fill rates, showed that patients of doctors who communicated better with them were significantly more likely to take their medicines as directed. (Stewart, MA. What is a successful doctor-patient interview? A study of interactions and outcomes. *Social Science and Medicine*, 1984:19(2), 167–175.)

Most telehealth devices are not this fancy. They are pretty much the same old standard tools, wired to output digital data. Years ago, I interviewed the guy who had designed the ophthalmoscope that acquired images of the retinas of astronauts who inhabited the space station. (How retinas do in microgravity was an important question.) When I inquired about this technology he bluntly told me, "It's not rocket science."

One higher-tech device to keep your eye on is Glass, previously Google Glass, worn as glasses and projecting a heads-up display right in the wearer's field of vision, like those cool displays we see in movies about jet fighter pilots or what the world looks like to the predator in the self-titled movie. Loyola University Health System in the Chicago area has announced a program in which they will send nursing and medical students, clad in these fancy glasses, into the homes of patients who have been recently discharged from the hospital. Experienced professionals back on the home planet will monitor the interaction via the audio and video capabilities of the equipment. The people on the front lines will also be able to receive instructions that show up on their side of the glasses.[15]

Of course, it is ideal if the data generated by telehealth systems can be directly incorporated into the electronic medical record. But even without solving all those vexing issues of data interfaces and database structure, remote delivery of health-care can have a big positive impact on many patients and the providers and systems that care for them.

There is no need to launch into a Tom Swift gee-whiz list of all the really cool gizmos that exist or are imagined for the telehealth toolkit. For now (and really, for always), the challenge is to identify problems and dig into the tool chest to see what implement(s) might be most handy to address them. Then choose the simplest, most reliable device for the job, which often turns out to be a less expensive one.

Thanks to the availability by phone of a nurse practitioner who worked in a big city hepatitis clinic, and to the care protocols she emailed me, I was able to care for all of the patients in my rural practice who were infected with the hepatitis C virus. This used to be a pretty complicated proposition, with decisions based on virus sub-type, viral count in the bloodstream, disease progression and general health. Until I developed an e-mail and phone-based telehealth "system" for managing hepatitis C, we had to send everybody with the disease to a gastroenterologist, preferably someone who subspecialized in liver disease. A formal program at the University of New Mexico, called Project ECHO, reported in 2012 that, for hepatitis patients treated by 21 outlying primary care doctors who participated in weekly video conference with a hepatitis expert, their outcomes were just as good as for patients treated at the academic medical center 200 miles away.*[,16]

House calls may even sometimes be the best way to meet a need. In the first year of a project called Independence at Home, a house call physician group in

---

* Harvoni, a combination of two antiviral drugs, has been on the market since 2014. A 12- to 24-week course of the drug will *cure* 95% of patients with hepatitis C, at the cost of $94,500.

Portland, Oregon saved Medicare $13,600 per patient and a group in Washington, D.C. saved $12,000 per patient, mostly due to fewer emergency room visits and hospitalizations.[17]

The Wide Range of Telehealth

Lyft, the second-biggest ridesharing service, has partnered with National MedTrans, a non-emergency medical transport benefit manager, to form Concierge, a company that uses Lyft's information technology platform to provide rides requested by healthcare organizations for their patients. The program has been piloted with Medicaid enrollees in New York City and with Medicare Advantage patients in California. Early results are encouraging. Wait times for rides have decreased by 30% and cost per ride by 32%. Uber, the biggest ride-sharing company, has followed suit by partnering with a company called Circulation to do the same sort of thing.[18]

In the realm of moving molecules (as opposed to electrons) in service of healthcare, drones are doing some of the lighter lifting: showering contraceptives over rural parts of Ghana (a World Health Organization initiative); transporting blood and other samples to laboratories across town; ferrying blood for transfusion to outlying medical facilities in Rwanda (by a California-based company called Zipline[19]); and delivering medications and medical supplies to people stranded by natural disasters all over the world, even in the United States.

Self-driving cars are becoming a reality. But most of us will still be riding in cars driven by humans for at least the next five or ten years. Robotic surgery is growing by leaps and bounds. But it is going to be a while before anybody dares perform surgery without a doctor in the room who can take over in case the electronic system fails. In the meantime, we gladly make use of the hazard warning and automatic braking systems that electronic technology has brought to our cars. And surgeons employ surgical robots to assist them in doing delicate procedures through tiny incisions on the patient with whom they share the operating room.

Here is the definition that Jeff Bauer and I came up with for our 1999 book, *Telemedicine and the Reinvention of Healthcare*,[20]

> Telemedicine is the combined use of telecommunications and computer technologies to improve the efficiency and effectiveness of healthcare services by liberating caregivers from the traditional constraints of place and time and by empowering consumers to make informed choices in a competitive marketplace.[21]

I think that definition still holds up pretty well, 180 tech-years later. (One person-year equals ten tech-years.) However, in keeping with the dictum to keep it simple,

I would like to restate the definition in a more compact form: **Telemedicine is the use of electronic information and communication technology to overcome barriers of distance and time when delivering healthcare.**

I use the words "telemedicine" and "telehealth" interchangeably. The latter term is perhaps a little better because it sounds a little broader, a little less doctor-centric. People use both words, which is fine with me, just so they do not try to limit it to mean what a doctor does with a patient in the exam room, only from a distance.* That is where the field started, with the goal of doing medical consults from afar.

Some of the first telemedicine efforts were with prisoners. The goal of corrections telemedicine programs is to avoid the need to choose between the costly alternatives of either bringing providers onsite or securely transporting inmates, along with the necessary driver and guards, to an outside facility for every medical consultation. In this case, the barrier to care is not time or distance, but prison walls, which are easily hopped over by electronic means.

Texas, the state with the largest incarcerated population, employs about 200 telemedicine units. Basic units cost around $2000 each. Around ¾ of the units have been upgraded, for $8000 or so, to include stethoscope, otoscope and the ability to transmit documents and radiologic images.[22]

---

* Let me insert a small (well, medium-sized) rant here. It seems that, at nearly every rural health conference I attend in my region, I encounter the same presentation about a telemedicine program that has been quite successful in providing early consultation on patients suffering an acute stroke. This is an important service, because the earlier clot-dissolving medication is administered to a patient with an acute stroke, the higher the likelihood of success in reducing or even reversing the brain damage that causes the long-term consequences of this affliction. According to current guidelines, by 4.5 hours, it is too late. Busting clots in the brain is tricky business. It can be done safely on the front lines. But is best performed in consultation with an expert.

For years, this tertiary hospital, which has excellent neurology and neurosurgery departments, has touted its ability to rapidly provide a telemedicine consult on any patient in the region who has had an acute stroke. The consultation includes distant viewing of the head CT scan by a neurologist, as well as a video conference at the bedside with the clinician and the patient, which means that a video connection has to be organized, including the requisite positioning of AV equipment and arranging for a broadband connection. What the clinician on the patient's side of the connection requires is for an expert to look at the CT image to say if the stroke is due to a clot or a bleed, because the last thing you'd want to do is to administer a clot-dissolving drug to a patient who is bleeding into her brain. Then the bedside clinician and the consultant need to discuss the case history (When exactly did the incident begin? Is there heart or kidney disease? Has there been recent surgery? and so on), as well as the physical findings (the extent of paralysis, the heart rhythm, etc.). This information can be exchanged perfectly well in a telephone conversation. The only thing that the video channel adds is the perception that fancy, high-powered telemedicine is being practiced here. It's worked. Thanks in part to its telestroke program, the tertiary hospital has sewed up a large share of acute stroke care in the region, which means transfer of many patients who really do need to see a neurologist and/or a neurosurgeon into the hospital's waiting arms. As usual, marketing trumps common sense.

Distance can present as big a barrier to obtaining needed services as prison walls. Rural family doctors are three times more likely to use telemedicine than their urban counterparts.[23] The US military has gone into telehealth in a big way. In 2014, military clinicians offered services in 28 medical disciplines in more than thirty countries located in 18 time zones.[24]

Barriers needn't be geographic or prison walls. Sometimes they are social. Telehealth setups that included two-way video, otoscope, electronic stethoscope and a skin camera were installed in 22 access points in Rochester, New York at inner city elementary schools, as well as in suburban childcare and elementary schools, all connected up with 10 primary care practices. Over 6500 acute care visits were delivered with this fairly basic technology over the course of 6 years. Insurers' (79% of the pupils were covered by Medicaid) records showed that emergency department visits decreased by 22% among these kids.[25]

A similar program in Howard County, Maryland has not only brought more immediate health services to the children at five elementary schools, but has led other pediatric practices that did not initially participate in the program to climb aboard the telemedicine train.[26]

Telemedicine is not just interactive video; nor is it communication that necessarily relies on a special data-gathering device. Telephone calls can fit under the telemedicine rubric.* So can faxes, text messages, emails, blogs, tweets, even telegrams, I suppose.

Over two years, out of more than 200,000 calls to a nurse triage line staffed by Mayo Clinic with RNs, 20,230 could be paired to insurance claims in the next seven days. Forty-six of these claims indicated that the caller had had acute appendicitis. In 91% of the cases, based only on what the patient told her on the phone plus professional judgment supplemented by triage protocols, the nurse strongly recommended that the patient seek face-to-face care in eight hours or less. When contacted later, only 40% of the people who had been instructed to get medical care posthaste said that they would have gone to a doctor right away without that advice.[27]

A study reported in 2015 in the *Journal of Pain and Symptom Management* found that *a daily phone call* to homebound hospice patients halved urgent staff visits and cut after-hours calls by two-thirds.[28] Another study, reported by health insurance giant Aetna in 2015, found that individuals with a recent cardiovascular event who had completed at least 7 out of 16 phone or video one-on-one calls with a

---

* Remember that the first words ever heard over a telephone, spoken 1876 by Alexander Graham Bell to his assistant, Thomas A. Watson in a lab across the hall, "Mr. Watson, come here. I want you." were for sort of a medical emergency. Bell had just knocked over a battery jar, spilling sulfuric acid on himself. Just three years later, the British medical journal *Lancet* ran a description of an American doctor who saved himself a midnight trip when he listened over the phone to the cough of an anxious mother and her child, then confidently declared that they did not have croup, and went back to bed. (Aronson, SH. The Lancet on the telephone 1876–1975. *Medical History*, 1977:21, 69–87.)

licensed social worker plus a behavioral coach over the course of 8 weeks had a 48% lower rate of all cause hospital days in the subsequent 6 months when compared to matched controls, who had not received the counseling and coaching on emotional wellbeing and adopting a healthier lifestyle. That comes to about 191 hospital days avoided in the intervention group over the course of 6 months. At an average cost of $4500 per hospital day, this program saved an estimated $864,000 with technology no fancier than simple phone and video calls.[29]

A study of 566 Kansas smokers reported that adding a video component to a tobacco cessation program-at-a-distance did not improve quit rates over delivering information, advice, counseling and encouragement by plain old telephone.[30]

An investigation that included 325 Chicago-area patients with major depression found that telephone-based cognitive behavioral therapy delivered over the phone was nearly as effective in reducing depressive symptoms as face-to-face sessions.[31]

The effectiveness of a telehealth intervention usually comes down to strength of the connection between the human beings at either end; on the telephone, that mostly means listening. When the Swedish National Board of Health and researchers analyzed data from the 33 malpractice claims that had arisen over the course of 7 years as a result of advice given by nurses on a telephone help line, they concluded that failure to listen to the caller was the number one reason for the adverse outcome. Whether in person or remotely, listening is where all good healthcare begins.[32]

The effects, even of apps that have been selected for good reasons by competent professionals, must be evaluated. Forty-six mental health apps that had been vetted by the professional staff at an Australian mental health center were made easily available to half of three hundred and eighty seven sixteen to twenty-five-year-olds who had sought assistance there. This was the intervention group. The other half of the study participants, who served as a control group, did not have access to the online toolbox. Both groups got counseling. Participants in the intervention arm of the study received weekly messages or emails encouraging them to log onto the website, with a link that guided them to apps that were particularly appropriate for them. The controls received general wellbeing messages.

After four weeks, there was no difference between the intervention and control groups in their mental wellbeing, as measured by standard psychological tests. In fact, a higher proportion of the study participants than of the controls had dropped out before the four-week reassessment, implying perhaps that the intervention might have been perceived as just another hassle.[33]

On the other hand, in a study reported in 1999 of 195 internet-connected patients who had received outpatient surgery at Beth Israel Deaconess Medical Center in Boston, the ones who had had access to the ambulatory surgery nursing website section that had information on managing immediate postoperative pain reported significantly less discomfort the night following their procedure and the next day than did the patients whose access did not include the pain module.[34]

There is strong evidence of the effectiveness of telehealth interventions to support self-care in diabetes and congestive heart failure.[35] Much more research needs to be done on how to make telehealth interventions work best and how they can contribute to the management of many more diseases.

Real-Time versus Store-and-Forward

A good place to begin categorizing telehealth is with the distinction between real-time and store-and-forward communication. "Real-time," also called "synchronous," means that there is a live person at both (or all) ends of a communication channel. Phone calls and interactive video conferences are examples of real-time contact.

It follows, then, that store-and-forward, also called "asynchronous communication," does not require that sender and receiver(s) be on the same channel at the same time. Email is the consummate example of store-and-forward communication.

Each way of communicating, synchronous and asynchronous, has its advantages. By providing the immediacy of inter-personal association, a real-time electronic connection allows for some of the intimacy of in-person contact. Think back to those late-night murmurings over the phone with your lover. These could have been even better if you had added video (assuming you'd brushed your hair).

Daily check-in phone calls with isolated patients may be quite therapeutic, in terms of the information gleaned in managing their medical problems, as well as simply providing human contact and emotional support. A compassionate relationship, in itself, is therapeutic. Super-charge an audio contact with a familiar face and the person-to-person connection will be that much stronger. Programs that provide simple in-home telepresence to very sick people for a period of time after hospital discharge regularly encounter resistance when they try to discontinue a service that has regularly brought a familiar face into the patient's home.

The Veterans Affairs General Medical Clinic in White River Junction, Vermont reported that they had been able to decrease total clinic visits by 19%, medication use by 14%, hospital days by 28% and intensive care days by 41% in 497 male patients over 54 years old simply by making regular phone contact with them at their homes. This intervention, which took place in 1988 through 1990, was performed by clinic physicians who asked patients about a standard checklist of symptoms. They called at intervals specified by protocol. Doctors were allotted an extra 60 minutes a week to make no more than 4 check-in calls to patients and document the encounters.[36] Giving the doctors the paid time to make their calls was a key to the program's success. (In a fee-for-service arrangement, this 60 minutes of doctors' time would have been written off as lost productivity.)

By 2012, the VHA's enhanced home telehealth program had reached over 119,000 veterans, facilitating independent living for 36% of them who would otherwise have required some level of domiciliary care. Hospital admissions decreased by 38% from the previous year and inpatient days by 58%.[37]

In the first year of a free confidential service to all Canadian Citizens that began in 2001, RNs fielded over one million calls in English and French, with translation support for 110 languages. In Ontario alone, it was estimated that the dial-a-nurse service had diverted more than 210,000 people from emergency rooms.[38]

Speaking of translation, there are many commercial translation services that offer audio, and lately video, links for translating from virtually any language you can think of into English and back. In one practice, I have accessed, by commercial language line, able medical translators for patients who spoke each of three different languages used in Somalia. Though somewhat cumbersome, the process worked just fine. Had we had a video channel for the patient, translator and me to share, I think it would have worked even better.

A more fully equipped consultation service has its place. One geriatric practice, consisting of 11 physicians and 17 advanced practice providers (PAs and NPs) who cared for 750 residents of 17 extended care facilities in Rochester, New York, was able, over the course of 2 years, to avoid transport to an emergency room or urgent care center in 75% of 301 acute illness consultations accomplished by telemedicine. The system featured a digital stethoscope and otoscope, an EKG machine, a high-resolution camera and a laptop computer.[39] Analysis did reveal the tendency for a doctor who was not in the room with the patient to stray from the best practice and follow a more "conservative" path, for example, to prescribe antibiotics for uncomplicated sinusitis "just to be safe."[40]

A number of studies have found that counseling and psychiatry services delivered via interactive video rival the effectiveness of face-to-face sessions.[41] Therapeutic alliances that are maintained by electronic means appear to be "non-inferior" to those that happen in person. The strength of the alliance is a strong predictor of the success of therapy.[42,43]

Between 2007 and 2009, 364 patients who screened positive for depression at 5 rural federally-qualified health centers (FQHC) were enrolled in a telemedicine study. Mental health services are generally quite scarce in rural areas and even harder to access for the non-moneyed folks who patronize FQHCs. None of the participating clinics had a mental health professional on staff. Half of the patients received the usual outpatient treatment from their primary care providers. This was the control group. The other half, the intervention group, had access, besides to their primary care provider, to a pharmacist by phone and to a psychologist and a psychiatrist by video conference. Both groups had nurse care managers who had been hired for the study to look after each practice's depressed patients. The intervention group was almost 8 times more likely than the control group to respond to depression treatment and nearly 13 times more likely to stay in remission.[44]

From 2004 to 20014 telementalhealth consults for rural residents covered by Medicare rose 45% per year. (Before you get too excited, that was from 2365 to 8710, still just a drop in the bucket.)[45]

All a patient needs for a video therapy session is a view of the provider's face. The provider is best served by two camera presets, one trained on the patient's face and one, to assess body language, on the patient's whole body. There are even papers that examine perception by the patient of eye contact with the consultant, based on the positioning of patient, professional, cameras and monitors.[46]

Some anxious people actually do better counseling with a face on a monitor than with a live person in the same room. These patients feel more comfortable discussing health matters when the setting feels less intimate. Research participants who were interviewed by Ellie, a virtual humanoid that had been "trained" to pick up non-verbal cues and respond to them, said they were overall more inclined to reveal sensitive information if they believed Ellie was autonomous, rather than if "she" was controlled by a person.[47]

* * * * * *

Avatars, fictional online personae, are popping up all over, including in healthcare. One interesting study that gave people the choice from among eight avatars of different ages, sexes and races to answer their questions about HIV/AIDS found that the users were at least as willing to open up to the avatars as they were to human experts. Not surprisingly, there was a large correlation between client race and the race of the chosen avatar. Overall, a white woman avatar was most popular.[48]

In 1998, Medicare released a set of rules that gave states the option to cover a narrow range of telehealth consultations in health professional shortage areas.[49] Only real-time encounters, with a patient at one end of the connection and a doctor simultaneously at the other, were covered by the Center for Medicare Services (CMS). Radiology and pathology interpretation, no matter the distance between patient and doctor, have never been counted by the government as telehealth. Some states today do allow for insurance payment for a limited range of store-and-forward consultations.[50]

Real-time is how you do things in an emergency. In the case of heart attack or stroke, every tick of the clock can mean heart muscle or brain cells lost.

If a situation is not emergent and there is no need for the sort of immediate interaction that counseling requires, it is harder to justify doing teleconsultation synchronously. Scheduling people, especially doctors, to simultaneously be at either end of a real-time connection can be quite a challenge, adding hassle and expense. Medicare's requirement that telehealth consults be done in real-time has put a significant crimp in the growth of telemedicine.

It is especially hard to free up physicians to do teleconsults in a smaller system with fewer doctors and staff. A larger contingent of people on duty in a big emergency room may provide the flexibility to free up one doctor per shift to be available for any teleconsults that might come in. The American military, with its deep and widespread resources, has been a pioneer at providing immediate consultation by electronic means from all sorts of hairy situations across the globe.

Electronic Intensive Care Units (eICU) have hit their stride in furnishing excellent moment-to-moment subspecialty backup for care delivered to very sick patients in out-of-the-way places. In 2016, Avera Health bragged that it provided eICU services to 10% of the nation's 1331 small rural critical access hospitals, located in 10 states, including 60% of the electronically monitored beds in its home state of South Dakota. Avera claims that its eCare services reduce ambulance and helicopter transfers from rural to urban sites by 18%, which comes to a chunk of change, most of it staying in the local healthcare system, where it is sorely needed. Not to mention that costs to family and friends, as well as worry, get significantly smaller if they can avoid all those trips to the city[51] to see their hospitalized loved one.

The eICU program at Emory University and affiliates reduced the average cost per stay of 8019 patients by $1486 during 15 months in 2014 and 2015, which came to $4.6 million. A large organization with a dedicated staff of specialty-trained nurses and doctors who watch patient monitors round-the-clock and react quickly to emergencies, sometimes even before they occur, can provide the same service to patients in a facility hundreds of miles away for little incremental cost than what it takes to add a few extra monitors in the control room to receive the distant data feed.

The challenge resides in getting staff on both sides of the channel to collaborate smoothly in managing the patients for whom they share responsibility. If clinicians on the monitoring end are allowed to directly give orders to the professionals at the bedside, rather than requiring that the orders be approved by a local doctor, patient length of stay in the ICU, a significant measure of quality of care (assuming that patients dying sooner is not the reason for earlier discharge), is reduced even further.[52]

A plastic surgery emergency consult service at the giant University Hospital in Newark, New Jersey reported that, over the course of one month, of 42 trauma referrals (mostly face and hand injuries), transmission from distant hospitals of a brief history plus up to 4 images (wound, x-ray, etc.) resulted in correct diagnosis 95% of the time. Transfer to the larger facility of one-quarter of these patients could have been avoided. What's more, surgeon response time, via this coordinated system was nine minutes, compared to 49 minutes for telephone consultation. Coordination was just as important to the success of this telehealth program as were the mobile gadgets.

In another study of 590 patients of 12 Connecticut community health centers whose primary care clinicians needed help from cardiologists, if the primary care providers had access to email consultation, 69% of their patients did not wind up having to see the heart specialist face-to-face. What's more, e-consultation took on average 5 days, whereas face-to-face took 24.[53]

A study done in Italy in 2004 provided 74 heart failure patients with telephone access to a nurse and a home single-lead (meaning able to assess rhythm only) EKG device connected to a modem, claimed to reduce hospitalizations by 89% from the previous year. I imagine it was more the nurse than the EKG that made the difference.[54]

A heart failure management program by Sentara Home Services in Virginia that included face-to-face and virtual video visits was able, for 44 enrolled patients, to reduce hospital admissions by 82% and ER visits by 77% over the course of 6 months. Again, I suspect that most of the improvement resulted from close contact with tuned-in nurses, not from having a video link.[55]

Using no electronic technology, an Australian study found in 1999 that just *one* post-hospital home visit by a nurse and a pharmacist a week after discharge, with referral to the primary care doctor if they saw fit, halved the hospital days, emergency room visits, and the death rate of the intervention group compared to the control group over the subsequent 18 months. Half of the time the visiting professionals found that the patient was not taking her medication as it had been prescribed on hospital discharge.[56]

Lest we get too enamored by care coordination services delivered by professionals, in-person or electronically, Allina Health, a health system serving Minnesota and Wisconsin, found that keeping watch on patients with chronic disease by laypeople whom they dubbed "care guides" after just *two weeks of training*, these patients were 31% more likely to meet care goals than the control group, who did not have the benefit of care guides to help them make and keep medical appointments and even to quit smoking.[57]

Over the course of a year, an hour-long interactive video consultation on 229 candidates for elective surgery whose medical condition might pose increased risk of complications reduced the last-minute procedure cancellation rate for medical reasons from 5.6% to 1.3%. Medications were optimized and preoperative studies were ordered remotely. The average patient lived 992 miles from the hospital in Brisbane, where they were to have their surgery. In other words, 10 people whose surgery was canceled were each saved 2000 round-trip miles and a few unnecessary days away from home and work, while the medical center got a corresponding boost in the efficiency of its surgical scheduling.[58]

Thanks to miniaturization, and portability, there's little need any more to drag around your pillow, blanky and teddy and toss and turn in a strange bed for a study in a sleep lab. A large share of the physiologic monitoring that goes into diagnosing and managing sleep disorders has moved from the sleep lab into the patient's own home, where it costs less and results better reflect the person's real-life sleep patterns.

Telehealth technology now allows audiology exams, including sophisticated hearing tests, checks of middle ear function and visual examination of the ear canals and drums, to be done from a distance. It is also possible to program hearing aids remotely.[59]

As a stand-alone service, remote automated consultation may take the form of sort of a doc- (or NP- or PA-) in-a-box supermarket walk-in clinic, which can keep patients out of expensive emergency rooms by addressing their relatively minor acute care needs. Some consultation services really are delivered now in boxes. The companies American Well and Computerized Screening, Inc. make private kiosks, equipped with cameras, vital sign equipment and even stethoscopes, which connect to a health professional, such as a nurse practitioner.

Walgreens announced in 2017 that it had opened a health kiosk, affiliated with the New York Presbyterian, "New York's No. 1 hospital," (their wording) serviced by emergency physicians at the Weill Cornell School of Medicine. The first site is at 40 Wall Street, with others in the planning stages.[60]

Less ritzy health kiosks are finding their way into malls and workplaces. A consultation may cost a cash customer as little as $15.[61] Health insurer Anthem installed 34 kiosks for 20 employers in 18 months, beginning in 2015.

It may be worth a doctor's while to do non-emergent telehealth consults if the encounters are bundled together. Some nephrologists, for example, do telemedicine patient rounds in satellite dialysis centers at the same time every day, with an assistant, or better a collaborating nurse, wheeling the cart that contains the telemedicine equipment from patient chair to patient chair.

On the High Plains of eastern Colorado, we sometimes provided telemedicine consults when face-to-face visits had been cancelled because the airplane that was to shuttle the specialist doctor to town had been grounded by a storm that was bad enough to keep her from flying but not to keep the scheduled patients away from the hospital. This was time that the doctor had already set aside, so the telehealth demands were not disrupting an otherwise packed schedule. Telehealth technology also gives itinerant surgeons the ability to do all-important post-operative rounds from afar.*

Years ago, for an anticoagulation clinic, my rural health center insisted on placing telehealth patients into the same schedule as in-person patients. All the consulting pharmacist had to do to see one of our patients from sixty miles away was to step in front of the video camera in the next cubicle. The staff at our site had already done the intake, gathered test results and placed the patient before the video camera and monitor. Today, the consultant would not even have to step into an adjoining cubicle. She could simply log into a secure line and use the video camera on the desktop computer in front of her to conduct the remote visit.

* * * * * *

The concept of telephone tag gets at the core challenge of real-time services, with the demand that two or more people be at the same (virtual) place at the same time. What we all love about email is that you do it on your own time. We complain about how much of our time email seems to gobble up. (A study of 46 primary care providers in 3 Texas clinics uncovered that they received, on average, 77 messages

---

* My experience working in rural hospitals convinced me that a competent generalist, backed by a good nursing staff, laboratory and radiology, could do about all of the rounding on out-of-town surgeon's cases just fine, so long as we could make easy telephone contact with the doctor. In such situations, the problem solved by fancier telehealth technology was mostly to assuage the insecurity or guilt of the operating doctor who had had the lesson drummed into him from the first day of training that the surgeon is *always* responsible for the care of his patients and must attend to them personally.

per day in their EHR inboxes.[62]) But it is our time. We always have the option of ignoring or deleting non-critical messages.

If I want a rheumatologist to look at the results of a blood panel I'd ordered on one of my patients, rather than calling her office, talking to the receptionist, waiting on hold, talking to the medical assistant, then finding that the doctor is at the hospital, I can, in a minute or so, email her (assuming we share a HIPAA-compliant channel) with the results attached, along with a brief description of the patient and my question. She can answer me from office, hospital or home, when she has a chance. If we need to discuss the case, she and I can agree, by email, on a time for the call.

There is a nationwide shortage of skin specialists. Because it lends itself so well to store-and-forward technology, dermatology is a field ripe for telehealth. Analysis of 965 consults performed by a Canadian teledermatology service in 2017 revealed that most of the consultations took the specialist 10–15 minutes to perform and saved nearly half the patients the need for a face-to-face visit. Ninety-five percent of the referring doctors rated the service good to excellent.[63]

Every dermatology diagnosis depends, in large part, on examination of the skin. A dermatoscope image displayed on a high-resolution monitor actually yields better images than the naked eye. Email the dermatologist pictures of skin lesions and rashes, along with a brief history that includes things like time since onset, itchiness, other diagnoses, medications and allergies, and she can diagnose most cases, looking at her laptop while eating corn flakes at the breakfast table. (Warning: unless you are a seasoned healthcare provider or have a naturally strong stomach, I do not recommend looking at images of icky skin lesions while eating.)

In a study published in *JAMA Dermatology* in 2016, researchers sent requests for online consultation on 62 fictional patients to 16 direct-to-consumer dermatology websites, at a cost of $35–$95 per consultation. Only 26% of the sites supplied the credentials of the consulting provider. The investigators found that, if the picture of the skin was alone enough to make a diagnosis, the consultants usually did pretty well. But when more clinical information, which could have been obtained face-to-face or by further email exchange, was needed to make the correct diagnosis, that communication rarely happened and the quality of care suffered.[64]

The problem is that Medicare and the other insurance providers still do not pay for most store-and-forward consultations.

A very low-tech telehealth cervical cancer screening program was quite successful among poor women in Madagascar (where health insurance coverage is not an issue because almost nobody has it). Women who had tested positive for papillomavirus, the cause of cervical cancer, were called into the clinic for further screening. A medical student inserted a vaginal speculum, painted their cervix with an iodine solution that could reveal abnormal tissue, and took a picture of the cervix with a smartphone. The images were forwarded to expert off-site physicians for interpretation. If indicated, an on-site physician later took cervical biopsies and brushings as directed by the interpreting expert. The minority of patients whose cervical testing results were concerning got the care they needed from highly trained experts.[65]

There was good agreement between the results obtained by novices who were backed up by distant experts, and results generated in-person by experienced doctors, which means that in Madagascar and other poor countries, many women, who might otherwise never attend to their cervical pre-malignancies or cancers, could be screened at little cost and hassle, saving much suffering and many lives. (Widespread vaccination of girls and boys against papillomavirus, the causative agent for cervical cancer, would be even better.)

Online medical consultations are popping up all over the place, both inside of systems and as entrepreneurial stand-alone services. Five to ten times a day Doctors Without Borders relays, via the internet, questions about challenging cases, submitted by providers in locations all over the troubled world and answered by a far-flung network of 280 consulting physicians.[66]

A number of other nonprofits and private companies, including Planned Parenthood, have begun offering contraceptive services through online consultations. Women answer questions about their health history, current health, sexual behavior and contraceptive preferences. When appropriate, the online encounter may result in a prescription of birth control pills, patches, vaginal rings or morning-after pills, along with education. It was determined long ago, based on strong data, that the negative medical and social consequences of unwanted pregnancy far outweigh the risk of using these low-risk contraceptive methods, even without a professional exam. For obvious reasons, online contraceptive prescription programs have generally done their best to stay out of the limelight.[67]

In Brazil, a program that provided abortion-inducing drugs to 370 women, at up to 13 weeks gestation, after they had completed an online consultation, allowed many women who otherwise did not have access to pregnancy termination services to receive abortion-inducing medications. The complication rate was low.[68]

In Iowa also, telehealth has brought medical abortion services to women in the first term of pregnancy who lived more than 50 miles from a site that performed surgical abortions.*[69] It should come a no surprise that the same battles that have occurred in state and federal courts over in-person access to pregnancy termination services are shaping up over providing those services from a distance.[70]

---

* At the other end of the family planning issue, a company called Cambridge Temperature Concepts claimed to have the same success rate at helping women become pregnant as in vitro fertilization, at a fraction of the cost. For £495 ($635 in 2011), a patient would receive a temperature sensor to wear in her armpit. The device was capable of taking up to 20,000 readings a day, which would be forwarded, via a PC, to the company's computers. Based on calculations made with these data, women (and their partners) received information about the ideal three-day window for conceiving during every cycle. Customers got a full refund if they did not become pregnant after one year of using the system. Cambridge Temperature Concepts is now called Sensii and they do still market a fertility product centered around a continuous temperature monitor with the new and improved name Duofertility. It hooks up with a smartphone. Prices start at £65.99 ($85 per month in 2017). The only evidence of effectiveness offered is a white paper published by the company itself. (Telemedicine Fertility monitor as successful as IVF. *The Wall Street Journal.* July 1, 2011.)

Telehealth systems are useful for teaching. Even the super-cautious American Board of Medical Specialties, which accredits post-medical school residency training programs, allows for proctoring of student doctors by distant preceptors via these technologies. Thanks to telehealth, student experience can be enriched by virtually bringing them to the bedside, examination room or operating room to observe interesting cases.

For newly-credentialed doctors, procedures can be telementored by distant teachers who can follow, on a split-screen, the goings-on in the endoscopy lab (including a view of the patient's face), while sharing with the newbie operator the view through the colonoscope. Ideally, the doctor with her hands on the scope will already have spent significant time practicing on one of the excellent setups used for virtual colonoscopy training, as well as having had a hand in some procedures live, with a teacher present in the room. (See Chapter 13, "Education.")

Since 2005, doctors at the University of Pittsburgh Medical Center have trained hundreds of surgeons in procedures performed on the base of the skull with scopes that fit through holes drilled through the bone. Sixty percent of the learners who come to Pittsburgh for the four days of training are from foreign countries. Beginning in 2011, a number of the attendees have taken advantage of video hook-ups that allow their mentors back at Pitt to see what they do through the scope so they can advise the newbies during the procedures. The teachers also have telestrators that let them draw right on top of the video pictures. In 2012, this telementoring setup cost about $15,000[71] per site, which would probably be recouped (at least in the United States) by getting paid for doing one or two of these procedures.

Everybody would like to have a personal clinician who knows them well and who can always see them on short notice. Some are concerned that the availability of remote consultation services will make it too easy for people to never select a primary care physician. In my humble opinion (IMHO in text message shorthand*), giving professional help to people who otherwise wouldn't consult a clinician is worth it. Telemedicine services present much less of a barrier to getting good care than a know-it-all neighbor does when she tells you, for free, that all you need to do for your incipient pneumonia is to eat a garlic clove, washed down by a tablespoon of apple cider vinegar, four times a day until you feel better (or you can't breathe).

Some telehealth services still require a person to be in the room with the patient, to serve as hands and nose for the clinician. The first telehealth clinic that I helped to grow was a wound care consult service, based in my practice in rural Colorado. We stumbled on the idea when the big referral hospital in our system pitched us about sending them patients for treatment in their underutilized hyperbaric chamber, a device that was initially developed to treat the bends in divers who ascend too rapidly from deep dives. These pressure chambers were later found to be of use in caring for some difficult-to-heal wounds by driving extra oxygen into the tissues.

---

* To my kids: See! I get it!

With two large nursing homes in our small town, we clinicians encountered a lot of hard-to-heal pressure sores and diabetic ulcers, which we did our best to treat. I might, a few times a year, refer such a patient to the wound care clinic at the tertiary facility an hour's drive away. Occasionally, one of those patients did receive hyperbaric treatments over the course of weeks or months.

The big hospital and our little hospital agreed to try doing a telemedicine wound clinic, to be staffed on their side by a wound care doctor, who came armed with a lot of specialized knowledge and a hyperbaric chamber. On our end, a medical assistant unwrapped the wound and positioned the patient so the camera could be focused on her wound or on her face, or else zoomed out to her whole body. A nurse practitioner then participated in a three-way video conversation with the patient and the doctor, with the MA looking on and soaking it all in. The NP knew the patient, so she could contextualize, for both patient and consulting physician, what was going on medically. She could report any odors emanating from the wound and, under the guidance of the doctor, scrape off ooze, pick off crust and trim dead tissue from the wound. Toward the end of the visit, the physician would instruct the patient, medical assistant and NP on treatments and dressings and, if indicated, schedule a follow-up appointment. Rarely was that appointment face-to-face with the far-away specialist. The next, all-important step was for the NP to instruct the nursing home staff, via written orders and sometimes a phone call, about day-to-day patient care, including how to clean and dress the wound, what complications to watch for and strategies for unloading pressure from the affected skin.

Our two half-day-a-month wound care clinics were busy from the outset. Rates of bedsores at the nursing home, a major quality indicator considered by all long-term care accreditors and watchdogs, were cut drastically. The nurse practitioner decided to get extra training in wound care and found that she could handle almost all of the cases without a consultant. If the NP was not available, her very capable medical assistant became a resource to all of us clinic providers when we needed immediate advice about choosing a dressing or a topical preparation for a skin wound.

Eventually, we found little further need for the telehealth wound care clinic. Referrals dried up as our local expertise expanded. The wound care specialist and the clinic providers had established a relationship that made for much more appropriate consultation when a patient did need it. Everybody (except, I suspect, for the hyperbaric unit business manager) was better off.

WoundMatrix unveiled a new mobile wound management telehealth system in 2015 that does about what ours did back in 2001. Their system is based on smartphones and tablets. As far as I can tell, except for making connections easier, the only significant thing the WoundMatrix system could do that ours couldn't was to automatically measure the area of a wound.[72] These days it is easier than ever to cobble together the pieces required to meet a particular clinical need without purchasing yet another expensive, stand-alone product that may or may not exchange data with one's other systems.

Studies have pretty overwhelmingly shown high acceptance of services delivered by electronic technology, even when there is not a clinical person to accompany the patient in the room. A 2016 survey by the Health Industry Distributors Association found that more than half of patients were "very satisfied" with their telehealth consults and 54% rated the experience as *better* than a regular face-to-face consultation.[73] Gains in accessibility and savings in cost more than compensated for not having another warm body in the room.

A 2016 survey of 500 mothers, performed by Blue Cross and Blue Shield of Georgia, found that 71% percent of the moms had recently lost more than two hours from a work or a school day taking a child to the doctor and 54% percent felt that video doctor visits would help them feel more confident about managing their family's wellbeing. Nearly all of the mothers expressed the wish that their children have round-the-clock access to a doctor.[74]

In my experience, the technology rapidly becomes transparent, just as the screen and surrounding movie theater dissolve into the background when you watch a movie.* How often do you, while talking on the phone, stop and say to yourself, "Wow! I'm actually talking to someone who is across the continent!"?

* * * * * *

The answer to meeting a clinical need is never, "Get a telemedicine system. Now what's the question?" You always have to start with lessons learned in Management 101. Do a solid needs assessment, followed by creative brainstorming, preferably with an array of stakeholders, as well as experts who know something about a range of delivery options, including telehealth. "Expert" means someone who knows something you need, not necessarily an expensive outside consultant.

Before starting a consultation service, there are numerous procedural and legal hurdles to clear, such as: professional accreditation and licensing; who will pay for the services and how much; and how malpractice liability will be addressed. The organization has to be very careful about how requests for consultation will be managed, with clearly specified: scope of services; procedures for detecting and referring urgencies; clinical documentation; distribution of workload; payment and insurance; etc.

Because it's their job, providers do worry that care dispensed at a distance could be of lesser quality. Administrators agonize over the service's palatability to patients and staff, as well as its financial impact. The technology is not that hard to figure out. The payer and regulatory environment can be fragmented and frustrating. If you are doing telehealth, make sure you have someone who understands how to clear these hurdles, which are ever-so-slowly being lowered. As usual, though, it is people who present the biggest barriers to change.

---

* Unlike novice moviegoers in the early 1900s who panicked and ran from the image on the screen of a train running toward them.

Chapter 11

Public Health

The future is already here. It is just not evenly distributed.

—William Gibson, author

I gather. young man, that you wish to be a Member of Parliament. The first lesson that you must learn is, when I call for statistics about the rate of infant mortality, what I want is proof that fewer babies died when I was Prime Minister than when anyone else is Prime Minister.

—Winston Churchill

Back in Chapter 6, "Economics," when I introduced the Institute for Healthcare Improvement's Triple Aim, did you notice that only one of the aims, improving the patient experience of care (including quality and satisfaction), is about individuals? The other two aims, improving the health of populations and reducing the per capita cost of health care, are from an aggregate point-of-view.

In medical school, as well as in almost all other programs that educate patient-facing health professionals, we learn to care for people one at a time. We may hear an occasional lecture on public health, or maybe even do a required rotation at a health department or some such institution. But the vast preponderance of health career instruction is about how to do the best job taking care of the patient before us. As a patient, you would want it that way. The trouble is, we professionals stay so busy feeding root systems, spraying for infestations and pruning, that we lose sight of the forest.

Even though today about two-thirds of Americans' medical care is paid out of Medicare, Medicaid, Veteran Affairs and other tax-funded coffers,[1] the reigning model for care delivery is still private, for-profit (which includes not-for-profit medical institutions that necessarily run a large share of their business through very profitable insurance companies). As I said in Chapter 6, "Economics," acute care is what yields the largest profit (or margin, if you call yourself not-for-profit). Prevention pays least well, paradoxically, because it gives the biggest bang for the buck.*

In 2016, only 4% of federal US healthcare dollars went to public health.[2] This should come as no surprise. The good news is that, thanks to the huge amounts of data being generated by everybody, from county health departments to Twitter, and to ever-sharper tools for making sense of these data, we are getting better at doing public health on a shoestring.

Since 2008, Australia has had program called "Let Them Know" (LTK) that allows people with venereal infections to notify sexual partners anonymously. The LTK website offers information on sexually transmitted diseases (STD) as well as materials with testing and treatment information for message recipients to take to their healthcare providers. I was not able to learn much on the effectiveness of LTK in tracing contacts and reducing the incidence of STDs. I did find that clinicians are great supporters of this simple and, I imagine, inexpensive program that runs on the power of the internet.[3] With all of the hooking up that social media make possible these days, it makes perfect sense to harness these same avenues of communication to address the public health issues that result from new ways of bringing people together.

The authors of a study published in 2014[4] showed that, by filtering Twitter for messages that seemed to be about flu symptoms, they could identify influenza outbreaks two to four weeks earlier than the Centers for Disease Control could with their usual method of analyzing data reported by health departments. "Google Flu Trends," which tabulates the location and quantities of queries about influenza, has also demonstrated some pretty good predictive power. In Japan, public health authorities tracked a flu epidemic by monitoring a prescription surveillance system.[5]

Analysis of tweet texts has been at least as accurate as the National Survey on Drug Usage for generating a map of prevalence of prescription opioid misuse, at a fraction of the time and cost.[6]

HealthMap, an online disease-tracking tool that includes news and social media inputs, identified an Ebola outbreak in Africa nine days before the World Health Organization recognized and announced the epidemic.[7]

Researchers found they could spot an eruption of norovirus within one day of its appearance by monitoring Baidu, the dominant Chinese internet search engine, for just two words, "noro" and "norovirus." Identifying a flare of this highly infectious

---

* A story that ran in the *New York Times* in January 2017 entitled, "Blame Technology, Not Longer Life Spans for Health Spending Increases," (Frakt, A. Blame technology, not longer life spans, for health spending increases. *The New York Times.* January 23, 2017) summarizes research that has found it is not the average American life span of 79 years, 3 years more than in 1995, that accounts for much of the huge increases in health care spending. Medical care of older people does cost more. From 65 to 74 years of age, they spend double the number of

agent early can save huge numbers of people, especially school children, from suf-fering with vomiting and diarrhea.[8]

Chicago's Department of Public Health uses a tool called Foodborne Chicago to screen Twitter for messages that are suspicious for food poisoning, then automat-ically sends the tweeters messages like "That doesn't sound good. Help us prevent this and report where you ate..." and invites them to provide more information to the Foodborne Chicago website. Beginning in 2013, during the first ten months of the program, out of 270 tweets suspicious for food poisoning, 193 tweeters accepted the invitation to supply more information, which resulted in 133 unan-nounced restaurant inspections that uncovered at least one critical violation in 20% of the sites surveyed. This compares to a 16% rate of critical violations on routine restaurant inspections.[9]

Seasonality of emotional issues is easy to follow on the web. Google Trends shows searches for anorexia, bulimia and schizophrenia decreased by 37% and 24% for suicide in the US summertime. Australia saw nearly mirror-image trends during the opposite months of the year, their summer.[10]

A mass cholera vaccination campaign in rural Haiti was supercharged to reach 45,417 people during three months in 2012, with the help of tablet computers and bar-coded patient ID cards. Data were uploaded and massaged nightly to provide a coded list of people and their Global Positioning System coordinates. The Red Cross paid for the program, which cost under $30,000, including training expenses for the health workers.[11]

In Philadelphia, researchers from the University of Pennsylvania equipped 300 people with a smartphone application that marked geolocations and asked them to record and forward every sighting they made of an automatic external defibrilla-tor. They then used these data to map 1400 defibrillators located in 500 buildings across the city. Among the effort's (not surprising) findings was that higher income areas had more devices.[12]

Propeller (formerly Asthmapolus) is a program whose mission is to help people manage their chronic respiratory disease. The system is based around an airflow meter, attached to a patient's inhaler, that measures how open her airways are. The user can not only see if she needs to do something immediately to control her disease, but the data are geocoded so she can learn in which locales her breathing tends to get better or worse, a tipoff to inciting factors like allergies or air pollut-ants. With the correct permissions, of course, researchers and public health officials can get their hands on highly detailed data to inform them about the health of the

---

healthcare dollars as the working age population; four times as much from 75 to 84; and six times as much once they reach 85. But today, they tend to stay healthier longer, putting off the most expensive end-of-life care for a few years, not extending it. Costly technology has con-tributed significantly to longevity at two ends of the age spectrum; at one extreme, in treating premature infants and at the other, in treating cardiovascular disease. Otherwise, technology has contributed greatly to cost with little measurable effect on population health.

public and of the environment, including identifying hotspots of disease incidence that merit further investigation.

Volume of pollution-related messages on the largest Chinese microblogging service, Sina Weibo, correlates well with particulate pollution levels.[13] Online searches for pet stores have been found to parallel multiple searches a little later for information on allergies; for fast food outlets with subsequent pursuit of the dope on heart attacks; for adult dating sites with inquiries about HIV and herpes infections.[14]

Tweets were found to be a sensitive barometer to public sentiment about the Affordable Care Act. A 0.10 increase in positive sentiment was associated with an 8.7% increase in activity at state-based health insurance marketplaces.[15]

Worldwide, local news reports have been sifted electronically to detect Zika outbreaks in places that lack the public health infrastructure to make reliable, timely official reports of disease incidence. Information channels, diseases to track and tools for turning data into information are multiplying at a rapid clip.

Guesses by large numbers of relatively uninformed people, sifted by fairly straightforward statistical techniques, can sometimes generate amazingly accurate results. Unanimous AI, a Silicon Valley firm established in 2014, has produced a system, "…that enables human groups to amplify their collective brainpower by forming real-time online swarms."[16] By polling a large number of people, the company claims to have predicted in 2016: the winner of the Stanley Cup, at odds of 542 to 1; the first four horses in order of finish of the Kentucky Derby; and the first World Series win of the Chicago Cubs since 1908, as well as whom they beat. Some call this phenomenon "hive mind," after the highly complex behavior of a bee colony (called by some a "superorganism") that emerges from the relatively simple behavior of each individual member of the hive. We have not yet begun to turn hive mind to addressing the problems of medicine and public health.

Artificial intelligence-driven software has shown great utility in public health, not just in tracking outbreaks of infectious diseases, but in predicting their spread and suggesting points of intervention to have maximum impact on controlling them.

Crashes, Gunshots and Other Illnesses

Non-infectious causes of human suffering are also amenable to data-intensive surveillance and interruption. There was even a report published in the journal *Psychological Science* in 2015 that demonstrated a correlation between location of coronary artery disease incidence and rate of public tweets expressing negative emotion. It makes sense. The more hostile and angrier an environment, the more likely that a person living there will suffer from a disease that researchers have clearly linked to the resulting emotions.[17]

Identifying crime hotspots for intensive policing is now a widespread, sometimes quite effective law enforcement strategy. Whether or not you consider assault and murder health problems (I do), they are addressable by using the tried and true tools of epidemiology, a discipline that dates its modern beginnings to 1854 when Dr. John Snow identified the Broad Street water pump as the source of cholera epidemics in a section of London.

For decades, experts have applied a public health approach to studying injuries and deaths that result from vehicular crashes. The National Highway Safety Board (NHSB) was formed in 1966. The agency's first director, a public health physician named William Haddon, set out to investigate interactions between host (human), agent (motor vehicle) and environment (highway) factors before, during and after crashes that resulted in injuries.[18] Thanks in large part to the data-driven, systematic approach to vehicular trauma initiated by Dr. Haddon and carried out ever since, fatalities per 100 million miles driven fell steadily from 5.5 in 1966, to 1.1 in 2011. That declining incidence curve has flattened out in the last few years, probably because most of the easier problems have been fixed.

The path to improved vehicular safety was not a smooth one. Seatbelts, which first made their appearance in 1955 Volvos, did not become required equipment in all US vehicles until 1966, as part of the same legislation that established the NHSB. Auto manufacturers had to be dragged, kicking and screaming, into adopting this standard, which it had clearly been shown could save many lives. The industry later resisted mandatory driver and passenger airbags, demonstrating once again that the major challenges to benefitting from a technology come not from the technology itself but from the people and institutions who will (or will not) manufacture, deploy and use it.

As time has passed, the American public's consciousness of safety issues has grown. Consumers have come to expect safer cars. Today, manufacturers compete in the public eye over the safety features of their vehicles.

Not so with firearms. The politically powerful gun lobby has seen to it that Congress not authorize the US Centers for Disease Control to spend one penny on studying the epidemiology of firearm violence. Guns accounted for 13,491 deaths in 2015, on a steeply rising curve, for the first time passing vehicular deaths.*

Sometimes just acquiring reliable data is the barrier to addressing health issues. (I consider illness, injury or death from any cause to be a health issue). The prohibition on collecting data on gun violence in the United States is one example. Poorer countries may not have the resources or will to support the public health infrastructure needed to collect data. Some sovereignties do not care to acknowledge the degree to which their population suffers from stigmatized diseases, like the denial of AIDS in sub-Saharan Africa, or from environmental causes, like China's official blindness, until recently, to the extent that air pollution in its cities and industrial centers causes illness.

---

* As this book was going to press, in the wake of the Marjorie Stoneham Douglas High School shooting in February 2018, Congress had, for the first time ever, provided some funds to allow the Centers for Disease Control to study gun violence.

Most of the time, the barrier to addressing human suffering from a public health perspective does not come from lack of data. It comes from lack of public will to do something about it. We are rolling in data. Every day we get more adept at turning those data into information that could guide the population to better health.

Getting health information into the hands of the poor must be a priority. It is no surprise that access to computers, broadband, online tools and the knowhow to use them is, like most every other good and service, unevenly distributed between the haves and the have-nots in our society, adding to the challenge of addressing social health inequalities. Ehealth efforts will never, in themselves, address the underlying structural problems that link poverty and ill-health. But ehealth will be part of the solution.

What we do not currently have is the political and business institutions, and the people to guide them, whose motivations are aligned with what's best for us. No amount of technology can fix that.

Chapter 12

Research

Any good scientist will tell you that the most important process is to ask the correct question.

—**Daniel S. Passerman, DO and
James P. Meza, MD, family doctors**[1]

My students are dismayed when I say to them, "Half of what you are taught as medical students will in ten years have been shown to be wrong. And the trouble is, none of your teachers knows which half."

—**Sydney Burwell
Dean, Harvard Faculty of Medicine, 1935–1949**

There is a wonderful cartoon I sometimes use when giving talks on medical informatics. It features a couple of elegant-looking people, a man and a woman, standing near each other on a sidewalk at night, under a street light. Each holds an elegant-looking dog on a leash. One person is saying (it does not matter which one), "There are some things you just can't get over the internet." The dogs are smelling each other's butts. Broaden the sense of the caption by substituting "from digital data" for the words "over the internet," and you could say that cartoon captures a major theme of this book. (When editing, I caught myself saying, "captures the essence of this book.")

In this chapter, I will discuss some of the endless things there are to learn from digital data, which doubles every year, meaning that in 2017 we produced as much data as in *the entire history* of humankind through 2016.[2] It should be clear by now just how much potential value lies in the uncountable heaps of medical and other data cached in vast digital coffers all over the Earth and in the cloud. We are still at the beginning of a revolution in medical science that is rooted in exploiting these riches.

For much of the last century, autopsy was one of the primary means of moving clinical science forward. As an intern, I got a positive mark in my record every time I was able to convince a family to allow an autopsy of their deceased loved one. Comparing patients' clinical course with what the pathologist found post-mortem has been a fundamental process for advancing medical science, medical education and quality of care.

Cook County Hospital in Chicago, where I trained, held a typical weekly clinical-pathological conference (CPC), where the poor intern or resident presented a brief summary of a deceased patient's history, physical findings, laboratory and radiologic data and hospital course, to the gathered medical staff. Then the pathologist would describe the corpse and project myriad stained microscopic slides of the patient's tissues, always leading up to a definitive pronouncement on what the medical problems were that really afflicted the patient and why she died. Sometimes the clinical team had gotten it right. Often we hadn't. There was much to be learned from the discrepancy between the ante- and post-mortem views of each case. And much entertainment (except for the clinical team that had erred in its diagnosis or treatment) to be derived from the drama. Many teaching institutions still put on regular CPCs.

Since those days, in the face of increased costs and much more sophisticated testing done while patients are alive, autopsy rates have plummeted. The medical record now serves as the corpse to be dissected and analyzed under the microscope in the quest to understand disease. Needless to say, a well-preserved corpse is much more valuable for research than one that is missing lots of pieces. The same goes for a complete and intact medical record.

As I explain in Chapter 1, "Logical Conclusions: How Medical Science Fits Into Western Culture," science, of which modern medicine is a branch, got its start in ancient Greece. Geometrizing, measuring and calculating, came to underlie the scientific worldview. Once we learned, beginning in the 1940s, to turn mathematizing into strings of ones and zeroes, represented as "ons" and "offs" of switches tied together in circuits that calculate at the speed of light, the digital revolution roared in upon us. Each day it roars more loudly.

Those ones and zeroes form the basis of classical digital computing, (as distinct from quantum computing.) (See Chapter 3, "Technology.") These days, analog, continuous information, like the tones and overtones that make up a musical performance or the colors, light and shading in a natural vista, easily succumb to algorithms, like MP3, MIDI, JPEG, MPEG, MP4, etc., which convert sound and pictures into digital information that can be stored, searched, manipulated, transmitted and reconstructed at will.

As discussed in previous chapters, not all things human are easily digitizable, but not for lack of trying. There are numerical scales in common use that measure depression, level of functioning, optimism, pain, dementia, health literacy and just about anything else you can think of. These sorts of data can be especially useful when tracking a condition or behavior over time.

This whole world of things that is reducible to ones and zeroes is now open to research by mining and analysis. Why is this?

First of all, it is because storing digital data has gotten to be very cheap. (See Chapter 3, "Technology.") We can salt away what seem to be endless quantities of information at little expense. Whole libraries fit on a few digital data cards. Using cameras and microphones, some people even attempt to make a continuous movie of their whole lives. And it's not like drawing a map that is as big as the territory they are mapping. They can compress their movie, fast forward it, run it backward, mark and index scenes to return to, label characters, insert special effects and so on. While a movie of one's life is not the same thing as life itself, it can capture and index a substantial share of the action. That is the second big thing about these new technologies, software that "knows" how to turn these large bodies of data into information.

Deb Roy, Director of the Laboratory for Social Machines at Massachusetts Institute of Technology and Chief Media Scientist at Twitter, along with his wife, Rupal Patel, Professor of Communications Sciences at Northeastern University, wired up their home for video and sound to record almost every moment of their newborn boy's life there. Using very sophisticated computer algorithms, they tweezed out of the 90,000 hours of video that they had recorded, the path by which their son had learned each of the 503 words he used by the age of two.

Dr. Roy delivered a fascinating TED talk on the project in 2011.[3] He wryly referred to his video archive as "the most extensive home movie collection ever." Based on their sheer length alone, the videos themselves surely are even more boring than most of the home movies we have been subjected to by doting parents and grandparents. It is the analysis that makes them interesting.

There was so much to learn from continuously monitoring the early language acquisition of just one child in such granular detail, done in the course of everyday life so that the technology itself had faded into near invisibility. One such finding was that, as the boy came closer to adding a word to his vocabulary, adults tended to pronounce it when around him in a more baby-talky way than they did before he had started making attempts to say it. This principle, heretofore only understood intuitively, was demonstrated fairly decisively by Baby Roy. The video held many other lessons about language acquisition that would not have been revealed without the sophisticated recording technology and techniques for analysis of big data. That was a decade ago. Technology and data analysis have, in the meantime, grown that much more powerful and less obtrusive.

I get the excited feeling that the sort of contribution the Bay Roy video made to language and cognitive science is just the beginning of what we will be able to learn in our brave new electronic world. Researchers will be recording and making sense of all sorts of data collected in the course of real life, not just in the laboratory.*

---

* See, for example, Neil H. Richards' 2013 *Harvard Law Review* article, "The Dangers of Surveillance," as well as George Orwell's dystopian novel, *1984*.

Pharmaceutical companies pay patients and doctors to record the conversations in their medical encounters. Then, the investigators turn natural language processing software loose on the data in hopes of generating insights into how to market to both groups.[4]

In 2015, the medical journal *Appetite* (Don't you love that title?) reported a study of 40 adults who wore body cameras through 742 eating episodes over the course of 15 days. The researchers analyzed the environmental and social context of eating. Among their findings was that people consumed more calories when they ate watching television. It is fishy though that, if you do the math, you'll find that only a little over one meal per day per participant was recorded.[5]

A significant share of basic medical science research is moving from the laboratory bench to the computer terminal. Molecules that could be likely candidates for binding to certain cell receptors and thus modifying diseases are screened by the thousands with the aid of computer programs that calculate the substances' estimated shapes before they are ever synthesized or injected into a lab rat.[6] (Incidentally, the problem of how molecules fold to produce three-dimensional shapes is one that quantum computers should be especially good at solving. [See Chapter 3, "Technology."])

Apple released in 2015 the Apple ResearchKit, which provides healthcare researchers with a platform that enables participants' iPhones to serve in all sorts of ways, many of them as yet unimagined, to collect and report data. At the time of the system's release, it had already been collecting data on breast cancer, diabetes, cardiovascular disease and Parkinson's disease, taking advantage of built-in sensors that include an accelerometer, microphone, gyroscope and GPS.[7]

Based just on the information we already possess, clinical research is due for a revolution. We should be able to answer an unending list of research questions once we figure out how to structure and query the gigantic amount of data that is locked up in electronic medical records.

The Alzheimer's Disease Neuroimaging Initiative provides one example that just scratches the surface of what can be learned by smart queries of a large database. This collaborative multicenter effort has merged clinical with brain imaging data and come up with a way to estimate the annual probability of progression of mild cognitive impairment to Alzheimer's disease, which ranges from 3% per year to 69% per year.[8]

In 2011, four large American drug manufacturers got together and donated to the National Institutes of Health data on 2.4 million chemical compounds from 4.7 million patents and 11 million journal abstracts, all packaged up for searchability by IBM with its Strategic Intellectual Property Insight Platform.[9]

In science, the larger the population you study, the more reliable the results. Kaiser Permanente of Northern California was able to reduce antibiotic use in newborns by up to 60% based on an algorithm that they derived from searching the clinical data of 600,000 mothers who delivered term babies.[10]

Developing the standards and interfaces that allow for patient data exchange between systems, as alluded to in Chapter 8, "Electronic Health Record," is a huge challenge. The more difficult task by far, though, is to generate the trust and consensus that must be in place before competing institutions and EHR suppliers will allow others to share their data.

The potential rewards are enormous. If you were a psychiatrist who, based on personal experience, had a hunch that some cold medications cause meltdowns in patients with schizophrenia, so you wanted to do a clinical study to check it out, think about how much time and money it would cost to: develop a study protocol; recruit enough patients with schizophrenia; establish a baseline of their functioning in the world; wait for them to get colds; randomly give placebos versus the real decongestant to the enrollees; reassess their function after receiving the medication; analyze the outcome; write and publish the paper; and have the results make a dent in best practice protocols and drug information resources. Unless the medications commonly caused severe side effects, such as psychotic breaks, in a significant slice of this population, it would hardly be worth the hundreds of thousands to millions of dollars it would cost to do such a study.

On the other hand, it should cost little to wring from the right database a reliable answer to the question about the possible relationship between decongestant use for respiratory infection symptoms and psychotic episodes in patients with schizophrenia.

Such a study would be deemed retrospective, that is, looking back on data that were not generated with the idea of researching this particular medical issue. Strength of evidence schemes would relegate such studies to class III or IV, third class or steerage, which is good for generating hypotheses to be researched by scientists who do have enough prestige to open the deep pockets that pay for the double-blind controlled experiments that travel first or second class. Retrospective studies are considered not so reliable for making clinical decisions. Big linked data and techniques for analyzing them have the potential to elevate enormously the value and status of the scientist who knows how to deftly wield a retrospectoscope.

In 2012, a team from Explorys, a spinoff of the Cleveland Clinic, was able to duplicate a study of abnormal blood clots in 26,714 Norwegians that had taken 14 years and millions of dollars to accomplish. Using the records in their EHR system, the Explorys scientists included 959,030 patients in their study at a cost that was equivalent to about $25,000 of donated researcher time.[11]

Using de-identified data, researchers from the University of Pennsylvania mined the UK General Practice Research Database (GPRD) to see how a retrospective study would measure up to the famous and very expensive Women's Health Initiative's (WHI) random controlled trial, which had provided the conclusive data that led to reversing positions on recommending hormone replacement therapy

(HRT) for nearly every post-menopausal woman. The Women's Health Initiative, one of the largest US prevention studies ever run, cost $625 million.*

The GPRD contained all of the electronic health records, from 1990 to 2000, of a representative sample of 5.7% of the entire English population, amounting to 905,234 women aged 50–79. That's a pretty darn big sample. Comparing women who had been exposed with those who had not been exposed to HRT, the scientists were able to support the conclusions of the Women's Health Initiative study that HRT increased women's risk of stroke, breast cancer and venous blood clots, and did not protect them at all from heart attack.[12]

It should be clear that big electronic medical databases blur the line between practice and research. With the right database, I could, after diagnosing a patient with a rare disease, see where all women in my region with the same diagnosis of about the same age as my patient were treated, and how they fared, so I can refer the patient to a doctor and a hospital that appear to be best suited to care for her. If I wanted to publish a report of this case or to tell the world about a cluster of cases turned up by my query that could raise questions about toxic pollution in the neighborhoods surrounding an old factory, I could just do it. I would not have had to start out by finding grant money or jumping through too many hoops with a research ethics board. If the suggestion of a link between pollution and this disease did appear to merit further exploration, I could then turn it over to someone with the means to do a formal research project on the question, complete with budget and institutional review board oversight (or do it myself if I knew how).

Research is described in the bioethics literature as an activity designed and intended to produce new knowledge. Clinical practice, supported by a robust information system, may not be designed to meet the definition of research, but it may produce new knowledge anyway. The separation of research from practice is another of the traditional underpinnings of healthcare that will be experiencing a seismic shift, with all the attendant ethical and practical dilemmas that such a readjustment generates. The term, "learning healthcare system," another of today's popular healthcare buzzphrases, makes room for practice and research in the same box, which describes best where I think we ought to go.

We will always need the gold standard double-blind placebo-controlled study for generating some medical information. For example, a drug company cannot very well ascertain, by data mining, what effects a newly-developed, as yet unpatented, drug has on 100,000 patients, because neither the company nor the FDA will want to turn an untested product loose on so many people. They must target instead a highly-selected study population that can generate a lot of high-quality data on each subject.

---

* On balance, even economically, the research paid off handsomely. The WHI website (admittedly a bit biased) claims that the study has saved $32.5 billion in healthcare costs. It was also worth it from the point of view of participating scientists who have published 1400 articles generated by the research.

To the dismay of researchers, effect sizes in placebo-controlled trials appear to be waning, probably because it is getting harder than ever to find treatments that make bigger than incremental improvements in therapy. A study of clinical trials reported between 1966 and 2010 in four leading medical journals found, first of all, a dramatically increased number of these gold-standard type studies and second, an effect size that had declined by about three-fourths. The authors of this paper suggested that researchers would get a bigger bang for their buck if they devoted more attention to comparing the safety, cost and tolerability of treatments with established efficacy, the sort of study that lends itself very well to data mining of medical records.[13]

When it comes to assessing more efficient ways of delivering care, such as by telehealth technology, making comparisons by data mining is a darn good research technique. Trouble is, "non-inferiority," does not ring the bells of the public, loosen the purse strings of grantors and investors, nor improve the mood of academic tenure committees in the way that "revolutionary" new outcomes that are demonstrated by prospective studies do.

Early in the stage of any clinical research project, investigators do a power analysis, which estimates the normal expected variation of some parameter (such as a scale of ability to function in a job for the schizophrenic patients in our make-believe study), the expected difference in findings between intervention and control group (for example, two points on a seven-point scale), and then calculates how many participants they will have to enroll to reliably measure the difference between the intervention and the placebo groups with a desired level of confidence that the results are real, that is, are not just the consequence of the normal random variation found in any population. The larger the study group, the greater the power, and the more faith can be put in the fact that the results stem from a legitimate phenomenon, rather than from a statistical fluke.

Recruiting and retaining enough participants to do prospective trials is often the biggest barrier to getting the power needed to perform a study. More than 40% of pediatric clinical trials registered with the federal government between 2008 and 2011 were either not completed or not published. Inadequate participant recruitment was the most frequent reason.[14]

The internet and social media can provide powerful tools to reach and cultivate patients for participation in medical research. For older kids, iTunes gift cards have been used very successfully as a recruitment tool.[15]

A 2017 review of 35 studies that reported on using Facebook to recruit medical research participants found an average cost of $14 per Facebook recruit, $1094 for television, $899 for print media, $636 for radio and $38 for email.[16]

Embedding alerts into the EHR, for example, a message from a group that is studying vaginal bleeding during pregnancy that pops up on the screen of a patient who has come to the emergency room with that problem, is another way to improve recruitment.

The larger the number of participants, the better the chance, all else being equal, that their data will sufficiently power a study to produce results that ultimately clinicians will have enough faith in to guide their practice. A lot hangs, though, on the words, "all else being equal." If a study's design is flawed, for example, by not taking confounding factors into account, you arrive at the old equation, *garbage in = garbage out.*

These days researchers have to worry that their data are contaminated by cross-talk on social media channels where study participants bump into each other and discuss their symptoms or side effects, thus interfering with their status as independent individual subjects.[17]

A great thing about doing a study retrospectively rather than prospectively is that do-overs are possible. Once a flaw in a study design is uncovered, a researcher can hopefully reprogram the query to compensate for the bias in the original analysis, provided, of course, that she is not just over-worrying the data to get the results she wants.*

In the example of our virtual study of schizophrenic patients who take cold medications, we might find that patients with more severe schizophrenia take fewer non-prescription drugs for their colds because they are incapable of getting to the drugstore themselves. So we could do separate statistical analyses on patients with a more and less serious disease, knowing they are taking different sorts of drugs to treat their cold symptoms.

Prospective studies, on the other hand, are designed to be run, analyzed and reported in that unwavering order, leaving researchers little or no leeway to turn back the hand of time so as to revise data collection, then adjust the analysis and results. For example, if our hypothetical scientists were, after-the-fact, to separately analyze patients who live in alternative care facilities versus in their own homes, there might not be enough study participants left in either group to provide the power needed to generate reliable results.

The first "completely internet-based" study reported in 2005 that, over an eight-week period, there was no difference in anxiety symptoms between patients who took the herbal remedy, kava, and those who took the placebo, as well as no reduction of insomnia in those taking the herb valerian, also placebo-controlled. There had been no problem recruiting the 1551 participants who hailed from 45 states. Participants got their pills by mail. They gave their informed content and took mood and sleep surveys online.[18]

Whether doing research by database mining or by real life controlled experiment, the same statistical principles hold when it comes to producing sound results.

---

* In doing research, one cannot just sift and sift data until one finds something interesting. If one has not been scrupulous about research and statistical methodology, sooner or later something will turn up, with no way of ascertaining what it really means. For example, if I run a historical correlation of the sales of each of 10,000 items in my supermarket with the price of some stock I'm thinking of purchasing, I am liable to find that the sales of at least one item, dill pickles for example, have tracked very well with the price of that stock. I would be a fool to invest in anything (except possibly in a cucumber growing or processing business) based on how pickle sales are doing.

The trappings may be different, but the armature on which scientific knowledge is hung stays the same. That's why science is so powerful. Though there are endless skirmishes about the details of method or the validity of one interpretation of the data over another, everybody who does science adheres to the same overall rules of how to acquire evidence and the statistical principles that must be used to weigh that evidence.

Both prospective and data mining studies are subject to the criticism of data torturing, that is, altering study design after the fact until one gets the results one is looking for. This is another of those "all things being equal" factors. Statistical methods can be like sausage grinders. One has to know when to stop turning the analysis crank, so as to extract an edible (i.e. scientifically valid) product rather than a homogenized mush that can be modeled into any desired form.

Colleagues are expected to test findings to the breaking point, whether they have been arrived at by using eyes, a microscope, ears or a computer. (Hopefully, the brain has been engaged all along.) If a finding does not hold up under scrutiny, it does not become part of the scientific canon.

A school of philosophy of science, initiated in the last century by Austrian-British philosopher Karl Popper, stakes scientific truth on the concept of falsifiability. What cannot be falsified stands as truth. Well, sort of. If there is not an imaginable scientific method that could prove a proposition false (like the existence of God), then that proposition just isn't in the realm of science. It may be true, but it is not scientifically true. Truths unearthed experimentally or by data mining may be falsified by experiments in the real world.

Validity of scientific results will, for as far into the future as I can see, depend on the understanding and integrity of researchers. All of our data and all of our meatspace and cyberspace tools are only as good as the people who employ them.

Dissemination

Over the course of my long career, the average time from medical discovery to its incorporation into practice has been around a decade, with little, if any, decrease in this interval over the years, in spite of a revolution in the technologies of dissemination. The study of when, why and how new knowledge into changes in medical practice has become a field unto itself, called translation science.

Except for the few patients who may benefit from a successful research protocol itself, the lag between when a medical advance is put on the books and when it is put into practice remains unconscionably long. The average delay between submission and publication of a research article is eight months. Sometimes a few years pass, consumed by reviews, revisions, rejections and resubmissions. The flow of scientific knowledge remains largely in the hands of large publishing houses. Globally, the academic publishing industry brings in $24 billion per year.[19]

Having seen a number of interventions come and go and come and go again, such as corticosteroids for acute stroke and various flavors of speed for weight loss, I've come to see that taking a long time to adopt a new practice is not necessarily a bad thing. If you wait long enough, there is a significant chance that you should not have done it anyway. Nobody would argue, however, that, in general, faster is better.

The physics community understood this when it launched arXiv in 1991, a preprint repository that stores submitted research papers and makes them available to everybody. (The "X" is the Greek letter, chi, pronounced "kai" and the name is pronounced the same as the English word, "archive.") ArXiv has since expanded to include astronomy, mathematics, computer science, quantitative biology and statistics. By 2014, the arXiv archive contained over 1,000,000 papers and was receiving 8,000 new ones a month. Moderators for each section review submissions. They apply somewhat laxer standards than those employed by the reviewers whose job it is to guard the status of eminent print journals, because the papers the arXivists allow to be posted are about to be reviewed and commented on by hundreds or thousands of online readers.*

ArXiv authors are initially vetted based on the papers they submit or whether they belong to a respected research institution. Once a paper is accepted, it is subject to review and comment in open online discussion by anybody else in the arXiv stable. Some papers are also submitted for print in traditional journals while some, even very famous and influential articles, such as Grigori Pearlman's 2002 proof of the mathematical Poincaré Conjecture 102 years after it had been posited, were not printed in a paper-and-ink journal, except after the fact.

A really cool feature of arXiv is that its papers are open for meta-analysis. That is, if a researcher wishes to agglomerate the data from multiple papers to see if they yield a bigger picture or more important findings, she is free to do so.

The diverse scientists who use arXiv are very happy to be able to get their work out to be looked at as soon as they feel it is fit for public scrutiny, rather than have to go through the lengthy process of reviews, revisions and negotiations that traditional journals routinely subject authors to. ArXiv has become so pervasive in the physics community that attempting to publish material plagiarized from the preprint server is virtually unheard of because doing so would do irreparable harm to the reputation of the plagiarizer.

Unlike on arXiv, it is usual practice for the identities of the reviewers of scientific papers in print journals to be kept anonymous, but not the names of the authors, which has produced in many fields a small group of people, protected by anonymity, who control the publish-or-perish fates of the intellectual masses, and worse yet, set the research agenda without wide input or consensus.

---

* Having more stringent gatekeepers is not necessarily a bad thing. A generalist clinician like me is always glad to know that acknowledged experts have reviewed the research results that I read.

Doing away with anonymous reviewing can enhance the process by which we add bricks to the scientific edifice. Having one's name openly attached to a comment about another's work goes a long way to keeping a person from criticizing research based on motivations such as professional jealousy, rather than on its intrinsic value.

A little junky science inevitably resides on arXiv. But the vast majority of what is found there is legitimate. All of it is subject to the bright lights of falsification.

Biology, and by extension, much of medical research, has been described as being either at a tipping point regarding preprints or in the midst of an existential crisis. There are currently a number of biology research preprint repositories. The foremost among them at the time of this writing is bioRxiv (pronounced "bio-archive"). Most of the early users have been scientists from computation-intensive branches of biomedical research: genomics researchers, bioinformaticists and lately, neuroscientists.[20]

As it is with their peers in other academic fields, getting published is the make-or-break factor to medical researchers' careers. The higher status the journal in which a study is published, the more weight it is given toward academic advancement of the author(s) and the higher the likelihood of winning further research grants. Authors may try and try to get their work into higher-ranking journals, like the *Journal of the American Medical Association* or the *New England Journal of Medicine*, before settling for having it appear in the *Lower Slobovian Journal of Improbable Results*, where it might be read by six people in six years.

The dark side of lowering barriers to publication of information is how much room it leaves for poor quality, misleading and wrong information to see the light of day, driven by publication-hungry authors and pushed out there by unethical publishers. Omics Online Publishing is a leading example of a company that makes the "predator market" in open-access publishing. They publish over 700 un-refereed online journals, many of them biomedical, with titles like *The Journal of Preventive Medicine*, filled with sketchy articles and easy to mistake for similarly-named well-respected journals like *Preventive Medicine*, which has been published by Elsevier since 1972.

Citation-hungry academics may choose to publish articles, rife with typos, in journals with overall poor quality control and murky statements of ownership. Studies sponsored by big pharmaceutical companies, including Novartis, Merck, Eli Lilly and GlaxoSmithKline, also appear in low-quality publications. Companies insist that sometimes they would rather have their findings disseminated as fast and as widely as possible and let the readers decide on their value than to have to follow the traditional slow, uncertain route to publication established by reputable journals.

Jeffrey Beall, the brave librarian at the University of Colorado who first hung the term "predatory" on the low-quality research publications he saw proliferating on the internet, even went so far as to compile a blacklist of suspect journals. Over the course of 6 years, the list grew from 18 to 1155. Beall quit disseminating his blacklist in 2014, I assume under legal threat. In the meantime, Omics has come under the scrutiny of the Federal Trade Commission.[21]

Legitimate online publishing is slowly making its way into healthcare. Virtually all print journals are simultaneously published electronically. There are a few research publications that are available exclusively online. I have followed *The Journal of Medical Internet Research* almost since its inception in 1999. This book owes a significant share of its substance to articles I have encountered in that online publication.

There is nothing yet in the realm of scientific medical literature that has the freewheeling ways of arXiv...for good reason. It would mean that prestigious print medical journals would give up a large chunk of their cachet, in terms of influence, subscription and advertising dollars. It costs $199 per year for a print subscription to the *Journal of the American Medical Association (JAMA)* and $189 for the *New England Journal of Medicine (NEJM)*. As a non-subscriber, if I want to download a single article, it will cost me $30 for 24-hour access to the edition in which a *JAMA* article appears and about that to pay to view one *NEJM* article.

As of 2017, about 200 German universities, who have affiliated into a group called Project DEAL, were, after two years, still locking horns with Elsevier, the largest publisher of scientific journals, in negotiations over cost and access. Project DEAL wants to halve the price of access to the 2500 Elsevier journals for libraries, as well as grant every corresponding author who is affiliated with a German institution full privileges to share her article with whomever she wants at no extra cost. Groups in Finland, France and the Netherlands are also negotiating with Elsevier to loosen its control of information that is the lifeblood of scientific research.[22] The momentum of the information revolution weighs the odds against Elsevier and other publishers whose profits are made by controlling access to information.

Funders of research are coming down more and more on the side of open access. So much of the research that appears in pricey medical journal publications is funded by governments spending tax revenues. In other words, the very people who ultimately pay for medical research are not free to see the results. The Bill and Melinda Gates Foundation, which by 2017 had given away $8 billion for medical research, making it the largest such charity in the world, announced in 2017 that the results of all research that it funds must be made available, free of charge, to anybody who wants it. They are following the lead of the second-largest medical research charity, the Wellcome Trust, based in England, which moved the year before to make the results of research it had paid for freely available, in at least two senses of the word "free," both widely and without cost.

Not only are research papers being made openly available, but there is a movement that is gradually gathering steam to open the raw data themselves, with full privacy protections of research participants (they used to be called subjects) of course, for study by other researchers. Especially in the face of research that is accomplished with public funds, arguments about the proprietary value of this information to the company or institution that possesses it, hold little water.

In the interest of medical science, as well, ultimately, of patients and the professionals who care for them, it would behoove medical researchers to follow their physicist colleagues and open not just their polished research findings, but their raw data to public examination. This would include data from studies that did not make it to publication, which would help to address the problem of publication bias. "Publication bias" refers to the natural tendency to publish studies that seem to say something that is new and exciting or to confirm what is already known, and to dismiss as less interesting work that fails to show statistically significant results. One could expect that many a sacred cow of medical science would be killed off by unpublished studies that failed to show significant results.[23,24]

Remember that establishing scientific truth requires openness to falsification. Without being able to look at the data themselves, too often we have to take the word of researchers who claim that their work is scientifically valid and worse yet, the word of their funders who may have a commercial interest in the research outcomes.

Even so far as reputable professional publications go, a large chunk of the current medical literature is still not very good. As ever more information becomes available to an ever wider audience, we will need interpreters who can help separate the reliable from the unreliable, and the significant from the evanescent, at least as much as we need researchers. We are still a long way from automating interpretation.

I myself subscribe to a number of online newsletters, where I read reports of recent research and rarely read the research itself. If it is a reliable source, I may start and end my perusal of an entry with the last little section, entitled something like "What this means for clinical practice." And that's just fine.

Chapter 13

Education

Power corrupts. Powerpoint corrupts absolutely.

—Edward Tufte, statistician and author of definitive
books on visual presentation of data

Be careful about reading books about health. You might die of a misprint.

—Mark Twain

I always love learning. I don't always like being taught.

—Winston Churchill

Baka ni tsukeru kusuri wa nai. There is no medicine that cures stupidity

—Japanese proverb

I see no reason to compare, yet again, the rate of increase of medical data, versus the limited ability of the human brain to absorb, store, make sense of information and then to access it appropriately when needed. No matter what your profession or field of interest, you have undoubtedly had the unpleasant experience of trying to drink from the information firehose.

I would like to explore here how to adjust the nozzle of that hose in ways that provide cool sips to the health practitioner when she needs them. Education is the process by which a clinician learns to manage the flow.

When I counsel young folks who are considering a medical career, I routinely tell them that the biggest challenge is not the heaps of academic stuff they have to learn how to consume and spit back out on demand. If they are admitted to medical school, they know how to do that. The challenge is to hang onto themselves while being crammed into the mold of an all-knowing, all-powerful doctor.

Things are significantly better than in my days as a medical student when, of our class of over 200, 5% were women, 5% people of color, and there was one openly gay man. We were like boys in the locker room. We understood that we were never to show weakness in this hyper-masculine atmosphere, which meant, among many other things, never saying, "I don't know." No matter how apparently trivial the question asked by a superior (as a medical student *everyone* is your superior), you were to try to answer it. If you came up short in naming all dozen items the list of traits of a particular congenital syndrome, a list you may never even have been told you were supposed to have memorized, you might be subjected to public ridicule, a practice called "pimping" in the parlance of medical training.

As a teacher, I came to recognize in my students and colleagues how pimping had impaired their ability to learn. Being unable to say, "I don't know," is a severe handicap to learning. Friends who worked with physicians outside of their medical practice have told me, for example, that this impairment makes physicians, on average, lousy investors and hard to train as pilots.

That's a scary thought, isn't it? Take a study published in 2013 in which 188 physicians were asked to address 4 simulated cases, 2 easy ones and 2 hard ones, in 4 sequential phases. After each phase, the doctors were asked for a list of possible diagnoses, what further information they would like to obtain (testing, consultations, etc.) and how confident they were in their diagnoses. Not surprisingly, they did better at coming to the correct diagnoses on the easy cases (55%) than on the hard ones (5%). They asked for more information on the hard ones. The surprise came in the physicians' estimates of their level of confidence in the veracity of the diagnoses they proposed. They were almost as confident in their answers to the hard cases, in which they had arrived at few right answers, as to the easy ones,[1] where they had been mostly right.

This sort of overconfidence in one's own skill sounds like a good argument for medical education that does not reward unaided memory and bluster. Rather, students ought to absorb (mostly from their mentors) a humble attitude, open to colleagues, to co-workers and to the medical literature; as well as embrace medical ordering and record-keeping systems embedded with as much intelligence as can be squeezed into them, while still keeping them usable. In medicine, what you don't know can hurt you and your patient. What you don't know you don't know can be especially pernicious.

Learning from Books and Lectures

By whatever means, every health care professional must acquire before she can practice, a baseline level of understanding of how the body works in health and disease. By a similar process, you have to understand some English before you can look up how to spell a word in the dictionary (unless you happen to be one of those Aspergery, non-English speaking, Scrabble champs who memorizes dictionaries). Some physicians with prodigious memorization skills can regurgitate amazing catalogs of medical facts. They may or may not be good doctors. In the end, real linguistic and medical ability depend much less on what you have managed to memorize and much more on what you have come to understand.

How then does one learn the inner language and logic of a vast field like medicine? I don't know. Before I had the slightest criteria by which to judge what was important and what was not, I tried to memorize everything.* It didn't take long before I quit attempting to commit it all to memory, by mnemonic device or other memory trick. I will, however, forever refer in my head to a wonderful dirty ditty that I learned in medical school when I need to come up with the names of one of the twelve cranial nerves. (Hint: Women learned a different mnemonic.)

As I have said many times already, it is the overall feel that a human being has for another human being, added on top of the medical science that applies to that person, that makes for an effective clinician. Compassion alone is not enough. You cannot be good at any type of healthcare practice if you do not understand enough of the science.

When I began serving in my first position as a director of continuing medical education (CME, which is education for practicing physicians) for a hospital, I found, to my dismay, that my job had been defined as putting on lecture-style conferences for the medical staff. The doctors would come into the conference room during the noon hour, eat a free lunch provided by a drug company sponsor, hear a talk, sign the roster and receive education credits that would count toward re-credentialing. (At least one learner would routinely sign-in, grab lunch and leave before the talk even started.)

It took a while to realize that this lax sort of program, with a sign-in sheet as the sole feedback mechanism buried in the whole CME effort, was worthwhile, just so long as I dropped the illusion that such "educational" conferences would have a measurable effect on the quality of patient care at our hospital, or even on the knowledge base of the medical staff. These were social events that conveyed the message that education and open discussion were important, a laudable, if not quantifiable overall outcome for an education program.

It still needs to be stated explicitly that the ultimate goal of professional education is to turn the learner into an effective agent for achieving greater health of individuals and of populations. Passively sitting in lectures, such as were the bread and butter of my first two so-called preclinical years of medical school and of the CME program I oversaw, is about the worst way to educate an effective agent.

Some live medical conferences get a boost in interactivity from audience response systems that allow attendees to vote on questions posed by the speaker, with responses instantaneously tallied and posted on a screen. Social media can also enhance the interactivity of live events. One report, published as far back as 2014, found that the number of tweets under the event hashtag before, after and especially during an anesthetists' conference in London, had sextupled over the year before. The airwaves were abuzz about learning points, which sessions to attend and access to notes and educational resources.[2]

---

* For example, when I studied biochemistry as a freshman medical student, I converted by some random mental process, the four DNA nucleotides, adenine, tyrosine, cytosine and guanine, into "A Tough Cookie Grandma," and the RNA nucleotides, with uracil in place of tyrosine, into "An Ugly Cookie Grandma." Obviously, I still remember these factoids, though I doubt that knowing them has ever, even once, done me or one of my patients a bit of good.

Learning from Patients and Peers

Medical and other health professional schools of today are getting away from the old lectures-with-slides format. Small group discussions, tutorials and problem solving now take up some of the time that used to be spent in the lecture hall. Interactive online materials are relied on more. Rather than schlepping around, reading and underlining thousand-page textbooks, students explore links to a rich variety of multimedia materials, available anywhere they have a computing device that can connect to the internet, which means just about everywhere.

As was typical, I spent the entire last half of medical school (the so-called "clinical years"), as well as all of my post-graduate training, in clinic and the hospital, where I got in-person experience out the wazoo. Experience is, in general, the best way to acquire knowledge, because the largest share of the self (which includes head, heart, hormones, gut and muscles) is involved in the learning.

Health professional educators are finding ways to insinuate experiential learning into the curriculum from the outset, not making their students wait up to two years to learn from/on patients, as I had to. Clinical experience might begin with just tagging along with a clinician and watching what she does in encounters with patients, participating a little in the conversation, maybe being guided through a simple exam or therapeutic maneuver, and asking lots of questions. As a student becomes more knowledgeable and capable, the level of involvement with patients is increased.

A study of Swiss internal medicine residents, reported in *Annals of Internal Medicine* in 2017, found that, in the course of a 11.6-hour shift (scheduled for 10 hours), the doctors-in-training spent 5.2 hours with computers and 1.7 hours with patients. So much for the ideal of learning from patients.[3]

Much of the art of teaching (and of curriculum design) is knowing how to make the adjustments of levels of involvement and autonomy at a rate that maximizes learning while always protecting the patient from the harm that can come at the hands of the inexperienced. That is where simulations come in.

I still have scary memories of the sorts of procedures I performed on patients as an intern. In those days, that was about the only way to learn, on human guinea pigs. The poor and people of color who frequented public hospitals, like the ones I trained at, provided a rich source of "clinical material" to be taught on. I get shivers when I recall the maxim we were expected to follow in learning medical procedures that went, "See one. Do one. Teach one."

Learning from Simulations

Way before medicine, aviation turned to the use of simulators to train people to perform the high-stakes task of flying an airplane. As early as World War I, the military trained pilots on the Ruggles Orientator, a pilot's seat mounted on gimbals that allowed it to pivot on all three axes, as well as to move vertically. Seat rotation and displacement were driven by electric motors attached to simulated flight controls. The device was employed to help meet the acute wartime need for trained pilots.

Since those days, there has been a constant effort to build ever-more-sophisticated flight simulators, with an ever-more-realistic and wide-ranging set of scenarios. Without having to leave the ground, pilots routinely work their way through every sort of equipment malfunction and emergency scenario that the people who build and fly airplanes can imagine.

Healthcare is catching up, slowly. I had my first encounter with simulation technology about 40 years ago, when I first practiced cardiopulmonary resuscitation on a CPR dummy. The first step was to shake this inert lump and shout, "Annie! Annie! Are you all right?" (the doll was named Resusci Annie) so as to make sure that she was really unresponsive. Annie consisted of a stiff plastic torso, covered by rubberized skin, connected by a semi-rigid neck to a head whose silicone rubber face was frozen into a spooky grin. The learner could practice hauling the jaw forward and tilting the head back in order to put the airway into alignment before blowing in air by mouth-to-mouth resuscitation (after having first cleaned Annie's lips with an alcohol wipe of any residue left by the previous trainee).

More advanced students could try inserting a laryngoscope into a model head, followed by a tracheal airway tube that had been lubricated with silicone spray. If the head was in the right position for mouth-to-mouth or if the far end of the tracheal tube was in the right place, blowing in air would inflate both balloon lungs.

Thanks to information processing power that lies at their core, today's simulators are much, much more realistic and effective.* Ever-more-sophisticated 3D printing systems turn out ever-more-lifelike tissues and body parts. Today's advanced simulators are programed with whole emergency scenarios that yield realistic patient responses to each intervention performed by the learner or team, based on sound physiologic parameters. Treatment paths, responses and outcomes can be recorded and reviewed, both for training and for trainee assessment.

Advances in simulation technology have given healthcare workers opportunities to practice catheterizing everything from urinary bladders to coronary arteries, complete with visual, auditory and tactile inputs. A neurosurgeon can rehearse a difficult tumor removal using real instruments on a virtual three-dimensional model of a patient's brain that has been re-constructed by a 3D printer from her CT and MRI scans.

---

* Though it is undoubtedly true that the more realistic a simulator the better the training, not every simulated experience needs to be sophisticated or high tech or even closely related to the educational goal to be of value. In a study of 42 surgical residents who had been sharpening their laparoscopic skills on a simulator, half of the residents were tasked with playing "Wii Sports Tennis," "Table Tennis" and "Battle at High Altitude," using both hands for 60 minutes a day, 5 days a week over the course of 4 weeks. When compared to the control group that had not spent 20 hours playing Wii games, these guys kicked butt on the laparoscopic simulator (and probably would have in ping pong high altitude combat too). (Gianotti, D, Patrizi, G, Di Rocco, G et al. Play to become a surgeon: Impact of Nintendo Wii training on laparoscopic skills. *PLOS One*, 2013:8(2), e57372.) (SPOILER ALERT) This is the premise of the book and the movie, *Ender's Game*, in which it turns out that young video gamers are actually battling real creatures on a faraway planet, not so farfetched considering what US military drone pilots are doing today all over the world.

A website called Second Life provides a set of development tools with which to construct a virtual world for exploration. In the medical realm, there are domains in which health science students can: explore caring for patients with diabetes or neurological disease; hear heart murmurs; learn about human genetics, including visiting a virtual apparel shop that boasts letting you "Wear your favorite chromosome!"; acquire some experience of what it's like to get around in a wheelchair; search PubMed (the huge database at the US National Library of Medicine); get a sense for the sorts of hallucinations that afflict people with certain mental health problems; and so on. These activities are designed to be way more engaging than reading a textbook.[4]

A simulator called SymPulse feeds a signal, via a cuff around the arm, that causes the wearer to experience Parkinson's type tremors and immobility. You don't have to be a health science student to receive a sudden large dose of insight into movement disorders from this apparatus, one example of a whole new class of gadgets called tele-empathy devices.[5]

Simulators can be used to teach groups too. For example, an emergency room crew can tune up their personal and teamwork skills in the course of handling any number of emergency scenarios on a realistic dummy whose breath sounds, heartbeat, blood pressure, urine output, pupillary reflexes and spoken words are powered by artificial intelligence. When carefully organized, group simulation exercises have the potential to reteach the "hidden curriculum" that is part of every health science student's education, by which she learned lessons, many of them nonverbal, mostly from role models, about the narrow boundaries that define her place in the medical hierarchy. (It occurs to me that "hidden curriculum versus explicit curriculum" is sort of parallel to "Story Versus Data" as presented in Chapter 5.) I have commented in Chapter 9, "Patient Care," that the pyramid of professional power and status, built of stone and standing over the ages, is one of the major barriers to teamwork and that fostering teamwork is a large part of the solution to improving most every process of patient care.*

---

* I am not the only one to recognize the need for team players in healthcare. When I sat on a medical school admissions committee a few years ago, we were told that we could assume that every candidate whom we would interview, having made it through the screening process, was smart enough to be a doctor. Committee members were instructed to look for signs that the candidate before us was a team player. Word always gets out about what criteria medical schools are emphasizing for admission to their next class (these things change like fashion) and the candidates—having made it thus far based on their ability to figure out what teachers want—alter their interview performance so as to meet those expectations. Needless to say, most everyone I interviewed that year told me about an experience that had been especially rewarding because of the collaboration among her teammates and herself.

Back in the seventies, my medical school, a state school with a large student body, didn't even interview me, which, all in all, probably didn't make much of a difference in the kind of doctors it turned out. There are always many more people who would make fine physicians than there are medical school slots for. Reforming how doctors are socialized in training is the key to making us productive contributors to problemsolving teams. Medical education is making some progress in that direction, driven not so much by curricular changes as by the feminization of the workforce, as well as the more collaborative ways of the generations of students that have followed my highly-competitive baby boomer cohort.

No matter how sophisticated the device, studies have shown that learning is deeper and lasts longer when a session on a simulator is followed by debriefing by a human. Having to answer questions such as: What did you find challenging about the experience? What did you learn? How will you change your practice based on what you learned? What will you study next? and How can the learning experience be improved in the future? addresses the meaning and emotional content of a lesson, which any skilled educator will tell you is as important as covering the intellectual content if real learning is to take place. Humans still depend on meanings and emotions for learning. Machines don't.[6]

Commercial and military pilots are required to log a certain amount of simulator time to maintain their pilot credentials. As far as I know, there are no doctors or other health professionals who, once they have finished their formal training (as if training were ever finished), are required to do simulations.* I predict this will change. Sooner or later, at least some medical professionals will have to pass tests on simulators in order to obtain or maintain certification. In the meantime, for the sake of credentialing, it behooves any clinician to keep up-to-date an (anonymized) database of patients seen, diagnoses encountered and procedures done to be used when applying for or renewing practice credentials, and maybe later, for recovering data to be used in research.[7]

It was not until 1969, when the American Academy of General Practice gave birth to the American Academy of Family Physicians (AAFP), that there was a single American medical organization whose credentials did not last a lifetime. The AAFP required that all doctors who had been certified by that organization be recertified every seven years, by examination and by showing that they had partaken of a certain amount of CME. The American Board of Medical Specialties has since mandated periodic recertification for all of the 24 medical specialty boards over whom they have dominion. Specialty boards also require earning a certain amount of continuing medical education credits in the interval. Many state medical boards, on the other hand, no longer require CME credits to maintain a license to practice.

Nobody would argue that a practicing professional ought to be able to demonstrate her competence at regular intervals during her career. It has just never been shown that mandatory CME makes for better physicians. Good physicians stay educated whether or not someone says they have to.

Teachable Moments

I read medicine all the time, but I rarely take a CME course for credit. Fortunately, there are relatively painless and free or inexpensive courses to be had online on almost

---

* Case simulations presented solely on computer screens have been tried out by some medical specialty societies for use in certification and recertification activities and tests. These exercises tend to be pretty lame. After a few years and heaps of complaints from its members, the American Board of Family Medicine has dropped computerized case simulations from its assessment armamentarium.

any subject. So, when I require credit hours to maintain one certification or another, I can get what I need off the internet. I doubt it makes me a better doctor, though.

The first principle of adult education is the supreme importance of exploiting teachable moments. The best time to learn something is when you need to know it.* Education without context may be enriching but it is generally not very effective when it comes to improving performance.

I came out of medical school hardly knowing any anatomy. I would have been motivated to learn a lot more on the subject, I'm sure, had I been headed for a career in surgery. Today I have pretty good anatomy chops because, over the course of practice, I kept looking things up in the copy of *Grant's Atlas of Anatomy* that has served me since medical school. (Anatomy doesn't change much from year to year.) In *Grant's*, I could usually find diagrams of anatomical relationships I needed to visualize in order to diagnose and treat the patient before me, things like which component of the shoulder joint was producing her pain or where to tap on a patient's leg to see if the numbness in a part of her foot was caused by an entrapped nerve. Even if I do not remember the exact anatomical details that accompany this particular sort of shoulder pain or foot numbness, the next time I see a patient with similar symptoms I will probably be able, as much by instinct as by conscious knowledge, to go right to the anatomical view in the reference material that will answer my question.

My knowledge of anatomy was accumulated over the course of countless teachable moments. But these teachable moments only fulfilled their promise when I made the time to take the atlas down from the shelf.

Today, thanks to resources that are accessible from the same computer screen as the record of the patient I am seeing, when I need to clarify a detail of anatomy, I no longer must excuse myself from the exam room, walk down the hall to my office, and haul *Grant's Atlas* down from the shelf. I can look things up from where I sit, getting right to the medical information resources I need on the same screen that displays the patient's medical record. And share that view with the patient.

This is medical education at its best, based on real teachable moments that arise in the course of doing my job. Engaging the patient makes it even better. If the medical information system is not easy to use simultaneously with the medical record, if it takes a number of clicks to shift gears, exit or minimize screens, and maybe even to log in or out, that is the equivalent of having to walk down the hall

---

* I do not consider the suggestion I saw in a nursing journal to load intensive care unit computer monitor screensavers with educational tidbits to be just-in-time, but rather, just-in-place, a phenomenon that invokes in me a certain antipathy. Think of the never-ending scoreboard and PA system ads you are subjected to at a professional ballgame, the commercials for additives and credit card deals displayed on monitors mounted on gasoline pumps, or the ads for real estate brokers plastered on your supermarket shopping cart. (Anderson, D, Dobson, N, Lewandowski, J et al. Using computer screen savers to enhance nurses learning in the intensive care environment. *Dimensions in Critical Care Nursing,* 2007:26(4), 160–162.) In order to function best, professionals need respite from their hyper-stimulating environment, not even more messages.

for a reference book, making it more likely that the teachable moment will slip away from me and my patient.

As I have said repeatedly, usability is by far the most important factor to consider when choosing any electronic information system. For these purposes, "Build it and they will come" should be replaced with "Build it with ample entrances, exits, aisles and legroom and with clear signage, and they will come." When medical information and patient data are well integrated, the boundary between practice and education blurs almost out of existence, in the same way that the line between practice and research becomes indistinct.

The American Board of Internal Medicine (ABIM), notorious for the head-breaking examinations it requires internists to pass for certification, has even begun to experiment with open-book (actually open-computer) tests that reflect how doctors really practice these days, with electronic information resources at their fingertips. In 2016, the ABIM invited a group of its diplomates to do a mock recertification exam with access to *UpToDate*, a widely used electronic medical information resource that I myself carry on my smartphone. The test must have gone pretty well because, beginning in 2018, recertification candidates will have the choice of doing an online Knowledge Check-in every two years or a full long-form reassessment test every ten.

I am an enthusiastic user of *UpToDate*. I appreciate the quality of the help the database gives me in caring for patients. As a bonus, the program keeps track of what topics I have looked up, which provided me with documentation of some badly needed CME hours in time for my most recent recertification deadline. Giving credit for time spent looking things up in teachable moments is not a gimmick. It makes great educational sense.

For some people and for some subjects, online interactive courses may be an effective educational alternative. A number of my friends and colleagues have taught online courses at college and graduate levels on all sorts of subjects, including medical ones. As they tell it, a well-designed distance education class can do more than just present materials, assign and grade projects and give tests. It can promote real discussion and even engage participants, who have never met face-to-face, to the extent that the class develops a genuine sense of community.

Nursing especially, with its many gradations of degrees and changing marketplace for its workers, has taken advantage of online education to advance nurses' education and their careers. Distance education has its American roots in the correspondence courses conducted by mail that resulted from the humanistic vision of adults as autonomous, self-motivated learners, promulgated by the likes of psychologists Carl Rogers and Abraham Maslow.[8]

Massive open online courses (MOOC), with unlimited registration and no fees, can attract large numbers of students. MOOCs come in all shapes and sizes and use the panoply of distance education technologies. Some courses will supply, for a fee, accredited continuing education credits to health professionals who complete the program. A MOOC can be a handy way for a professional to accumulate needed credits and even to learn something in greater depth than a brief online education course allows.[9]

A report from China in 2007 stated that doctors, many of them un-credentialed and practicing in remote villages, had been enrolled in video courses in 6000 classrooms in 8 provinces. Fees for the 3-year course were about 3400 yuan, $448 apiece. The doctors who had done the video training scored better on a test of medical knowledge than their peers who studied in the traditional way, in hospital classrooms.[10]

As I said in the Chapter 9, "Patient Care," one of the best ways to change professionals' behavior is to provide them with data that actually help the clinician to do a better job. Three hospitals in Philadelphia found that including the cost of medical tests in their automated physician order entry system, without some sort of comparative feedback, had none of the impact they hoped it would have on the frequency of ordering expensive studies.[11] On the other hand, I have seen for myself how the staff on the wing of a long-term care facility that had the highest rate of patient eye infections as the result of lax handwashing started washing their hands religiously once they saw the graph that compared their unit's infection rate to the rates on other units. Merely posting regularly in the surgeons' lounge cesarean section rates, broken out by doctor, has repeatedly been shown to result in a lowering the number of C-sections performed in an institution. In other words, when properly used, data are an educational tool.

The overarching theme here is that the more closely education is associated with practice, the better it works, especially when the goal of education is to promote better patient care, not to enhance the ability to regurgitate memorized lists of facts. Electronic information tools can bring timeliness, proximity and relevance to the educational endeavor and ultimately, actually make healthcare better.

Chapter 14

The Connected World of Patients

"What hurts, Tillie?"

"*Everyting.*"

"Well, better you should tell me what doesn't hurt."

"*Notting.*"

(The doctor chuckles.)

This is a transcript from memory of a patient interview I was lucky enough to sit in on during the outpatient medicine rotation I did in my fourth year of medical school. The encounter happened in the office of a wise old general internist on Chicago's north side. His patient was an elderly Jewish woman.

Doctor G proceeded with unhurried questioning and a gentle exam, until he arrived at the conclusion that the patient had consulted him about her standard arthritic aches and pains and sluggish bowels, no worse than usual. Mostly she just needed to see him for reassurance, which my mentor provided with great good humor, backed by the understanding that came from having known and cared for this woman and her husband for decades. Encounters such as this one are the reason many physicians, especially us generalists, chose careers in medicine.

Patient Portals

If that encounter between Tillie and Dr. G were to happen today, the physician might instead have received a message documenting Tillie's multiple complaints, forwarded to him by the practice's triage nurse who had been the first to open the patient's correspondence after it arrived via the patient portal.* The doctor might then decide to talk to Tillie on the phone or even over a two-way video connection. He could choose to send orders for blood tests to the lab; a request for x-rays to radiology; and transmit to the patient an email message advising that she get these done. He could order prescriptions for her too, using the online prescription subsystem of the practice's EHR.

In the process, Dr. G would have documented everything in the electronic record, some of it automatically: a summary of the conversation, tests ordered, prescriptions and patient advice given, and even automatic reminders to staff and patient for follow-up phone calls and office appointments. All of the ordered testing would be logged into the system, which would automatically send reports to doctor and staff, flagging any results that were abnormal or never received.

Given that the encounter between Dr. G and Tillie happened over forty years ago, of course, none of these electronic options were available, not to mention that even today it would be pretty unlikely that a middle-aged doctor and an elderly lady would choose to conduct their business electronically. They both knew that what she needed was for her doctor to see her, listen to her and touch her. Anything less than face-to-face contact would not have worked as well.

These days, most doctors have used at least a part or two of an electronic record system in their practice. Some of them, even some middle age docs, have actually exploited enhanced modes of communication that reside in an EMR system to bolster patient care.

The AARP publications that I regularly receive are replete with features that tout to us oldsters the advantages of using a computer, including to help choose when and where to get what sorts of medical care, and to enhance and monitor its effectiveness. Studies show surprisingly high uptake of computer technology among seniors. According to one report, in 2015, 62% of Americans over 65 had searched for health information online. Eighty-three percent believed they should have full online access to their medical records.[1]

Near the other end of the age spectrum, when 572 college freshmen were queried about seeking help for emotional problems, 63% said face-to-face methods (physician, counselor, therapist, professor) would be okay and 75% liked online methods (education, self-help apps, therapy, chat room or forum, Instant Messenger, Reddit,

---

* This smooth flow of information might have been short-circuited anyway because there should have been explicit instructions on the opening page of the patient portal to use a real-time channel, like phoning the on-call doctor or, God forbid, calling 911, in case of an emergency, which Tillie considered her sluggish bowels to be.

Twitter and Facebook).[2] Parenthetically, 99% of these students owned a laptop computer, 85% a smartphone and only 29% a desktop computer.

In a 2014 survey, 93% of Americans ages 21 and over said they desired email contact with their doctors. A quarter of those even admitted they'd pay $25 per email if they had to.[3] Technology Advice Research reported in 2015 that 26%–41% of 24–35 year olds wanted their physicians to offer online services, including appointment scheduling, test result reporting, bill paying and secure messaging.[4]

Four focus groups of pregnant women told researchers that the standard schedule of prenatal visits is not designed to meet their needs for information. Traditionally, women see their prenatal care providers only once a month through the first trimester, which is when they typically have the most questions. They plug these holes with information obtained elsewhere, much of it online, some of it of low quality.[5] When I used to deliver babies, I gave every expectant mother in my practice a really good book about pregnancy and childbirth at the first prenatal visit. It was well worth the investment. These days, email contact with the practice, as well as a webography of reliable information sources, can go a long way toward meeting those informational needs.

Numerous studies have reported that patient-initiated emails to providers save money by reducing use of other types of healthcare. Not surprisingly, the same research has revealed that patients with higher out-of-pocket healthcare expenses are significantly more likely to resort first to communicating with their provider by email if such a channel is available.[6]

Let's change the opening scenario now. In the course of interviewing a millennial who has consulted me about her inability to concentrate, I ask, "Tell me when you keep an eye out for electronic messages."

"Always."

"Well, then tell me about when you don't keep an eye out."

"Never, except when I sleep. (But I leave the ringer on so I can hear when a message comes in.)"

Needless to say, this patient is likely to be well-primed to do a share of relating to her doctor online. But, in the course of our therapeutic relationship, I would need to consider the meta-message that might come with accomplishing most of our transactions electronically, crowding out face-to-face interaction, thereby exacerbating what is missing from her young life, direct human contact with friends, family and physician too. Perhaps this patient would benefit, just as much as Tillie did, from having the doctor in the same room with her.

Personal Health Record

Though many healthcare institutions act otherwise, HIPAA mandated in 1996 that "Accessing and maintaining copies of one's health information for one's own purposes is a right, not a privilege." This was 23 years after Shenkin and Warner had editorialized in the *New England Journal of Medicine* that giving patients their medical records might improve their healthcare.[7]

Patients certainly desire access to their medical records. Eighty percent of people surveyed in 2017 said that they not only wanted access to the words in their records, but also to see the radiology images therein.[8]

In 2009, the United States Institute of Medicine came out in favor of the personal health record (PHR), which is a document (paper or electronic) that belongs to the patient, not to one or to a dozen different institutions, and includes all of her health data. The patient is free to annotate and amend the record. The PHR is considered a crucial strategy in the effort to engage patients in their own care, a cornerstone of visions of efficient health care that is oriented toward wellbeing. (See Chapter 9, "Patient Care.")

An electronic personal health record that belongs to an individual patient, maintained on her own slice of the cloud or in a personal digital device of choice, is a much skinnier target than the thousands or millions of records that may reside in the single system of a large healthcare organization.[9]

As part of the OpenNotes research project, 87% of 13,564 patients in Boston, Seattle and central Pennsylvania, who said they wanted internet access to their medical visit notes, did look at their record at least once during the subsequent 19 months. In a follow-up survey, two-thirds of these patients believed they were able to take better control of their care as a result of being able to see their records, including adhering more closely to their medication regimens. One-third shared the notes with others. One-third had privacy concerns. Only 1%–8% said that the records had caused confusion, worry or offence. Ninety-nine percent of patients wanted continued access to their records and no doctor in the program chose to stop participating.

Twenty-eight percent of physicians at another OpenNotes site, Beth Israel Hospital in Boston, said that they had been less candid in their patient encounter notes once patients were encouraged to become active participants in documenting their care.[10] Lack of candor in medical documentation is not a good thing.

Opening records to patients necessarily constrains how things ought to be stated. Clinicians must strive to replace medical jargon and abbreviations with plain English (e.g. "right eye" instead of OD; "shortness of breath" in place of "SOB;" "red" instead of "erythematous") and to use language that does not sound pejorative (e.g. substitute "overweight" for "morbidly obese" and "concerned" for "demanding"). Mention of scary but unlikely possible diagnoses should generally be kept away from patients so as not to induce unnecessary worry. Unsubstantiated opinions about psychological issues or faked symptoms must be withheld from a patient, at least temporarily, so as not to harm the therapeutic relationship. If the patient reads that the provider has low expectation for success of her therapeutic plan, it can induce a nocebo effect and become a self-fulfilling prophecy. A nocebo, the opposite of placebo, is an intervention paired with the belief that it is not going to work, so it doesn't.

How then are clinicians to keep track of things like unlikely scary diagnoses or opinions that the patient is faking? This is an issue to discuss with the EHR vendor and possibly a health information professional or with an attorney with special expertise in matters of health information privacy. Remember that, according to HIPAA, patients have a near-absolute right to read their own medical records. Providers need to figure out now how to live with that fact. The answer is not to hide behind the perceived safety of objectified data in the form of checklists, thereby losing the all-important stories. (See Chapter 5, "Data Versus Story.")

The general impression has been that, as clinicians get used to having their patients read their notes, and see the positive effects that the ensuing dialogs have on engagement and care, they feel less need to shelter their documentation from patient view. A fundamental shift in relationship between patient and provider is likely to result from widespread use of open medical records, uncovering a multitude of complex issues that will have to be worked out over time.[11]

Some participants in the open record movement have taken the further step of allowing patients to directly add to and comment on their own records. Surely there is the potential headache of records bloated by compulsives who record every day's steps taken, the composition of every meal eaten, the duration of every night's sleep and the quality of every bowel movement. There will also be doubting patients who seek to match wits with the provider in the documentation. Mostly, though, getting direct patient input into the record will be a good thing, improving accuracy of the data it contains and nudging the locus of control in the patients' direction.

I have one word of warning about giving the patient the final word on what goes into the medical record. Instinctively, we human beings try to look our best in others' eyes, which explains some of the tiresome aspects of small message services (SMS) like Facebook, where people routinely choose to post items that make their lives appear to be wonderful. For the same reason, airlines that fly small shuttle planes routinely add 10%–20% to the weights people wishfully report before boarding. We still need a way to distinguish between the information that a patient adds to her PHR and what a health professional records.

There remains a small percentage of OpenNotes physicians who believe that patients perusing their own medical records complicates their care without improving it, leading to longer office visits, more phone calls and emails to the doctor out of concern for what they had read.[12]

One study of Kaiser Permanente patients in Colorado found that those who had been granted online access to their medical records from 2005 to 2010 made 0.7 more clinic visits, 0.3 more phone calls, 0.02 more after-hours clinic visits, 0.01 more emergency room visits, and had 0.02 more hospitalizations per member per year. That is not a lot. But it does at least cast a shadow of a doubt on the claim that open access to medical records will reduce utilization.[13]

Besides being more accurate and comprehensive than the sorts of documents most patients and their providers are stuck with today, the PMR could be a linchpin for involving patients in their own care. Patient engagement is a cornerstone to efforts to improve healthcare quality and outcomes. Using a minimalist definition of a PHR, keeping track of personal health information with the help of the internet and communicating with a healthcare provider by email, 17% of US adults appeared to be on their way to having a PHR in 2013. Based on data acquired beginning in 1998, the authors of the paper in which this figure was reported, optimistically estimated that it would be another 10–20 years before a full PHR is truly the norm.[14]

It does not take a full-fledged PHR to make progress in patient care. Thirty percent of patients who were asked to review their medications on an online feedback form did so and eighty-nine percent of them requested changes to their lists. The reviewing pharmacist responded favorably to 68% of these changes. In other words, for very little effort, the veracity of medication lists, a major impediment to efforts for achieving continuity of care (See Chapter 9, "Patient Care"), was improved in over half of the patients who reviewed them online.[15,16]

The journal *BMJ* carried a report in 2016 that documented the reactions of 27,703 patients to having been granted open access to their charts, as well as of their 113 primary care doctors in three US practices. The data were collected in 2010 and 2011, so we can probably assume that today's better connected consumers and professionals would be that much more sanguine about open access. About one-third read their doctors' notes and 7% contacted the office about what they'd read, which 29% of the time was about a perceived error in the record that they reported later had been corrected successfully 85% of the time.

During this interval, 37% of patients with open record access said they had come to feel better about their doctors and the rest felt about the same. After a year, 53% of doctors opined that patient satisfaction had increased and 51% believed patients trusted them more.[17]

Empowerment

Historians say that the Protestant Reformation would not have been possible without invention of the moveable type printing press, introduced in Europe by Johannes Guttenberg in the mid-fifteenth century.* One of the first works he printed was, of course, the Bible. Though just a tiny fraction of the population was literate in those days, this technology, which hugely reduced the cost of replicating texts, got the actual written word into many more hands than those of a

---

* Examples of wood, ceramic and metal moveable type, dating back as far as the eleventh century have been found in China. But our story is focused on the West.

few clergymen who had been solely entrusted with interpreting and disseminating the word of God.

Books, newspapers and magazines came along in rapid succession, as well as the ideal of universal literacy. Information had always been power. And now it was being disseminated. Telegraph, telephone, radio and television brought information transmission at the speed of light. Today, new electronic media and channels seem to be rolled out every week. Everybody has more information.

Theoretically, that means everybody has more power. It is well beyond the scope of this work to discuss the uses and abuses of power that we face in a world that is drowning in information. Suffice it to say that laypeople really can be more empowered regarding their own health and healthcare if they choose wisely from the gobs of information that are available to them and use it well. That's how I felt when I went to the car dealer with a printout in hand of data, downloaded from the internet, telling me exactly what the dealer's wholesale price was and what deals and rebates were available at that moment for the vehicle I wanted.

A 2017 search of 295 healthcare institution websites that were supposed to provide price information found that only 17% actually delivered geographically relevant cost estimates on four procedures—upper gastrointestinal endoscopy, brain MRI, cholesterol blood panel and hip replacement—in the first two web pages.[18]

In spite of the high opinion that we generally hold of our healthcare providers, based on a representative survey of 1000 participants in 2008, Kelton Research estimated that 38% of American adults had doubted the opinion of a medical professional based on information obtained online. Not surprisingly, younger adults were more doubting than their elders.[19]

There is a big difference between purveying a car and purveying care. I'm not suggesting that patients arm themselves with information so they can treat healthcare providers as they would car salespeople. In the world of too much information, we need smart professionals more than ever, people whom we can trust to make sense of the facts and apply them to our particular situation.

"Collaboration" ought to be the operative word. Knowledge is even more powerful in collaborative relationships than in adversarial ones. Without trust, which is a consummately human quality, knowledge is of lesser use.

The Choosing Wisely campaign has employed an interesting strategy to change health professional behavior. Since 2012, the program has been educating healthcare providers, as well as consumers, with a widely circulated and publicized list of tests, treatments and procedures that are generally not recommended, accompanied by the strong suggestion to patients that they discuss it with their provider should she order one of these. More than 70 bona fide medical specialty societies, in collaboration with the publishers of *Consumer Reports*, had, as of 2016, generated a list of 470 recommendations, such as avoiding routine PSA tests in asymptomatic men and routine pap smears for teens. Though these recommendations account for just a fraction of overuse, early studies indicate they have had a significant effect on utilization in places where Choosing Wisely has been pushed. An EMR, of course, provides ample opportunities to build in alerts and routines that guide clinicians and patients to choose wisely.*,[20]

Easy access to information has even affected relationships among physicians. Now that I can prepare myself with a few minutes' review of a subject before I discuss a patient with a subspecialist consultant, I feel that much more equal when standing on her home turf. Because information that used to be theirs only is now universally available, every specialty finds it harder to defend the exclusivity of its territory. Likewise, lines between different health professions and between different specialties are becoming less distinct.

Giving everybody access to the same information is a crucial step toward adopting the sort of teamwork, including with patients, that will go a long way toward solving the problems that plague American healthcare.

Information Seeking

Whatever communication occurs at a distance between patients and me, it is but a few drops compared to the gushers of information delivered by myriad other channels that connect them to the world. They are on the internet, looking things up or just browsing. They converse with friends, co-workers and some strangers by way of texting, voice calls and video calls like Skype and FaceTime. They may regularly check into social media sites, like Facebook, Twitter, LinkedIn, Tumblr, Pinterest and Instagram. They may follow certain blogs, occasionally post comments on them and maybe even write a blog themselves.

The average US adult seeks online health information three times a month. Patients with multiple sclerosis do so seven times a month.[21] In 2013, the Pew Research Center found that 77% of online health information pursuit began with a search website like Google or Bing, 13% with a medical information website like WebMD, 2% with Wikipedia and 1% with a social network like Facebook.[22]

Of these websites, only the material on WebMD is vetted from the outset. Lack of expert review would be okay if folks had a way to sort reliable from unreliable information. Unfortunately, too many people do not possess this skill. In a study published in 2016, researchers turned a group of diabetics loose to find answers to

---

* For every dollar spent on the Choosing Wisely campaign, direct-to-consumer marketers are probably spending hundreds or thousands to convince people to get total body scans and other tests that are much more likely to lead to further worry, expense and possibly complications than to any health benefit. (See "number needed to screen" in the Glossary.) It goes without saying that the $6.4 billion that pharmaceutical companies spent in 2016 on direct-to-consumer advertising of prescription drugs has a similar and much more toxic effect on the health and on the pocketbooks of the American public. (https://www.usatoday.com/story/money/2017/03/16/prescription-drug-costs-uptv-ads/99203878/)

questions about managing their disease. Only 40%–65% of answers obtained from internet sources, and 45%–63% of answers that came from laypeople, were judged by experts to be valid.[23]

As of the end of 2013, Wikipedia contained 155,000 medical articles, 1 billion bytes in over 255 languages, buttressed by almost 1 million references. All of this information was supported by just 300 core members, half of whom were healthcare professionals and 85% of whom had a university education.[24]

A 2016 report of the results of 20 Google searches for information on the human papilloma virus vaccine, which is unquestionably safe and unequivocally protects women from cervical cancer and men from penile cancer, found that about one-third of the top 5–10 search results portrayed the vaccine in a negative light.[25] Anti-vaccination groups have made very effective use of the internet and social media to spread their dangerous beliefs. Whether or not information is valid or the outcome liable to be salutary or harmful, the means to disseminate information confers influence and power.[26]

In an article that appeared in *The Journal of the American Osteopathic Association* in 2014, 19 doctors declared their disapproval of the information they found under the main Wikipedia article on 9 of the 10 most costly medical conditions in the United States.[27]

One can always find on the internet information that confirms one's prejudices. As search engines, endowed with AI, get better at finding for us what we *like to* see and hear (and purchase), we run the risk of creating echo chambers that isolate us from the information we *ought to* see and hear in order to broaden and deepen our understanding.

A study led by Stanford University researchers reported in one newsletter under the header, "IS BEAUTY MORE IMPORTANT THAN BRAINS?" that 42% of consumers judge the credibility of a health website primarily on its visual appeal, not on its content. You should be relieved to know that another study found that a website's looks were much less important to experts in the field, less than 8% of whom even noticed the layout.[28]

The Health on the Internet (HON) Foundation began in 1995 with the mission of promoting the quality of online health information. A website must meet a set of criteria in order to qualify for HON certification. These criteria have to do with quality of the editorial process and assessment of the validity of the material presented. The HON code has been translated into 35 languages and has been used in 90 countries. Currently, there are more than 8000 websites certified under the HON code, a drop in the bucket.[29]

Five percent of all Google searches, which comes to nearly two hundred million a year, are for health information. In recognition of this fact, Google has partnered in a big way with Mayo Clinic to present high quality medical information to laypeople via internet browser and the Google mobile app. They claim that over 11 physicians will have viewed and approved every item presented by Google Health, much of which comes from elsewhere via hyperlinks to reliable sites. There are many illustrations, also doctor-approved.

This is the fullest application yet of Google's Knowledge-Graph strategy, a structural framework upon which to hang information. When you type in a search term that is a symptom, treatment or medical condition, an illustrated box pops up on the right of the results page with links to more information.[30] The site is meant to be ad-supported. I have not been able to ascertain whether the Google Knowledge-Graph enhanced health tool has been a success, either in service terms or in financial ones.

Reputable, well-funded organizations dedicated to addressing broad classes of problems, like the American Cancer Society, the American Diabetes Association or the American Heart Association, are good places to find trustworthy disease-specific information, decision aids, links to other information resources and organizations, etc. Hundreds of groups, connected to bona fide professional organizations and dedicated to serving patients with specific diseases, like amyotrophic lateral sclerosis (ALS), cystic fibrosis and chronic fatigue, maintain patient-friendly websites. Providing names and web addresses of such sites on handouts and as hyperlinks on its patient portal, is a significant, easy-to-offer service that any healthcare practice can do for its patients.

Using "medical" as a search term for YouTube videos, the site responded that there were "about 13,900,000 results," which presents just as big a challenge as text-based information in separating wheat from chaff. Some of the information is indexed under channels, with offerings produced by the likes of the National Library of Medicine and Harvard Medical School. The same general strategies apply for finding reputable videos as for seeking out any other medical information on the internet. (See Chapter 9, "Patient Care—Evidence-Based Medicine and Best Practices.") There is even a YouTube channel for "doctors and other health IT stakeholders to share success stories related to the use of health IT."[31]

Thanks to cellphone technology, many, many more inhabitants of the less developed world are now connected. Cell phones may turn out to be great levelers in this country too. A 2012 study published by the Pew Research Center found US African Americans, Latinos and college graduates were the biggest users of this modality for obtaining health information.[32] There is evidence, though, that poorer kids waste even more time playing with electronic gadgets than their more privileged counterparts, sort of damned if you do damned if you don't.[33]

Social Media

I've learned that if I want to greatly improve the odds of communicating with my children, it is best to text them. Phone calls are too easy to screen and email is not immediate enough. I suspect, though, that texting is just the channel du jure. Perhaps texting is already passé and I just haven't figured that out yet.

Short message services (SMS) have done some good things. They are being experimented with extensively as messaging platforms that can point people in the direction of healthier lifestyles or better management of chronic diseases. So far not too much has come of it. (See "Pushed Messages" below.) Notably, though, the day that Facebook added organ donor status to its profiles in 2012, 57,451 customers signed up.[34]

I do fear that texting and the other forms of instant messaging that generations after me are so tied to carry a risk of creating a hyper-vigilant state, of being always on the lookout for the next message. The structure of some SMS is held up as a model for creating and maintaining an addiction.* Scientific studies that correlate the amount of time spent with social media with isolation, depression and insomnia continue to accumulate.[35] Members of Generation Z, born between the mid-1990s and mid-2000s, who have been online almost from birth, are especially at risk.

The *American Journal of Epidemiology* published in 2017 a widely-noted study of 5208 participants in a Gallup survey that showed higher numbers of Facebook links clicked and user status updates entered correlated with lower self-reported physical and mental health, as well as life satisfaction. Even body mass index (weight/height^2, a measure of obesity) went up with increased Facebook use.[36]

Being bombarded by messages may be especially toxic to healthcare providers, diminishing our ability to listen deeply to patients, which bodes ill for the care patients receive and for the satisfaction of the professionals who deliver it. For older adults, on the other hand, time spent on the internet may decrease loneliness.[37]

There's also the problem of boundaries. I have reluctantly chosen to engage in the world of social media in order to help market this book. But I really don't like it. Ever since this man who grew up in Chicago found himself as one of two general practitioners in a town of 2000 people on the plains of eastern Colorado, the week after his face and mop of curly hair ran on the front page of the newspaper, he has

---

* Snapchat rewards take the form of tallies of messages and length of message streaks. They are time-pressured and without bounds. Snapstreaks last only as long as each person in a dyad has sent a message to the other in the last twenty-four hours. The user has constant access to a running total of messages she has sent and received. This reward system is considered a model for inducing addictive behavior. Here are the titles of the first seven articles (besides ads) that popped up in a Google search of "Snapchat addiction" on October 25, 2017: "Confronting my daughter's addiction to Snapchat;" "16 Signs You're Addicted To Snapchat;" "I Am A Snapchat Addict Who Is Over Snapchat;" "10 Signs You Are Addicted To Snapchat;" "How To Help A Child Who Is Addicted To Snapchat;" and "Talk to your teen about Snapchat Ghost Mode, and track their time."

had high regard for anonymity.* I've had to learn how to regulate how much of myself I put out there. Social media is one place where, in the past, I chose to draw the line.

On the other hand, self-revelation can be an extremely powerful tool in the therapeutic relationship. It's one of the things I ask health science students to pay attention to when they see me interacting with patients. Comparing a mother's worry about her child to anxiety I've had about my own kids or revealing to a person struggling with quitting smoking that I used to be a smoker can go a long way toward establishing trust and credibility. At the opposite extreme is the seductive patient who, for obvious reasons, I insist call me Dr. Ringel, not Marc.

There is a huge potential downside to using social media in one's professional life. As of 2012, only 9% of medical schools and residencies checked applicants' social media sites as part of the review process. I'll bet that percentage has grown a lot since then. Applicants beware,[38] especially if you've belonged to a fraternity!

Besides loss of privacy, using social media always carries at least some risk of opening oneself to trolls and all sorts of other internet miscreants whose mission is to sow discord, miscommunication and unhappiness, as well as to steal passwords and address books. This subject is covered in greater detail in Chapter 6, "Security and Privacy." Just keep in mind that the more ways you are connected, the more ways there are to get to you.

"Nudging" is the concept of affecting behavior change through subtle messaging. Recently, the American electorate has experienced plenty of spin, malicious hacking and outright lies by politicians, inside and outside our country, who seek to nudge our voting behavior one way or another, supercharged by use of big data and multiple channels of communication.

How about using these methods to nudge people into healthier behaviors, like increasing how much exercise they get? No problem, except perhaps if the personal data used to tailor individually effective messages are obtained and used unethically. How might people with religious objections to childhood immunizations feel about well-intentioned attempts to nudge them to get their kids vaccinated?

---

* I was particularly freaked out by the stares I encountered, for example, one Sunday noon early in my two-year National Health Service Corps tour of duty. As I walked into one of the town's four restaurants, which was full because church had just let out, every head to the right turned to the left and every head to the left turned to the right to follow me as I progressed down the center aisle to my table at the rear of the establishment. After lunch I called my mentor, an older family doctor who had practiced for years in rural Illinois. (It was southern Illinois, so he spoke with a bit of a drawl.) Here's what he said.

"Marc, try not to kill anybody for the first six months. After that, you can walk down Main Street nekkid. Half of the people will say, 'I don't believe Doctor Ringel would do that.' And the other half will say, 'Aw, that's just good ole Doc.'" My friend was right (though I didn't put his idea about public nudity to the test). Those stares had been curious and friendly. Still, I don't enjoy living in a fishbowl, at least not all the time.

It is not hard to imagine a contemporary equivalent of the Temperance Movement or the War on Drugs, which did little to improve the health of the population while bringing in their wake organized crime, exploding jail populations and other social evils that we have yet to get over. Even with the best of intentions, decisions on which behaviors to nudge and how to nudge them need to be made within the context of the culture, by people who understand its values.

Online Ratings and Reviews

As of 2014, there were 40 or 50 online doctor rating sites. A survey of 2000 US adults performed by the AMA found that one-quarter of them had consulted at least one online review site before seeing a doctor and over a third of those people said that their choice had been affected by what they had read on the website(s). Few of the respondents, however, had submitted ratings themselves.[39]

An analysis of 3617 online reviews of 300 doctors in 4 different cities found that 53% were rated 2 stars or fewer out of a maximum of 4 or 5. Forty-three percent of the bad evaluations mentioned poor "bedside manner." Thirty-five percent complained about poor customer service. Twenty-two percent questioned the doctor's medical skills.

There are two things to take note of in these data. First, over half of the people who had bothered to register reviews were unhappy with the doctor. Second, connection with the doctor appears to be the make-or-break issue when it comes to patient satisfaction.[40] Analysis of data from one site, RateMD, indicated that punctuality and staff attitude were the most important factors in determining customer ratings.[41]

A retrospective review of data from the Medical Board of California found only a very small difference between online patient ratings of doctors who had been on probation between 1989 and 2015 and those who had not been in trouble with the Board.[42] The *Journal of Medical Internet Research* carried a study in 2016 that showed no correlation between the online ratings of 614 cardiac surgeons practicing in 5 states and their risk-adjusted mortality rates, an objective measure of their patients' surgical outcomes.[43]

On the other hand, a study performed in 2013 demonstrated a correlation between a hospital's Facebook rating and its readmission rate. Readmissions are considered a negative indicator for quality, reflecting hospital discharges made before the patient was well enough to be released and/or poor planning for follow-up after discharge. In this report, the higher the rating, the lower the readmission rate.[44] (See Chapter 9, "Patient Care.")

In 2013, researchers found a strong negative correlation between Facebook likes for the 40 New York City hospitals that maintained Facebook pages and their 30-day mortality rates, which are adjusted for case severity. In other words, the more "likes", the fewer deaths.[45]

There is very little consistency among hospital rating sites. In 2015, not one hospital received a top rating from all four of the big ones, Consumer Reports, Healthgrades, U.S. News & World Report and The Leapfrog Group. Of 844 hospitals reviewed, only 10% earned top marks from even two sites. And 27 hospitals that received the highest grades from one organization received the lowest from another.[46]

That's not such a bad thing, anyway. There is little evidence that publicly disclosing quality ratings has much effect on actual quality of care. Based on data from millions of hospital admissions, Hospital Compare, Medicare's public quality reporting system, was found to have minimal to no impact on mortality from heart attack, pneumonia and heart failure, the three conditions they focused on from 2005 to 2008.[47]

Like any other measurement that smart professionals get our hands on, we learn to game the rating system. Four articles published in the professional literature between 1996 and 2005 made a strong case that sicker and poorer patients had suffered reduced access to cardiac procedures due to administrators' and doctors' desire to improve their outcome statistics for cardiac care.[48]

Like it or not, rating sites are here to stay. So are social media, which also rate and rank healthcare institutions and professionals. If you are a health professional about to bite the bullet and get into the social media game, here is some basic advice.

- Do a "Google" search on yourself to see what's out there already.
- Get a professional headshot.
- Start with doing a profile for a site like LinkedIn or Doximity, a sort of electronic résumé. This is an important step toward getting a higher Google ranking and making a good first impression.
- Then adopt, slowly, and only if you want to, other websites as they seem to meet your professional goals to: educate patients; grow the practice; express opinions about healthcare reform; or whatever.
- Be absolutely certain that no protected patient information ever finds its way into your posts.
- Encourage patients to review you at online sites.
- In the case of a bad online review, pay attention, fix what you can and call the complainer to talk personally. Never get into a shouting match, in person, on the phone or online.
- If a complainer is anonymous and defamatory (i.e. making statements that could be found to be objectively false, not just opinions), you can even get a court to issue a subpoena to the internet service provider to supply the author's identity and proceed from there.[49]

Sooner or later most of us will have to make an appearance on social media, if for no other reason than to counter bad influences. Just don't expect to provide much competition to the 70 representative brands of cigarettes that, as of 2014, had 238 Facebook pages, or the 46 brands listed in Wikipedia and the over 120,000 pro-tobacco videos on YouTube.[50]

Online Groups

One shouldn't automatically discount information available on the internet and social media just because it was put out there by laypeople and might never have been seen, let alone blessed by healthcare professionals. Real people with real diseases and real symptoms who take real medicines with real side effects may have a whole lot to contribute to others' understanding of their own medical problems. Patients don't have to be mini-doctors to offer to each other (and to their providers, if they'll listen) a wealth of expertise about coping with their illness.

Online groups may have an activist dimension, where electronic communications are employed to organize and mobilize campaigns to enhance research, services, insurance coverage or anything else that lies within the scope of a group's concerns. The content of support group conversations may, in itself, also be useful to research in terms of what it reveals about the real issues and coping strategies of people grappling with a health problem day-by-day.

There are affinity groups for people suffering with most any medical problem you can think of, both common and rare. Registries of people with diseases like Down syndrome and muscular dystrophy that are maintained by professional organizations offer secure listings of members in online databases, general information and personal updates and, if desired, access to participation in research studies. Some of these registries are in the process of linking, with patient permission, to biorepositories that contain genetic and other data, thereby supercharging research in the field.[51]

The website, PatientsLikeMe, boasts 500,000 members who have 2700 different medical conditions. These people have recorded over 40,000,000 disease data points about themselves. The site gives folks with similar medical problems the opportunity to learn from and support each other.

PatientsLikeMe participants can also do research. One user-initiated study examined the use of lithium, a longtime staple in the treatment of bipolar disease, to see if it slowed the progression of the neurodegenerative disease amyotrophic lateral sclerosis (ALS, "Lou Gehrig Disease"), as had been claimed in one study. By pairing a sample of 348 people with ALS who were taking lithium with a control group of people who weren't taking the medication, the PatientsLikeMe study was able, in just 9 months, to show pretty decisively that this drug, which can be toxic to kidneys and thyroid, was of no value in slowing progression of ALS.[52] That is just one of over 100 studies PatientsLikeMe has published to date.

I Had Cancer is a website where people can share their cancer experience and search for peers by type of cancer, geography, age, gender and time of diagnosis, as well as initiate or join ongoing conversations with peers.

There was even a report in 2015 out of Australia that an online support group for rural physicians had showed a positive effect on psychological wellbeing among the connected doctors. The docs' biggest complaint about their online experience was slow internet connection speed.[53]

There is plenty of room for support groups to do harm too. There are pro-eating disorder websites for potentially lethal conditions like anorexia nervosa, where individuals may find reinforcement of their dangerous food-related behaviors and encouragement from fellow sufferers to keep at them.[54]

Besides participants with bad information, there is the hazard of trolls. Many groups are moderated in order to protect participants from ill-intentioned actors. Knowledgeable people monitor discussions, seeing to it that exchanges among users are within the bounds of the subject matter and of civility.

Social media are important elements in driving illicit drug sales.[55] And "legitimate" drug sales too. Pharmaceutical companies employ people to hype their products on social media and websites. Bona fide drug companies follow online discussions looking for "digital footprints" that allow them to target people for advertising. They run their own online health forums and have their own pages on Twitter, Facebook and YouTube. Many of these marketing nudges may not be recognized as such by unsuspecting potential customers.[56]

Self-Care

The cover of the first edition of the *Whole Earth Catalog*, published in 1968, famously pictured a satellite image of, what else, the whole Earth. It was an invitation to think big. At the same time, the publication reviewed real tools for use here on our home planet, from garden shovels to manuals for electrical wiring and home birthing. This big book, whose full title was, *Whole Earth Catalog: Access to Tools*, served as a guide for the part of the countercultural movement of the sixties and seventies that focused on how to exert control over one's own life, (especially, but not solely, by adopting a self-sufficient rural lifestyle).

Dr. Tom Ferguson, editor of the medical section of the *Catalog*, founded a magazine in 1975, called *Medical Self Care*, that was based on Whole Earth ideas about tools for empowerment. The magazine featured regular reviews of tools for self-care. *Medical Self Care* ceased publication in 1989. Today there is greater need than ever for good, reliable information about the myriad healthcare tools, many of them digital, that are available to consumers.

The journal *BMJ* reported on a study of one class of such tools, 23 free online symptom-checkers. Users enter their symptoms and a computerized algorithm provides a tentative diagnosis and suggests if they need to seek further care. When it came to recognizing the severity of the afflictions that underlay 45 standardized patient vignettes submitted to the symptom-checkers by the study's scientists, the programs correctly identified emergency conditions 80% of the time, and non-emergencies 55% of the time. They were right about only 33% of cases amenable to self-care (which is the cautious side they ought to err on, instead of suggesting that someone doesn't need medical care when she really does).

These electronic mavens did terribly at arriving at a diagnosis, which they got right just one-third of the time and only managed to list in their top 20 diagnostic possibilities 58% of the time. Since this study was performed in 2014, we can assume that, thanks to AI, online symptom checkers have become at least a little more accurate since then. Whether they are precise enough to rely on solely is still an open question.*

In 2016, the Hacking Medicine Institute, a spin-off from MIT, debuted a modern version of the Whole Earth concept for assessing the efficacy and safety of digital health products, called Ranked.[57] In May 2017, I counted 30 product reviews on the site. In 2016, the Apple Store alone featured 150,000 healthcare apps.

Simple wearable devices that continuously monitor and report things like heart rate, steps, posture, distance traveled, activity, sleep, and so on, are all the rage. Engineers at the University of California, San Diego even announced in 2016 that they had developed a wearable tattoo that sends blood alcohol levels to a cellphone or other monitoring station.[58]

I have little doubt that a good deal of progress in telehealth will be consumer-driven, especially as more generations of digital natives come of age. As of 2016, 40% of millennials (18–34 years old) owned a wearable physiologic monitor, 29% of Gen Xers (35–54) and 10% of baby boomers (55–70). One out of three millennials had downloaded a health app in the 30 days prior to taking this survey of four thousand fifteen American adults.[59]

A report published in the *Journal of Medical Internet Research* in 2015 found that 46% of people who had downloaded a health app had stopped using it because

---

* I was relieved to find that when the same vignettes with the same constellation of symptoms were presented to 234 physicians and doctors-in-training, the human beings did more than twice as well as the computer in arriving at the most probable diagnosis (72.1% vs. 34.0%). (Semigran, HL, Levine, DM, Nundy, S et al. Comparison of physician and computer diagnostic accuracy. *JAMA Internal Medicine*, 2016:176(12), 1860-1861.)

One fascinating study found that participants who were distracted with tasks like memorizing random digits for three minutes after they had gone through a computerized medical decision aid program made better decisions than those who had been tasked with deciding immediately and than those who had been asked to think about their decision for three minutes before they gave their answer. Which gets to something we already know, that good information and conscious processing are not all that goes into making a good decision. (Manigault, AW, Handley, IM, Whillock, SR et al. Assessment of unconscious decision aids applied to complex patient-centered medical decisions. *Journal of Medical Internet Research*, 2015:17(2), e37.)

of cost, privacy concerns or waning interest.[60] Still, the market intelligence firm, Tractica, predicts that by 2020 annual sales of wearable medical devices will reach nearly 100 million units worldwide, accounting for $17.8 billion in revenue. Accenture, a business management consulting firm, estimated that in 2016 fewer than 2% of patients were using mobile health apps[61] that a hospital had provided for them.

There are big problems with the reliability of the data these gadgets collect, as well as a severe lack of scientific literature on how to use the information to actually improve health status.

The Nightscout Project is a great example of consumer-driven healthcare technology that appears to be of real value. In 2013, the parents of a 4-year-old boy with newly diagnosed type I diabetes decided that they needed to be able to follow the data that his continuous glucose monitor (CGM) generated every five minutes, including when their child was at school. The boy's father was a programmer who succeeded in linking the monitor output to the cloud through a smartphone. Parents of other diabetic children "heard" the father's tweet (if it had been me, it would have been a crow) about the successful data transfer and Nightscout was on its way.

The parents formed themselves into a private Facebook group called "CGM in the Cloud." They created a website, where they posted the program's code, conversed with and advised each other. They made and shared tweaks and enhancements to their open-source product, such as sending remote alerts for high and low blood sugar levels. Within 18 months, CGM in the Cloud boasted 15,000 members in the United States and 4000 members abroad.

The last words on the opening page of the Nightscout website carry this disclaimer:

> All information, thought, and code described here is intended for informational and educational purposes only. Use of code from github.com is without warranty or support of any kind.
>
> Each element of the system can fail at any time rendering the system unusable. There is no password protected privacy or security provided by these tools; all data you upload can be available for anyone on the internet to read if they have your specific URL to view your data. Please review the LICENSE found within each repository for further details. This is not a project of the Dexcom company….
>
> **Do not use any of the Nightscout information or code to make medical decisions**. [bolded in original][62]

The line between what health professionals do and what laypeople do for themselves is getting hazier. I suspect that, thanks to information technology, we've seen just the beginning of epic battles over who can do what to whom, as reflected by the clumsiness of the above disclaimer.

In a research trial, 118 veterans with diabetes, aged 50–70, were paired with peer mentors, matched by age, race and sex, who had achieved good control over their blood sugar. The mentor would call once a week to see how her partner was doing. After six months of receiving these calls, patients' glycohemoglobin had decreased an average of one percent, which indicates a significant improvement in average blood sugar. Glycohemoglobin levels decreased about half as much (0.45%) in mentor-less patients who were promised monetary rewards for lowering their number and hardly at all (0.1%) in the control group.[63] As is so often the case, human contact is what made the difference. The only electronic technologies employed by this self-care group were the telephone and the target patient's glucose monitor.

Remember Me! is an example of fancier technology, based on a smartphone, designed to improve function for people with memory loss. The app combines stored pictures, as well as GPS data, all stitched together via the cloud. When a person whom the user knows is nearby, the app alerts her by flashing pictures of the acquaintance that have been stored on the phone. The developers have even planned a "call this person" reminder feature, based on data like stored birthdays.[64] Clever though the app is, I don't think it's caught on yet. When it comes to self-help apps, we still hardly know what will work and, if it does work, if it will catch on.

There are a lot of crappy apps to be avoided out there. One of the most outrageous ones I've heard of is "AcneApp," which sold 11,600 downloads on iTunes for $1.99 each, claiming to cure acne with the cellphone light. An Android version, "AcnePwner," was downloaded 3300 times. The FTC did fine both of the companies that produced these worthless software products and required that the apps be removed from the market.

There are plenty more medical apps to avoid. Most may be harmless in themselves, but they could cause untold problems by providing people with a reason not to get the care that would really help them.[65]

There are smartphone apps that tout their ability to diagnose malignant skin lesions without the help of a professional. When three such apps, which each cost under $5, were tested against 188 skin lesions, 60 of which were known melanomas, two were accurate 70% of the time and one just 7% of the time! Melanomas, the scariest of skin cancers, can kill you. How early this malignancy is diagnosed and cut out makes a huge difference on prognosis.[66] This is definitely not a diagnosis you want to trust to an app that misses three of ten malignancies, let alone nine of ten. In 2015, the FDA fined makers of two melanoma detection apps, "MelApp" and "Mole Detective," $20,000 each and took their products off the market.

One mobile dermatology app targeted to consumers that has shown some promise is Sunface, a free program for mobile phones that ages a person's selfie in proportion to a projected amount of sun exposure over the years. The more sun, the older the skin looks. When the app was tried out on students at two German high schools, the aged selfies were reported to have made a big impression on the adolescents, hopefully motivating sun avoidance and protection behaviors and, ultimately, resulting in less skin damage and malignancy over the lifetime of these fair northern Europeans.[67]

We must always keep in mind that, especially in healthcare, the answer is never, "get an app" or "get a new electronic device, now what's the problem." Many creative solutions take place in meatspace, not cyberspace. People with disabilities, sometimes with the assistance of occupational therapists and industrial designers, have devised all sorts of material world hacks such as: putting a Lazy Susan on a refrigerator shelf to make all items on it easily reachable; attaching small bumps to the answer button on the phone to facilitate picking up calls by people with low vision; rounding out sharp, hazardous edges on furniture with rubberized putty; wrapping rubber bands around cups to make them easier to grip. Identifying a challenge and thinking creatively about how to meet it, not searching for ways to use cool technology, is where all patient problem solving always needs to begin.[68]

Pushed Messages

Text messages can be sent to remind a person of a doctor's appointment, to take a medication, check blood sugar or blood pressure or mood. Timed reminders work best in the short-term. One study found triple the concentration of chlorhexidine, the cleaner that reduces bacterial counts on the skin that is prescribed for pre-elective surgery showers, in patients who had had received SMS text, voicemail or email reminders, than in those whose memories had not been jogged by electronically-delivered messages.[69]

Reminders that are sent over a longer period about, for example, taking chronic medications or thinking positive thoughts, are more likely to be ignored. A study of 1139 Finnish patients with schizophrenia, a particularly challenging group to get to take their medications, revealed no reduction in hospitalization or use of other medical services in those who received individually tailored SMS reminders to take their medications.*,[70]

In light of how overwhelmed we all are with information and messages, it is not surprising that sending regular electronic reminders via any channel is not very effective. (See discussion of alarm fatigue in Chapter 9, "Patient Care.") An article published in the *Annual Review of Public Health* in 2015 summarizing an exhaustive search of the medical literature, came up with just 15 systematic reviews, which had evaluated just 89 individual studies of text messaging that appeared

---

* Developers are quite busy producing apps designed to help people with mental health problems. For example, "T2 Mood Tracker," a smartphone app designed for use by people with depression or anxiety, tailors the level of service to match a user's level of engagement with the program, starting with reminders and reporting of mental state and escalating to educational information, as well as graphically displaying the person's own data. [http://t2health.dcoe.mil/apps/t2-mood-tracker]

to be scientifically valid. Based on this scant set of studies, it did appear to the authors of the paper that, as of now, text messaging has a positive effect on efforts at smoking cessation, weight loss, amount of exercise, management of some chronic diseases and adherence to medication regimens.

There is some evidence that nagging-by-text-message may slightly increase rates of breast, cervical and colon cancer screening,[71] as well as rates of influenza immunization.[72] This is encouraging news. But we don't have nearly enough information yet to know how to translate an idea for an SMS health intervention into a program that is likely to work, nor do we have the long-term studies that would tell us if these strategies have a significant effect on people's health and quality of life.[73] The process is still mostly trial-and-error.

Crowd Sourcing, Games and Virtual Reality

Researchers from Spain and South Africa found that, in the form of a game, lay-people could do quite well at counting malaria parasites in a thick blood smear, a measure fundamental to managing that tropical disease. The amateurs received one minute(!) of training as to what the parasite looks like. Then, presented in a competitive game format, they were asked to click on as many parasites in a digitized image as they could in one minute(!). Statistically, combining the clicks of just 13 seekers resulted in an accuracy rate of over 99%(!), rivaling that of experienced laboratory technicians.[74]

After viewing an optional 2-minute-and-36-second video, the crowd-sourced Stall Catchers program will let you contribute to Alzheimer's research by labeling blockages of capillary blood flow in microscopic videos of mouse brains.

CrowdMed received $2.4 million in venture capital to launch their product, a website that crowdsources difficult diagnoses. It is a version of a prediction market, run on the same principles as a financial exchange or a sports betting establishment. A stable of "medical detectives," most of whom are health professionals and a few of whom call themselves "medical aficionados," work on a case and come up with a list of possible diagnoses. The detectives who get it right are rewarded out of the fee of $149–$749 per month, paid by the patient, as well as moving up in their ranking, which gets them more shots at higher-paying cases. The more a customer pays, the greater the number of higher-ranking detectives get assigned to her case and the greater the detectives' possible reward.

Fancy software combines the various detectives' opinions into an overall list of diagnoses, each with an attached probability of being right. The patient and her doctor decide which diagnosis(-es) is/are correct. And that determines which detectives get the rewards. The company claims on its website that 75% of patients say that CrowdMed's diagnosis was eventually confirmed.

Wii game technology has been successfully used to help maintain the mobility of patients with Parkinson's, and all sorts of others in need of getting a move on.[75]

For the able-bodied, internet-enabled GPS monitors, either as stand-alone units or as features of smartphones, allow them to compete at hiking, running, climbing and cycling, without ever meeting face-to-face.

When I was a kid, what we saw on television and at the movies was our version of virtual reality. On rare occasions the viewing experience at a movie theater would be enhanced by some gimmick like release of scents of roses or sulfur at the appropriate moments, or vibrators that shook the seats, or a ghost that was reeled on a rope across the ceiling in front of the screen during especially scary scenes. For one horror flick, a man carrying a clipboard asked patrons to sign a release form absolving the theater from liability should they suffer a heart attack from fright while watching the show. That was a sort of virtual reality that brought the movie experience right out into the theater lobby. Most of the time, though, we got just picture and sound, enhanced, year by year, ever more vividly, with bigger screens and more speakers to help movie theaters compete with the television sets in our homes. Still today, the vast majority of media experience for most of us is limited to plain old audio and video, which still work quite well.

Virtual reality (VR) systems routinely provide more immersive experiences than visuals and sound. Headsets give 3D worldviews that change with moving your eyes or your head. More advanced systems are linked to limbs and hands too, allowing the user to move around and to manipulate objects in the virtual world. Some even provide haptic feedback, meaning that, for example, the VR glove you're wearing lets you feel the virtual vase that you grasp and pick up. This medium is in a very early stage of development, still a long way from the holodeck that broke the monotony of those long voyages on the Starship Enterprise.

These days it is mostly your average, non-professional, non-military young person who is driving the market for virtual reality. Every year the online games they play become more immersive, engaging a larger share of the senses. In Chapter 13, "Education," I touched on simulation technology for professional education. Smart clinicians and educators will tap into the burgeoning range of off-the-shelf VR products, and into their clients' ever-growing comfort with the experiences that VR provides, when they choose to develop systems that really do help people take care of themselves. If health professionals are really smart, we will follow the lead of those we seek to serve into this brave new world of electronic technology.

Coda

We have covered a lot of territory, from emotional entanglement to quantum entanglement. The underlying dialectic has stayed the same over thousands of years. On the one hand is lived human experience, while on the other, an objectified, quantified, world. The latter brings the wonders of science and technology, including all the marvelous ways that modern medicine ameliorates suffering. The former is just life in all its messiness and richness.

As information technology gets more powerful, it can capture and mimic more of the messiness and richness of the material world. Just look at how computer animated films have evolved from that first dance scene of "Beauty and the Beast" that wowed us in the 1991 Disney animated film to the 3D digital extravaganzas of today that stand on the verge of immersing the audience in virtual reality.

But, like the scents that those dogs in the cartoon I described in the first paragraph of Chapter 12 pick up from each other, there is still so much that is just not reducible to strings of zeroes and ones. Some of these things are common-sense navigation of the material world. Some are feelings that it takes a human body to feel. Some are creations that come from deep within the human psyche (or, if you prefer, from the divine spirit or from out of the clear blue).

Philosophers, scientists and technologists debate endlessly whether machines will ever achieve the sort of flexibility, creativity and consciousness that characterize the human being. I am not about to enter that debate. For the purpose of this work, suffice it to say that if such a singularity occurs, it will happen well beyond my lifetime.

In the meantime, we need to employ our uniquely human ability to understand and empathize in ways that produce maximum benefit for humankind and for our threatened planet. Information technology provides a set of ever more powerful tools to be harnessed in service of our wellbeing.

"To be harnessed" are the key words in that last sentence. These days it too often appears that technology has taken the lead in healthcare and is dragging us poor humans along behind it. My main goal in writing this book has been to examine how we might re-envision the healthcare enterprise with people at its center and technology as its servant.

I am not very optimistic about the likelihood of making Americans' life and health much better in the short term. The misalignment between our profit-motivated non-system and people's real healthcare needs has shown no signs of diminishing over the nearly five decades that I have been involved in American medicine. If anything, the polarization that has afflicted the body politic in recent years has made it less likely than ever that we can fix healthcare soon.

I, however, find myself to be less pessimistic in the medium-to-longer-term. The informational tools at our disposal are so much more powerful and the cost for using them so much less that, when an inflection point does come (probably at the hands of aggrieved consumers), we will be in a great position to know what must be done. The big question is, of course, if we will have the political will to do it.

Here I am yet again talking about the human and political barriers, not the technological barriers that keep the healthcare system from serving the people. Technology itself is the easy part. People are the hard part. We're emotional, untidy and really, really interesting.

Glossary

[*Terms in italics* appear elsewhere in the glossary.]

3D printing—a computer controlled process whereby a three-dimensional model is built up by stacking successive thin layers of material on top of each other.

accountable care organization (ACO)—a group of doctors, hospitals and other health care providers who come together with the goal of delivering coordinated high quality care to their Medicare patients. ACOs were created by the *Affordable Care Act* as a vehicle to move health care delivery away from fee-for-service and toward value-based care.

Affordable Care Act (ACA)—a sweeping healthcare reform law, passed by the US Congress in 2010, and the center of acrimonious political debate ever since. The ACA led to providing health insurance to a large proportion of the previously uninsured population. Known as *Obamacare*, by both cheerleaders and detractors.

analog—a measure of a continuous quantity, such as what you obtain with a wooden ruler or a mechanical speedometer. Until you get down to microscopic scales, most everything in our experience of the material world is analog. Vinyl records are analog. Compare to *digital*. CDs are *digital*.

analytics—statistical analysis of data collected, in healthcare including, but not limited to, claims and cost data, pharmaceutical data, clinical data from electronic medical records and patient behavior and sentiment data.

app—a program that resides on a smartphone. There are thousands and thousands of apps, with more added every day, that do everything from identifying a song playing on the radio to notifying an investor the moment a stock reaches a pre-determined critical price. Medical apps, some useful, some harmful, mostly un-vetted, are also proliferating at a breakneck pace. For good and for bad, mobile apps are a cornerstone of consumer-led medical technology innovation.

application program interface (API)—provides data for applications that did not create or originate the data. APIs are the software that allow the same data to be used by different programs.

artificial intelligence (AI)—an electronic device that appears capable of "learning" and "problem solving" in a way that mimics human cognitive function. A more formal definition of AI is the ability of a device to "perceive" its environment and take action to maximize its chances of succeeding at some goal. Some members of the AI community use as a working definition, "whatever computers cannot do yet."

arXiv—an archive of *preprint* scientific articles that began in the world of physics in 1991.

asynchronous—see *store-and-forward*.

augmentation—in robotics, machines that work to enhance human performance. Compare to *automation*.

augmented reality—integration of computer-generated information with the user's experience of her environment. Compare to *virtual reality*.

authentication (of credentials)—ensuring that users of an information system are the persons they claim to be.

automation—in robotics, machines that do work without the presence of human operators. Compare to *augmentation*.

avatar—a fictional online persona with roots in online gaming. One chooses or creates a fictional profile for use online. An avatar need not match the sex, race, or even the species or home planet of the person behind it.

biome—a term borrowed from ecology that describes the sum-total of organisms that live together in a niche. Gut, mouth, skin, vagina and nasal passages each hosts its own biome. Biomics is the study of biomes.

blockchain—a continuously growing ledger of encrypted data recorded among many machines, first conceptualized in 2008. Thanks to their distributed nature and underlying cryptography, it is nearly impossible to tamper with data held in a blockchain.

blog—derived from "weblog," a recurring set of internet posts that readers may subscribe to if they think the writing offers something interesting. The larger the number of followers a blogger has, the higher her status, higher her imputed influence and higher her commercial value. Though the odds are slim, people have blogged their way to wealth and stardom.

blogosphere—the virtual world in which blogs exist. Though it doesn't have set boundaries, there is a medical blogosphere, consisting of writers about health and medicine.

bring your own device (BYOD)—generally a complicating factor for any organization whose members want to use at work the personal smartphones, tablets, etc. that they are most comfortable with.

byte—eight binary digits, encoding 128 (2^8) possibilities. The usual unit measure of electronic memory.

capitation—an arrangement for paying a fixed amount for all of the healthcare that a person in the covered population receives over a set period of time, thereby motivating contracted providers to control the resources they expend in furnishing that care. Compare to *fee-for-service*.

care management—oversight and coordination, by a designated professional or team, of the care that a patient receives, often from multiple sources, as well as self-care activities, in pursuit of optimal outcomes. See *disease management*.

Centers for Medicare and Medicaid Services (CMS)—the huge federal agency, within the Department of Health and Human Services, that administers Medicare and Medicaid. Previously known as the Health Care Financing Administration (HCFA).

classical computing—electronic computing that is accomplished by moving around plain old, un-entangled electrons. Contrast with *quantum computing*.

clinical pathologic conference (CPC)—a standard teaching event for physicians in which the clinical course of a patient is compared to autopsy findings. Presenting at a CPC is one of the scariest things an intern can experience. See *retrospectoscope*.

clinical guidelines (also called clinical practice guidelines)—a set of recommendations, usually narrow in scope, that specify a best approach to a medical issue. The Institute of Medicine issued this definition in 2011. "Clinical practice guidelines are statements that include recommendations intended to optimize patient care that are informed by a systematic review of evidence and an assessment of the benefits and harms of alternative care options."[1]

clinician—a health professional who has direct contact with patients and has immediate responsibility for choosing diagnostic and therapeutic measures. For the purposes of this book, it usually means nurse practitioner, physician or physician assistant.

cloud—a shared electronic resource, such as servers, storage, applications and services. A cloud may be internal to an organization and accessed over its intranet or external and its resources accessed over the internet. The term probably owes its origin to ARPANET, the internet's precursor, which, as far back as 1977, used cloud symbols to indicate networked hardware.

community-engaged research (CER)—collaboration between a community and researchers to create and disseminate knowledge and strengthen the community. Ideally, CER is based on and results in a strong ongoing relationship between communities and academicians.

computerized physician order entry (CPOE)—a process whereby physicians (and other clinicians) enter orders for patient care directly into a computer, rather than writing them freehand or issuing them verbally. CPOE provides the opportunity to build safeguards and prompts into the process of delivering patient care.

confidentiality—ensuring that information is not accessed by unauthorized persons.

continuing medical education (CME)—formal education consumed by physicians after finishing their training.

cookbook medicine—a disparaging term leveled at patient care guidelines that appear to discount the clinician's judgment in delivering care.

copy-and-paste—a quick, easy to perform function of word processing in which text that appears in one place is duplicated in another. Copy-and-pasted notes in medical records may be perceived with the same jaundiced eye as are plagiarized paragraphs in term papers.

crowdsource—the process of soliciting input from a number of individuals and processing their answers electronically in an attempt to answer a question. The technique is sometimes amazingly accurate, even when the people polled have minimal expertise regarding the question asked.

cyberchondria—unfounded anxiety about one's health brought on by information obtained on the internet.

cyberspace—a term coined in 1982 by prescient science fiction writer William Gibson to describe the virtual world of electronic existence. Compare to *meatspace*.

dark web—the part of the World Wide Web that employs software that allows users and website operators to remain anonymous. Used extensively for clandestine operations, both legal and illegal.

data—the stuff that computers and electronic computing devices process and exchange and hopefully turn into *information*.

data mining—doing a study by extracting from a *database* data that have already been collected. Compare to *prospective study*.

database—a structured set of *data*.

digiceutical—information-technology based therapy, such as remote monitoring of mood or activity coupled with tailored messaging, to address emotional issues or promote healthy behaviors.

digital—information encoded in discrete units, as opposed to as continuous quantities. Virtually all electronic computing is performed digitally. Compare to *analog*.

digital immigrant—anybody who used to listen to cassette audio tapes. Opposite of a *digital native*.

digital native—a term coined by educator Mark Prensky in 2001 to describe children who have grown up with digital technology. Their understanding of the electronic devices that surround them is likened to the intuitive grasp that native speakers have of their own language. Linguists have determined that twelve years is the maximum age for learning to speak a language without a detectible foreign accent. Opposite of *digital immigrant*.

digital phenotyping—a new hot term in the psychiatric literature that depends on measures, frequently derived from smartphone interactions with patients, to quantify aspects of their behavior.

disease management—*care management* of a particular medical problem, usually severe, complicated and chronic.

double blind—a feature that lends credibility to a medical study because neither participant nor researcher knows who gets the real treatment and who gets the placebo. Blinding is meant to block the bias that can be introduced into research findings by expectations of both the participant and the scientist. When paired with a *prospective study*, design, double blinding is considered the gold standard for generating reputable results.

electronic health record (EHR)—the preferred term (this year) for the *electronic medical record (EMR)* because it implies a wider range of information. As far as I'm concerned, it is okay to use either term. For me, the main drawback of the phrase "electronic health record" is that, when I abbreviate it, the spell checker in my word processing program repeatedly rearranges EHR to read HER.

electronic medical record (EMR)—see *electronic health record*.

entanglement—this well-demonstrated, counterintuitive result of quantum physics says that under certain conditions the qualities of particles remain correlated, even after being separated by large distances. Einstein called entanglement "spooky action at a distance." Entanglement is the driving principle of *quantum computing*.

epidemiology—the study of the patterns, causes and effects of health and disease conditions in defined populations.

evidence-based medicine (EBM)—the conscientious and judicious use of current best evidence from clinical care research in the management of individual patients.[2]

exabyte—one quintillion (10^{18}) *bytes*, one billion *gigabytes*.

Fast Healthcare Interoperability Resources (FHIR)—(pronounced fire), the most recent update of *Health Level-7* standards for healthcare data interchange, based on a logical model that should remove some of the current barriers to patient data sharing.

fee-for-service—care delivered on a per-unit basis. The primary driver of inflation of medical costs. The more you do under a fee-for-service model, the more you get paid. Contrast to *capitation* and *value-based care*.

folksonomy—a classification system derived from tags that users have attached to electronic information. A folksonomy may be less scientifically valid than a *taxonomy* that is written by experts, but it is likely to better reflect how users of a system actually see and use its information.

gamification—pursuing a therapeutic endeavor using a system that is experienced by the user as a game with challenges and rewards.

garbage in = garbage out—an old saw in computerese, which states that *information* is only as good as the quality and reliability of the *data* upon which it is based.

genome—the sum-total of an individual's native DNA and RNA. Genomics is the study of genomes.

geocoding—tagging data with an exact location. Especially useful for doing population health studies and interventions.

gigabyte—one billion (10^8) *bytes*.

grading of recommendations assessment (GRADE)—the most widely used scoring system for lending an overall weight to suggestions for best practice, based on the strength of the underlying scientific evidence. See *strength of recommendation taxonomy*.

haptic—in virtual reality environments, it refers to the sense of touch. Haptic feedback, for example, feeling the virtual softball you hold in the glove on your virtual hand, is still in the early stages of development. Olfactory and gustatory (smell and taste) feedback will come later yet.

Health Insurance Portability and Accountability Act (HIPAA)—a law passed by Congress in 1996 that specifies data privacy and security standards for personal medical information. There are hefty penalties for HIPAA violations.

Health Information Technology for Economic & Clinical Health Act (HITECH)—federal legislation enacted in 2009 that first spelled out the concept of *meaningful use* for health information technology, and started the healthcare industry and the feds down a very expensive path to computerizing medical records.

Health Level-7 (HL7)—a set of standards, widely adopted, including internationally, for transferring clinical and administrative data between software applications. Since its inception in the late eighties, HL7 has been updated multiple times. It is virtually ubiquitous in the healthcare software world. See *Fast Healthcare Interoperability Resources (FHIR)*.

hidden curriculum—"those aspects of medical education where professional identity, including values, skills and attitudes, are shaped and modeled."[3] Though first named in an article about education of physicians, the concept applies to all health professionals, as well as to most every type worker who must undergo most any kind of job training.

HIPAAnoia—in spite of clear guidelines for appropriate sharing of *private health information* that are part of in the *Health Insurance Portability and Accountability Act*, the considerable penalties, including criminal ones, for not adhering to the act's privacy and security standards, have led to inordinate reluctance on the part of many healthcare workers and institutions to share patient data.

hive mind—collective intelligence that either brings out the wisdom of the group or leads to deadening conformity of thought. *Crowdsource* is an example of hive mind.

homophily—the tendency to listen to and affiliate with people like oneself. Homophily, supercharged by social media, is considered to be one of the driving forces in the fracturing of consensus in American society and politics today.

Hype Cycle for Emerging Technologies—Gartner, a technology consulting group, branded this graphical representation that divides adoption of new technology into five phases: trigger, peak of inflated expectations, trough of disillusionment, slope of enlightenment and plateau of productivity. Gartner publishes an annual report in which they estimate where on the graph new technologies fall. The same principles hold for medical treatments. One wise old commentator suggested, "Use a drug while it is new and still works."

IMHO—in my humble opinion. One of the most common text message abbreviations.

influential—a sociology term that refers to an individual who holds sway in a group or organization, not necessarily based on rank or title. Identifying and recruiting influentials to the cause is often a crucial step to making a program work.

infodemiology—science of distribution and determinants of information on the internet or in a population, with the ultimate aim to inform public health, including public policy.

information—answers to specific questions. It lies between *data* and *knowledge*. *Data* are compiled and processed to yield information. Information is abstracted to yield *knowledge*.

integrity—refers to data or information that has not been altered by unauthorized persons.

interoperability—the ability of computers and software systems to make use of the same *data* and/or *information*.

killer app—a world-changing software application. The electronic spreadsheet, Pacman and the Amazon shopping cart come to mind.

knowledge—what a cognitive observer makes of *information*.

landline—the wire connections that all telephone service used to depend on.

law of diminishing astonishment—technologies that wow us when they are introduced quickly lose their ability to amaze us. See *Hype Cycle for Emerging Technologies*.

machine intelligence—see *artificial intelligence*.

machine learning—field of study that gives computers the ability to change their behavior to better accomplish a task without being explicitly programmed; a subclass of approaches to *machine intelligence*.

massive open online course (MOOC)—a course of study made available over the internet without charge to a very large number of people [Google online dictionary].

meaningful use—a concept brought into existence in 2009 by the *Health Information Technology for Economic & Clinical Health Act* that specifies levels of functionalities that electronic health records must achieve in order to qualify users for different degrees of rewards. Meaningful use has been a moving target and a motivator for much gaming of the system by vendors and by users.

meatspace—the everyday world that we humans inhabit. Contrast to *cyberspace*.

Medicare Access & CHIP [Children's Health Insurance Program] Reauthorization Act (MACRA)—federal legislation passed in 2015 that outlines a quality-based program for reimbursing clinicians. Like *accountable care organizations*, it is another complicated policy initiative devised by the feds to move medical practice away from quantity-driven fee-for-service toward quality-driven care.

megabyte—a million (10^6) *bytes*.

metabolome—the sum-total of the small molecules—including amino acids, nucleic acids, sugars, fatty acids, vitamins, co-factors, glycoproteins and many others—that are found in an individual. Metabolomics is the study of metabolomes.

meta-analysis—a scientific analysis that employs statistical techniques to combine the data of multiple studies. By obtaining a larger sample size, a meta-analysis strives for outcomes of higher validity than each individual study could provide.

mobile health (mHealth)—healthcare delivered or facilitated by a portable electronic device.

model—an abstract representation of reality. A key tool for advancing scientific knowledge.

Moore's Law—first put forth in 1965 by Gordon Moore, co-founder of Intel, it states that the number of transistors on a memory chip doubles about every two years. Almost in defiance of the fundamental laws of physics and the economic law of diminishing returns, Moore's Law continues to hold, more or less, today.

multi-morbidity—more than one medical problem in the same person, one of the biggest challenges in healthcare today, for clinicians and for electronic information systems. Nearly three out of four people over 65 have two or more serious medical problems and one in four of younger people do.

Nationwide Health Information Network (NHIN)—a glimmer in the eye of the drafters of the *Health Information Technology for Economic & Clinical Health Act* that seeks to facilitate secure information exchange among providers of healthcare by promulgating a set of standards and policies for health data interchange. *See regional health information organization.*

neural network—software that learns by pruning and reinforcing connections among elements of the system. Patterned on how animal brains learn, neural networks have been especially useful in visual pattern recognition and speech recognition and generation.

Nike net—see *sneaker net.*

non-inferior—in many studies of clinical care, the researcher will hope to show that a new, often less expensive way of doing something, with a new drug or by telemedicine for example, is just as good as doing it the established way.

nudging—affecting behavior change through subtle messaging. Not etymologically related to *noodging*, the Yiddish word meaning "pestering," but at risk of being perceived that way.

number needed to screen (NNS)—an estimate, given the incidence of the sought-after condition in the target population and the sensitivity and specificity of the diagnostic procedure, how many patients would have to be tested in order to turn up one patient who really does have that condition. Similar to *number needed to treat.*

number needed to treat (NNT)—a statistical measure that estimates the likely clinical impact that an intervention, such as a drug or a surgical procedure, is expected to have on a population. It better reflects the value of the intervention than pure incidence or outcome data by specifying how many patients with condition x would have to be treated with intervention y in order to achieve outcome z. For example, one estimate of NNT for cholesterol-lowering statins to delay one death in the general population under 50 years old has been set at about 1000 for men or 5000 for women (http://austinpublishinggroup.com/cardiovascular-disorders/fulltext/jcd-v2-id1018.pdf), which means that 999 men and 4999 women who took this drug would be exposed to its side effects (including muscle inflammation and possibly increased risk of diabetes) without receiving its benefits. See *number needed to screen.*

Obamacare—See *Affordable Care Act.*

-omics—the attempt to study the totality of a biological system at a certain level of abstraction. See *biome, genome, metabolome, proteome.*

ontology—a formal explicit specification of shared conceptualization that is often a crucial first step in designing an *application program interface*. If well-constructed, an ontology is less mutable than a *taxonomy.*

open source software—computer instructions that any person is free download, use and tinker with. Open source products have the advantage of many brains working to extend them and make them better, and the disadvantage that come with having no rigid central authority to (try to) assure that everything works as it should.

p-hacking—dredging data until you turn up something that looks meaningful. The "p" refers to the p-value, a statistical estimate of how likely it is that a research finding is valid, rather than the result of random chance. P-hacking is bad science.

personal health record (PHR)—ideally, the sum total of health information, controlled by the person to whom it belongs.

pimping—the common practice in medical "education" in which a trainee is questioned and ridiculed publicly if unable to provide a satisfactory answer. The resulting humiliation, which is supposed to motivate a student to study even harder, is a central reason why so many physicians are deemed impaired learners, unable to admit when they don't know something. See *clinical-pathological conference*.

plain old telephone service (POTS)—see *twisted pair* and *landline*.

population health—the health of a group. Traditionally, American medicine has focused on individual health. Population health must be considered in developing health policy and healthcare systems. The *Affordable Care Act* took some small steps in that direction.

power analysis—a preliminary process in doing clinical research that estimates the number of research participants that will be needed for a study to achieve a desired degree of confidence in the results.

predatory journal—a publication, usually online, that publishes academic articles for a fee, sometimes with minimal to zero quality control.

preprint—online publication of an academic article. *ArXiv* is the archetypal preprint repository.

privacy—control over who has access to medical information.

prospective study—a research project that is designed first then run in real time. Compare to *data mining* and *retrospective study*.

protected health information (PHI)—under US law, especially the *Healthcare Information Portability and Accountability Act*, the contents of a patient's medical record and payment history, all of which may be released only to narrowly specified recipients under clearly-defined circumstances.

problem-oriented medical record (POMR)—a system devised by Larry Weed, MD, in the days before electronic medical records, to organize clinical information in a way that makes it most useful in the course of caring for patients. Some features of the POMR, especially the permanent problem list, are still relevant today.

proteome—the sum total of the proteins that make up an individual. Proteins, which are encoded for in the *genome*, are the principle building blocks of living cells. Proteomics is the study of proteomes.

publication bias—the prejudices that lead authors, journals and research sponsors to bring to light articles that present new findings and confirm old ones and to bury studies that conclude the author's thesis (hunch) was wrong or that something doesn't work as expected.

quadruple aim—the *triple aim* plus adding the goal of improving the work life of health care providers, including clinicians and staff. [Bodenheimer, T., Sinsky, C. From triple to quadruple aim: Care of the patient requires care of the provider. *Annals of Family Medicine*, November–December 2014:12(6), 573–576. http://www.annfammed.org/content/12/6/573.full]

quality improvement (QI)—a point of view and set of skills that seeks to change how a business or clinical process is organized and delivered so as to produce the best outcome at the least cost. QI leans heavily on teamwork, data and creative problem solving. Peter Drucker, the management expert, famously said, "If you can't measure it, you can't manage it." Sometimes this hyperbolic emphasis on measurement gets in the way of efficiency and common sense.

quantum computing—devices and methods that make use of entangled bits of matter to do computations that are many orders of magnitude faster than today's most powerful supercomputers can do. Quantum computing is in its infancy. See *entanglement*.

qbit—the basic unit of information in a quantum computer, which, thanks to quantum strangeness, remains indeterminate during the computation, rather than a 0 or a 1, as in a classical computer.

real-time—communication with live people on both the sending and the receiving ends of a channel. Conferences may link more than two sites in real time.

real-time location system (RLTS)—technologies that track the location of objects or people.

regional health information organization (RHIO) (pronounced ree-oh)—a group of users who agree on a set of procedures and protocols for electronically sharing *protected health information* among them. Considered a precursor to a *Nationwide Health Information Network*. Also called regional health information exchange.

research participant—what we used to call "research subject." The term implies more equal footing between researchers and the human beings they study. Way better than "guinea pig."

retrospective study—research conceived and performed after data have been collected. *Data mining* is a principal tool of this type of research. Compare to *prospective study*.

retrospectoscope—a virtual medical instrument that allows one to see the right answer in retrospect. Every medical trainee learns of its power. See *clinical-pathologic conferences*. Contrast with *prospective study*.

robotics—a branch of technology that designs and employs machines to do work, more or less flexibly and autonomously.

security—the ability of a system to protect information and system resources with respect to confidentiality and integrity.

sensitivity—the likelihood that a test will identify what it is looking for. Sensitivity varies inversely with *specificity*. That is, the more sensitive a test, the more likely that it is falsely positive. A significant piece of the art of medical practice lies in knowing how to weigh sensitivity and *specificity* to best serve a particular patient in a particular situation.

server farm—a collection of internet servers in one place, sometimes numbering into the tens of thousands, usually tied together to provide *cloud* services.

singularity—the theorized moment when machine intelligence surpasses human intelligence, setting machines on a rapid evolutionary path that brings them to far outstriping the capabilities of human beings. Some futurists view this possibility through dystopian lenses, some through utopian lenses, and some argue against its possibility. Nobody knows if and when it will happen.

skeumorph—a reference to a previous era that is held over in a new technology, either for lack of vision or for reassuring users that there is still something familiar about a new technology. Think of the Ventiports, the non-functional ornaments that have graced the front fenders of Buicks since 1948.

small message service (SMS)—text messaging, most often mobile device to mobile device.

snail mail—postal service (as opposed to email). This disparaging term emphasizes the slow speed and inefficiency of moving atoms versus electrons.

sneaker net—a term developed in the old days when the most efficient way to move data or a program from one device to another was to copy it onto a floppy disk and walk it down the hall where it could be uploaded on a second machine.

specificity—the likelihood that a positive result means that a test has identified what it is looking for. Specificity varies inversely with *sensitivity*. That is, the more specific a test, the more likely you have missed a case. A good share of the art of medical practice lies in knowing how to weigh *sensitivity* and specificity for a particular patient in a particular situation.

store-and-forward—communication that does not require sender and receiver to be simultaneously present. The system stores the message for retrieval at such time as the receiver chooses to retrieve it. Email is the quintessential example of a store-and-forward messaging system. Also called *asynchronous*.

strength of recommendation taxonomy (SORT)—a scoring system developed by the American Academy of Family Physicians for giving an overall weight to suggestions for best practice, based on the soundness of the underlying scientific evidence. See *grading of recommendations assessment*.

synchronous—see *real-time*.

taxonomy—a formal classification system for a set of data. The plant classification system developed by Swedish botanist Carl Linneaus in the 18th Century is the prototype of modern biological taxonomy. Compare to *folksonomy*.

tech year—approximately ten people years, reflecting the rapid pace of technological development. (I made up this term.)

telehealth—see *telemedicine*.

telemedicine—use of electronic information and communication technology to overcome barriers of distance and time when delivering healthcare.

terabyte—a million million (10^{12}) *bytes*.

translation science—the scientific study of turning research findings into medical practice.

triple aim—improving the patient experience of care (including quality and satisfaction); improving the health of populations; and reducing the per capita cost of health care. [Institute for Healthcare Improvement]

troll—an evil creature who posts messages on the internet with the intention of causing disruption.

tweetation—a journal article mention on Twitter. A hip modern measure of impact factor of an academic publication. (I include this word mostly because it is so poetical and outrageous.)

twisted pair—the two wires, active and ground, that run between a home or office phone and the telephone pole outside it to provide the standard *landline* connection to the telephone network. "Twisted Pair" would also, in my estimation, make a good name for a punk rock duo.

usability—the effectiveness, efficiency and satisfaction with which users can achieve specific tasks employing the system or device in question.

value-based care—healthcare services delivered and reimbursed on the basis of quality and outcomes. Compare to *fee-for-service*.

vaporware—promises by vendors that their systems can perform certain functions that clients find out, often too late, they can't.

virtual reality (VR)—a computer-generated simulation that is composed of more than just audio and two-dimensional video. Three-dimensional video, scenes that vary with eye, head position and body motion and *haptic feedback* are enhancements that can add to the realness of a VR experience.

wiki—a website that allows collaborative editing of its content and structure by its users. [Google definition.]

wisdom—beyond *data*, *information* and *knowledge*, lies the sort understanding that, thus far, only an experienced human being has been able to achieve.

References

Chapter 1

1. Quoted in Bennett-Woods, D. *Nanotechnology, Ethics and Society.* Boca Raton, FL: CRC Press. 2008.
2. Ibid.
3. Wikipedia. https://en.wikipedia.org/wiki/Koch%27s_postulates. Accessed December 9, 2017.
4. Laplace, Pierre Simon. *A Philosophical Essay on Probabilities.* 1814. Truscott, FW and Emory, FL, trans. Dover Publications, NY, 1951, p. 4.
5. Engel, GL. The need for a new medical model: A challenge for biomedicine. *Science.* 1977:196(4286), 129–136.
6. Antonovsky, A. Islands rather than bridgeheads: The problematic status of the biopsychosocial model. *Family Systems Medicine.* 1989:7(3), 243–253.

Chapter 2

1. Milneson, Michael. *Demanding Medical Excellence.* Chicago: University of Chicago Press. 1999.
2. http://qz.com/179897/more-people-around-the-world-have-cell-phones-than-ever-had-land-lines/
3. Sax, D. Our love affair with digital is over. *The New York Times.* November 19, 2017, SR-10.
4. Quoted in Solon O. Smartphones won't make your kids dumb—We think. *Scientific American* [online]. June 25, 2016. http://www.scientificamerican.com/article/smart-phones-won-t-make-your-kids-dumb-we-think/?WT.mc_id=SA_MB_20160629
5. Solon, Olivia. Smartphones won't make your kids dumb—We think; Mosaic—The science of life. *Scientific American.* http://www.scientificamerican.com/article/smart-phones-won-t-make-your-kids-dumb-we-think/?WT.mc_id=SA_MB_20160629
6. Evans, JA. Electronic publication and the narrowing of science and scholarship. *Science,* 2008:321(18), 395–398.
7. Stephen J Greenberg, MSLS, PhD, Coordinator of Public Services, History of Medicine Division, National Library of Medicine, National Institutes of Health, Department of Health and Human Services.

8. http://www.ncbi.nlm.nih.gov/pubmed/4037559
9. Hoogendam, Arjen, Anton FH Stalenhoef, Pieter F de Vries Robbé et al. Answers to questions posed during daily patient care are more likely to be answered by UpToDate than PubMed. *Journal of Medical Internet Research.* 2008:10(4), e29.
10. Siebert, JN, Ehrier, F, Gervaix, A et al. Adherence to AHA guidelines when adapted for augmented reality glasses for assisted pediatric cardiopulmonary resuscitation: A randomized controlled trial. *Journal of Medical Internet Research.* 2017:19(5), 1–13.
11. Levinson, D. Information, computers, and clinical practice. *Journal of the American Medical Association.* 1983:249(5), 607–609.
12. Alan Lembitz—COPIC
13. Victoroff, Michael S, Drury, Barbara M, Campagna, Elizabeth J et al. Impact of electronic health records on malpractice claims in a sample of physician offices in Colorado: A retrospective cohort study. *Journal of General Internal Medicine.* 2013:28(5), 637–644.
14. Finnegan, J. Doctor who doesn't use computers loses legal battle to regain her medical license. *Fierce Healthcare.* November 28, 2017.
15. Kyrillidou, M, Cook, C. The evolution of measurement and evaluation of libraries: A perspective from the association of research libraries. *Library Trends.* 1977:56(4), 312–321.
16. Just, BH, Marc, D, Munns, M. Why patient matching is a challenge: Research on master patient index (MPI) data discrepancies in key identifying fields. *Health Information Management.* 2016 Spring; 1–13.
17. Kaushal, R, Kern, LM, Barrón, Y et al. Electronic prescribing improves patient safety in community-based practices. *Journal of General Internal Medicine.* 2010:25(6), 530–536.
18. Kaushal, R, Shojania, KG, Bates, DW. The Impact of Computerized Physician Order Entry. *Journal of the American Medical Informatics Medicine Association.* 1999.
19. The Leapfrog Group. *Preventing Medication Errors in Hospitals.* 2016.
20. Sander, U, Emmert, M, Dickel, J et al. Information presentation features and comprehensibility of hospital report cards: Design analysis and online survey among users. *Journal of Medical Internet Research.* 2015:17(3), 1–16.

Chapter 3

1. Mapping Broadband Health in America. www.fcc.gov/health/maps
2. http://www.telecompetitor.com/pew-u-s-smartphone-ownership-broadband-penetration-reached-record-levels-in-2016/
3. https://www.statista.com/chart/2072/landline-phones-in-the-united-states/
4. https://www.akamai.com/us/en/multimedia/documents/state-of-the-internet/q4-2015-state-of-the-internet-executive-review.pdf
5. Zwart, CM, He, M, Wu, T et al. Selection and pilot implementation of a mobile image viewer: A case study. *Journal of Medical Internet Research.* 2015:3(2)e45, 1–9.
6. Verghese, A. The Doctor's bag for the new millenium. *The New York Times.* October 8, 2012.
7. Trauma Center in a Backpack. *Federal Telemedicine News.* June 26, 2013.
8. Zwart, CM, He, M, Wu, T et al. Selection and pilot implementation of a mobile image viewer: A case study. *Journal of Medical Internet Research.* 2015:3(2)e45, 1–9.

9. Mato, PD, White, LM, Bleakney, R et al. Diagnostic accuracy of an iPhone DICOM viewer for the interpretation of magnetic resonance imaging of the knee. *Clinical Journal of Sports Medicine.* 2014:24(4), 308–313.

10. See Jaron, Lanier. *You are not a Gadget.* New York: Vintage. 2011.

11. ORTHOMONITOR Introduced by Kinematix. *Federal Telemedicine News.* October 19, 2014.

12. Pogue, D. The good, the bad and the weirdest "Internet of Things" things. *Scientific American.* July 1, 2016.

13. *Wired* [online]. February 7, 2017. https://www.wired.com/brandlab/2017/01/sensor-based-economy/?mbid=nl_2717_p3&CNDID=46084762

14. McConnon, A. *How 3-D Printing is Changing Healthcare. The Wall Street Journal.* September 12, 2017.

15. Sweeney, E. Despite federal push to offer EHR access, patient engagement is low. *FierceHealthcare.* March 16, 2017.

16. Giardina, TD, Baidwin, J, Nystrom, DT et al. Patient perceptions of receiving test results via online portals: A mixed-method study. *Journal of the American Medical Informatics Association.* 2017:0(0), 1–7.

17. Woods S, Schwartz, E, Tuepker, A et al. Patient experiences with full electronic access to health records and clinical notes through the My HealthVet Personal Health Record Pilot: Qualitative study. *Journal of Medical Internet Research.* 2013:15(3), 1–12.

18. http://www.motherjones.com/politics/2015/10/epic-systems-judith-faulkner-hitech-ehr-interoperability

19. healthmgttech.com, October 2016, p. 11.

20. Adler-Milstein, J, Pfeifer, E et al. Information blocking: Is it occurring and what policy strategies can address it? *Milbank Quarterly.* 2017:95(1), 117–135.

21. http://www.motherjones.com/politics/2015/10/epic-systems-judith-faulkner-hitech-ehr-interoperability

22. Study: HIEs can help significantly reduce unnecessary ED tests. *iHealthBeat.* July 23, 2015. ePub

23. Vest JR, Kern, LM, Campion, TR et al. Association between use of a health information exchange system and hospital admissions. *Applied Clinical Informatics.* 2014:5, 219–231.

24. State of the Enterprise/Private Health Information Exchange Industry. Black Book Market Research 2015 User Survey, p. 77.

25. Patrick, C. We've spent billions to fix our medical records, and they're still a mess. Here's why. *Mother Jones.* October 21, 2015. http://www.motherjones.com/politics/2015/10/epic-systems-judith-faulkner-hitech-ehr-interoperability

26. https://www.cirrusinsight.com/blog/much-data-google-store

27. Hsu, J. It's time to think beyond cloud computing. *Backchannel.* August 23, 2017.

28. DMR publishing. http://expandedramblings.com/index.php/email-statistics/

29. LaRocque, JR, Davis, CL, Tan, TP et. al. Patient preferences for receiving reports of test results. *Journal of the American Board of Family Medicine.* 2013:28(5)759-766.

30. Survey: Patients consider digital tools when selecting providers. *iHealthBeat.* January 16, 2015.

31. Ammenwerth, E et al. The impact of electronic patient portals on patient care: A systematic review of controlled trials. *Journal of Medical Internet Research.* 2012:14(6), 1–12.

32. Smith, PA. There's a new crash dummy in town. *Scientific American* online. February 1, 2016.

33. Lewis-Krause, G. The great AI awakening. *The New York Times Magazine*. December 18, 2016.

34. Oberije, C, Nalbontov G, Dekker A et al. A prospective study comparing the predictions of doctors versus models for treatment outcome of lung cancer patients: A step towards individualized care and shared decision-making. *Radiotherapy Oncology*. 2014:112(1), 37–43.

35. Goldzweig, CL. Electronic health record-based interventions for improving appropriate diagnostic imaging: A systematic review and meta-analysis. *Annals of Internal Medicine*. 2015:162(8), 557–565.

36. Mullard, A. The drug-maker's guide to the galaxy. *Nature News and Comment*. September 26, 2017.

37. http://time.com/4656011/artificial-intelligence-ai-poker-tournament-libratus-cmu/

38. https://www.wired.com/2017/02/ai-learn-like-humans-little-uncertainty/?mbid=nl_2317_p1&CNDID=46084762 and Texas Hold 'Em cham-pion. https://www.wired.com/2017/02/libratus/?mbid=nl_2117_p3&CNDID=46084762

39. Gómez Grajales, CA. *Statistics Views*. June 23, 2015. http://www.statisticsviews.com/details/feature/8065581/The-statistics-behind-Google-Translate.html

40. Hartnett, K. Artificial intelligence learns to learn entirely on its own. *Quanta*. October 18, 2017.

41. Simonite, T. Google's learning software learns to write learning software. *Wired* (online). October 13, 2017

42. Levin, S, Toerper, M, Hamrock, E et al. Machine-learning based electronic triage more accurately differentiates patients with respect to clinical outcomes compare with the emergency severity index. *Annals of Emergency Medicine*. 2017 electronic preprint, 1–10e2.

43. Reardon, S. AI algorithms to prevent suicide gain traction. *Nature*. Online December 13, 2017.

44. Stinson, L. The surprising repercussions of making AI assistants sound human. *Wired*. May 12, 2017.

45. Molteni, M. Thanks to AI, computers can now see your health problems. *Wired*. January 9, 2017, p. 6.

46. Bedi, G, Carrillo, F, Cecchi, GA et al. Automated analysis of free speech predicts psychosis onset in high-risk youths. *Schizophrenia*. 2015 (15030), 1–7.

47. Esteva, A, Kuprel, B, Novoa, RA et al. Dermatologist-level classification of skin cancer with deep neural networks. *Nature*. 2017:252, 115–125.

48. Rajpurkar, P, Irvin, J, Zhu, K et al. CheXNet: Radiologist-level pneumonia detection on chest X-rays with deep learning. ArXiv; 11/14/17, arXiv:1711.05225v2.

49. Radiologists struggle to ID gorilla on a CT lung scan. *FierceMedicalImaging*. February 14, 2013.

50. Donde, J. Self-driving cars will kill people. Who decides who dies? *Wired* [online]. September 21, 2017.

51. http://standards.ieee.org/develop/indconn/ec/ead_v1.pdf

52. O'Neil, C. *Weapons of Math Destruction: How Big Data Increases Inequality and Threatens Democracy*. New York: Crown Publishing Group/Penguin Random House. 2016.

53. Simonite, T. AI experts want to end "Black Box" algorithms in government. *Wired* [online]. October 18, 2017.

54. Greenmeier, L. Could AI be the future of fake news and product reviews? *Scientific American* [online]. October 16, 2017.

55. Emspak, J. How a machine learns prejudice. *Scientific American*. December 29, 2016.
56. Matsakis, L. Researchers fooled a Google AI into thinking a rifle was a helicopter. *Wired*. [online] December 17, 2017.
57. Verghese, H, Shah, NH, Harrington, RA et al. What this computer needs is a physician—Humanism and artificial intelligence. *JAMA*. 2017 [online]. December 20, 2017.
58. http://www.nytimes.com/1988/07/20/us/farm-population-lowest-since-1850-s.html
59. Biesheuvel, T. 500,—Tons of Steel. 14 Jobs. *Bloomberg Business week*. June 17, 2017, 17–18.
60. https://www.youtube.com/watch?v=TvKAN_UPVY4
61. Nelson, E. Why American jobs have a higher risk of automation than jobs in Germany, the UK, and Japan. *Quartz*. https://qz.com/598380/the-us-just-dropped-its-biggest-bomb…
62. https://en.wikipedia.org/wiki/DARPA_Robotics_Challenge
63. https://www.youtube.com/watch?v=8P9geWwi9e0
64. Barrie, A. Teddy bear-faced robot is built for battlefields. *Fox News*. March 29, 2012.
65. Stewart, J. Why these German researchers became self-driving cars. *Wired* [online]. November 5, 2017
66. Metz, R. Better than opioids? Virtual reality could be your next painkiller. *Technology Review*. July 18, 2016.

Chapter 4

1. Feinstein, AR, Horowitz, RI. Problems in the "evidence" of evidence-based medicine. *American Journal of Medicine*. 1997:103(6), 529–535.
2. David, Schenck, Larry, Churchill. *Remen NR in Healers: Extraordinary Clinicians*. Oxford, UK: Oxford University Press. 2011.
3. J Meza, JP, Passerman, DS. *Integrating Narrative Medicine and Evidence-Based Medicine: The Everyday Social Practice of Healing*. Boca Raton, FL: CRC Press. 2011.
4. https://www.theguardian.com/science/2012/may/07/quest-connectome-mapping-brain
5. http://www.industrytap.com/knowledge-doubling-every-12-months-soon-to-be-every-12-hours/3950
6. https://en.wikipedia.org/wiki/Jacobellis_v._Ohio
7. http://www.techrepublic.com/article/ibm-watson-the-inside-story-of-how-the-jeopardy-winning-supercomputer-was-born-and-what-it-wants-to-do-next/
8. http://www.businessinsider.com/ibms-watson-may-soon-be-the-best-doctor-in-the-world-2014-4
9. https://www.youtube.com/watch?v=r5AZwkz8zLU
10. https://en.wikipedia.org/wiki/Computational_humor
11. Weiner, JP, Yeh, S, Blumenthal, D. The impact of health information technology and e-health on the future demand for physician services. *Health Affairs*. 2013:32(11), 1998–2004.
12. Kaplan, SH, Greenfield, S, Ware, JE. Assessing the effects of physician-patient interactions on the outcomes of chronic disease. *Medical Care*. 1989:27(3), S110–S127.
13. Porter, S. Reducing hospital admissions: Small primary care practices shine in national study. *Annals of Family Medicine*. 2014:12, 578–579.

Chapter 5

1. Safran, C. *Testimony to the House Ways & Means Subcommittee on Health*, 2004. Quoted by e-patient Dave. The invisible stakeholder: Why America needs a patient-in-chief in https://participatorymedicine.org/epatients/2010/01/patientin-chief.html.
2. Sorum, P. Patient as author, physician as critic: Insights from contemporary literary theory. *Archives of Family Medicine*. 1994:3, 549–556.
3. Gawande, A. *Being Mortal: Medicine and What Matters in the End*. New York, NY: Picador-Macmillan. 2014.
4. Yadav, S, Kazanji, N, K C N et al. Comparison of accuracy of physical examination findings in initial progress notes between paper charts and a newly implemented electronic health record. *Journal of the American Medical Informatics Association*. 2016:0, 1–4.
5. Anthes, E. Hospital checklists are meant to save lives—So why do they often fail? *Nature*. July 28, 2015. ePub.
6. Davis, DA. Accuracy of physician self-assessment compared with observed measures of competence: A systematic review. *Journal of the American Medical Association*. 2006:296(9), 1094–1102.
7. Cohen, MD, Hilligoss, B, Kajdacsy-Balla Amarai, AC. A handoff is not a telegram: An understanding of the patient is co-constructed. *Critical Care*. 2012:16(1), 303–308.
8. Hampton, JR. Relative contributions of history-taking, physical examination, and laboratory investigation and diagnosis and management of medical outpatients. *British Medical Journal*. 1975:2, 486–489.
9. Singh, H, Giardina, TD, Meyer, AN et al. Types and origins of diagnostic errors in primary care settings. *JAMA Internal Medicine*. 2013, E1–E8.
10. O'Neill, T. Are electronic medical records worth the costs of implementation? *American Action Forum*. August 6, 2015, ePub.
11. Roghanizad, M. Ask in person: You're less persuasive than you think over email. *Journal of Experimental Social Psychology*. 2017:69, 223–226.
12. https://press.rsna.org/timssnet/media/pressreleases/pr_target.cfm?ID=389
13. Tai-Seale, M, Olson, CW, Chan AS et al. Electronic health record logs indicate that physicians split time evenly between seeing patients and desktop medicine. *Health Affairs*. 2017:36(4), 655–662.
14. Wang, MD, Khanna, R, Najafi, N et al. Characterizing the source of text in electronic health record progress notes. *JAMA Internal Medicine*. Online May 30, 2017, e1–e2.

Chapter 6

1. How much will the US health IT market be worth in 2017? *Cognitive Medical Systems*. August 22, 2016.
2. http://www.cfrinc.net/cfrblog/it-spending-in-healthcare-on-the-rise-growing-fast-towards-2019
3. Dieleman, JL. Factors associated with increases in US health care spending, 1996–2013. *JAMA*. 2017:318(17), 1668–1678.

4. Large U.S. employers project health care benefit costs to surpass $14,000 per employee in 2018. *Globe Newswire*. August 8, 2017.
5. http://apps.who.int/gho/data/view.main.182
6. https://www.ncbi.nlm.nih.gov/pmc/articles/PMC1292086/pdf/jrsocmed00151-0028.pdf
7. http://ob-efm.com/2434.htm
8. http://www.cochrane.org/CD006066/PREG_continuous-cardiotocography-ctg-form-electronic-fetal-monitoring-efm-fetal-assessment-during-labour
9. http://www.theunnecesarean.com/blog/2010/3/18/united-states-cesarean-rates-by-year-1970-to-2007.html
10. http://www.huffingtonpost.com/2015/04/14/C-section-rate-recommendation_n_7058954.html
11. http://transform.childbirthconnection.org/wp-content/uploads/2013/06/LTM-III_NMSO.pdf. p. 85.
12. Stelfox, H, Gandhi, TK, Orav, EJ et al. The relation of patient satisfaction complaints against physicians and malpractice lawsuits. *The American Journal of Medicine*. 2005:118, 1126–1133.
13. Berwick, DM. Measuring physicians' quality and performance. *JAMA*. 2009:301(22), 2485–2486.
14. Slabodkin, G. Lack of payer, provider info sharing complicates shift to value-based care. *The Resource for HIT Leaders*. July 3, 2017.
15. Telehealth use of medicare and medicaid. *GAO Highlights*. July 2017.
16. Terry, K. Telehealth visits raise costs due to more use, study shows. *Medscape Medical News*. March 6, 2017.
17. Wright, JD, Tergas, AI, Hou, JY et al. Effect of regional hospital competition and hospital financial status on the use of Robotic-Assisted surgery. *JAMA Surgery*. 2016:151(7), 612–620.
18. McNickle, M. 5 most powerful green IT practices. *Healthcare IT News*. September 14, 2011.

Chapter 7

1. healthmgttech.com, April 2017, p. 5.
2. http://www.prnewswire.com/news-releases….300451690.html
3. Shaw, G. The healthcare data breech that took 14 years to uncover. *FierceHealthcare*. August 18, 2017.
4. Seth, TR. *Unix System Security Tools*. New York, NY: McGraw Hill. 1999.
5. https://arstechnica.com/tech-policy/2009/09/your-secrets-live-online-in-databases-of-ruin/
6. Deleger, L, Molnar, K, Savova, G et al. Large-scale evaluation of automated clinical note de-identification and its impact on information extraction. *Journal of the Medical Informatics Association*, 2012:20(1), 84–94.
7. Tanner, A. Strengthening protection of patient medical data. *The Concord Review*. January 10, 2017, p. 24.
8. Dwoskin, E. Brokers trade on sensitive medical data with little oversight, Senate says. *The Wall Street Journal* [online]. December 18, 2013. https://blogs.wsj.com/digits/2013/12/18/brokers-trade-on-sensitive-medical-data-with-little-oversightsenate-says/

9. Malin, BA, Emam, KE, O'Keefe, CM. Biomedical data privacy: Problems, perspectives and recent advances. *Journal of the Medical Informatics Association*, 2012:20(1), 1 5.

10. Caine, K, Hanania, R. Patients want granular privacy control over health information in electronic health records. *Journal of the Medical Informatics Association*, 2012:0, 1–9.

11. Azaria, A, Ekblaw, A, Vieira, T et al. MedRec: Using blockchain for medical data access and permission management. 2nd International Conference on Open and Big Data. 2016, 25–30.

12. Holdhaus, E. Bitcoin mining guzzles energy—and its carbon footprint just keeps growing. *Wired* [online]. December 6, 2017.

13. Hoofnagle, C et al. How different are young adults when it comes to information privacy, attitudes and policies? Annenberg School of Communications Departmental Papers. 2010.

14. Barrett, B. Don't get your kid an internet-connected toy. *Wired* [online]. December 20, 2017.

15. http://www.darkreading.com/attacks-breaches/major-cyberattacks-on-healthcare-grew-63--in-2016/d/d-id/1327779

16. Sweeney, E. 6 in 10 healthcare organizations have a dedicated cybersecurity executive, and it makes a big difference. *Fierce Healthcare*. August 9, 2017.

17. ISMP survey shows provider text messaging often runs afoul of patient safety. Institute for Safe Medication Practices [online]. November 16, 2017. http://www.ismp.org/newsletters/acutecare/showarticle.aspx?id=1182

18. Frequently Asked Questions About Cyber Liability/Data Breach Insurance. *Financial Fast Facts*. COPIC Financial Group, Ltd. 02/17.

19. Hassidim, A, Korach, T, Shreberk-Hassidim, R et al. Prevalence of sharing access credentials in electronic medical records. *Health Informatics Research*, 2017:23(3), 176–182.

20. Intagliata, C. Biometric identifies you in a heartbeat. *Scientific American* [online]. October 6, 2017.

21. Dunietz, J. Cryptographers and geneticists unite to analyze genomes they can't see. *Scientific American* [online]. August 22, 2017.

22. Molteni, M. 23andMe is digging through your data for a Parkinson's cure. *Wired* [online]. September 13, 2017.

23. Greenberg, A. Biohackers encoded malware in a strand of DNA. *Wired*. August 10, 2017.

24. Retail pharmacies use discount programs to collect customer data. *iHealthBeat* [online]. November 24, 2015.

25. Truven Health Analytics. Data Privacy, Part 2. January 2015.

26. https://arstechnica.com/tech-policy/2009/09/your-secrets-live-online-in-databases-of-ruin/

27. Vallina-Rodriguez, N, Srikanth, S. 7 in 10 smartphone apps share your data with third party services. *The Conversation*. May 29, 2017. https://theconversation.com/7-in-10-smartphone-apps-share-your-data-with-third-party-services-72404

28. Xia, W, Heatherly, R, Ding, X. R-U policy frontiers for health data de-identification. *Journal of the American Medical Informatics Association*, 2015:0, 1–16.

29. http://www.forbes.com/sites/kashmirhill/2012/02/16/how-target-figured-out-a-teen-girl-was-pregnant-before-her-father-did/ - 6164c3cd34c6

30. Paul, D. Your own pacemaker can now testify against you in court. *Wired* [online]. July 29, 2017.
31. Winters, D. Inside China's vast new experiment in social ranking. *Wired* [online]. January 2018.
32. http://theconversation.com/why-you-should-donate-your-data-as-well-as-your-organs-when-you-die-72555

Chapter 8

1. Hripcsak, G, Albers, DJ. Next-generation phenotyping of electronic health records. *Journal of the Medial Informatics Association*, 2013:20(1), 117–121.
2. Beasley, JW, Wetterneck, TB, Temte, J et al. Information Chaos in primary care: Implications for physician performance and patient safety. *Journal of the American Board of Family Medicine*, 2011:24(6), 745–751.
3. Smith, PC, Araya-Guerra, R, Bublitz, C et al. Missing clinical information during primary care visits, *JAMA*. 2005:293(5), 565–571.
4. Holmes, C, Brown, M. Healthcare provider attitudes towards the problem list in an electronic health record: A mixed methods qualitative study. *BMC Medical Informatics and Decision Making*, 2012:12:127.
5. Simborg, D, Starfield, BH, Horn, SD et al. Information factors affecting problem follow-up in ambulatory care. *Medical Care*, 1976:14(10), 848–856.
6. Office of the National Coordinator for Health Information Technology. 2016 Report to Congress on Health IT Progress. www.healthit.gov
7. O'Neill, T. Are electronic health records worth the costs of implementation? *American Action Forum*. August 6, 2015, ePub.
8. Alvarado, CS. Electronic Health Record Adoption and Interoperability among U.S. Skilled Nuring Facilities in 2016. ONC Data Brief No. 69. August 2017, pp. 1–14.
9. Beresford, L. Doctors spending over $32,000 on health information technology. *Medical Economics*. September 28, 2016.
10. Terry, K. Who spends more on health IT, hospitals or private practices? *Medscape*. August 4, 2017.
11. Barkholz, D. Hospitals can expect financial pain from EHR installs. *Modern Healthcare*. July 26, 2017.
12. Verdon, DR. Physician outcry on EHR functionality, cost will shake the health information technology sector. *Medical Economics*. February 10, 2014.
13. Survey of physicians shows declining satisfaction with electronic health records. *American College of Physicians*. August 10, 2015, ePub.
14. EHR Software Buyer View 2015. softwareadvice.com/medical/buyerview/her-report-2015
15. Postmortem of the hospital electronic health record replacement frenzy. *Black Book Market Research*. April 29, 2016. p. 4.
16. Total cost of that NHS IT FIASCO to taxpayers: £10.1bn. The Register. August 22, 2013.
17. Block, L, Habicht, R, Wu, AW et al. In the wake of the 2003 and 2011 duty hours regulations, how do internal medicine interns spend their time? *Journal of General Internal Medicine*, 2013:28, 1042–1047. Online.
18. Sinsky, C, Colligan, L, Li, L et al. Allocation of physician time in ambulatory practice: A time and motion study in 4 specialties. *Annals of Internal Medicine*, 2016:165, 753–760. Online.

19. Pelland, KD, Baier, RR, Gardner, RL. It is like texting at the dinner table: A qualitative analysis of the impact of electronic health records on patient-physician interaction in hospitals. *Journal of Innovation in Health Informatics*, 2017:24(2), 216–223.

20. Hysong, SJ, Spitzmuller, C, Espadas, D et al. Electronic alerts and clinician turnover: The influence of user acceptance. *American Journal of Managed Care*, 2014:20, SP520–SP530.

21. Shanafelt, TD, Dyrbye, LN, Sinsky, C et al. Relationship between clerical burden and characteristics of the electronic environment with physician burnout and professional satisfaction. *Mayo Clinic Proceedings*, 2016:91(7), 836–848.

22. Shanafelt, TD, Hasan, O, Dyrbye, N et al. Changes in burnout and satisfaction with work-life balance in physicians an the general US working population between 2011 and 2014. *Mayo Clinic Proceedings*, 2015:90, 1600–1613.

23. Kosiorek, D. Using your medical practice's HER data for analytics. *MGMA Connection Plus*. 2017. http://www.mgma.com/practice-resources/mgma-connection-plus-on…

24. Casalino, LP, Gans, D, Weber, R et al. US physician practices spend more than $15.4 billion annually to report quality measures. *Health Affairs*, 2016:35(3), 401–406.

25. Mendelson, A. The effects of pay-for-performance programs on health, health care use, and processes of care. *Annals of Internal Medicine*. January 10, 2017. p. 13.

26. Bodenheimer, T, Sinsky, C. From triple to quadruple aim: Care of the patient requires care of the provider. *Annals of Family Medicine*, November/December 2014:12(6), 573–576. http://www.annfammed.org/content/12/6/573.full

27. Edwardson, N, Kash, BA, Janakiraman, R. Measuring the impact of electronic health record adoption on charge capture. *Medical Care Research and Review*, 2016:74(5), 582–594.

28. Paper-based thinking, and beyond. *EHR Watch*. February 19, 2013.

29. Belden, JL, Koopman, RJ, Patil, SJ et al. Dynamic electronic health record note prototype: Seeing more by showing less. *JABFM*, 2017:30(6), 691–700.

30. Hill, RG, Jr, Sears, LM, Melanson, SW. 4000 clicks: A productivity analysis of electronic health records in a community hospital ED. *American Journal of Emergency Medicine*, November 2013:31(11), 1591–1594.

31. Ratwani, RM, Fong, A, Puthumana, JS et al. Emergency physician use of cognitive strategies to manage interruptions. *Annals of Emergency Medicine*, 2017:70(5), 683–685.

32. 25 quotes that show just how fed up physicians are with EHRs. *Becker's Health IT and CIO Review* [online]. October 2, 2015.

33. *PRWeb*. October 17, 2014.

34. Middleton, B, Bloomrosen, M, Dente, MA et al. Enhancing patient safety and quality of care by improving the usability of electronic health record systems: reconditions from the AMIA. *Journal of the American Medical Informatics Association*, 2013:0, 1–7.

35. Middleton B et al., Ibid.

36. www.ihealthbeat.org/articles/2015/12/2physician-residents-pre…

37. Chen, L, Guo, U, Illipparambil, LC et al. Racing against the clock: Internal medicine residents' time spent on electronic health records. *Journal of Graduate Medical Education*, February 1, 2016:8(1), 39–44.

38. https://en.wikipedia.org/wiki/Transistor_count

39. Celi, LA, Davidzon, G, Johnson, AEW et al. Bridging the health data divide. *Journal of Medical Internet Research*, 2016, 18(12), 9.

40. Beckman, HB, Frankel, RM. The effect of physician behavior on the collection of data. *Annals of Internal Medicine.* 1984:101, 692–696.
41. Ratanawongsa, N. Association between clinician computer use and communication with patients in safety-net clinics. *JAMA Internal Medicine,* 2016:176(1), 125–128.
42. Gillespie, L. Jobs for medical scribes are rising rapidly but standards lag. *Kaiser Health News* [online]. December 7, 2015.
43. Bowman, D. Med schools prep students to avoid device distractions. *FierceHealthIT.* March 30, 2012.
44. King, J. The role of health IT and delivery system reform in facilitating advanced care delivery. *American Journal of Managed Care,* 2016:22(4), 258–265.
45. Karsh, B-T, Weinger, MB, Abbott, PA et al. Health information technology: Fallacies and sober realities. *Journal of the American Medical Informatics Association,* 2010:17, 617–623.

Chapter 9

1. https://www.ncbi.nlm.nih.gov/pubmed/15827845
2. Clinical Evidence Concise, #11. *BMJ.* BMJ Publishing Group, London, 2004. p. vi.
3. Zoler, M. Opinion-based ACC/AHA recommendations raise concern. *Family Practice News.* March 15, 2009, p. 9.
4. Weiss, R, Charney, E, Baumgardner, RA et al. Changing patient management: What influences the practicing pediatrician? *Pediatrics,* 1990:85(5), 791–795.
5. Ioannidis, JPA. Why most published research findings are false. *PLoS Medicine,* 2005:2(8), 696–701.
6. Patsopoulos, NA, Analatos, AA, Loannidis, JP. Relative citation impact of various study designs in the health sciences. *JAMA,* 2005:293(19), 2362–2366.
7. Hendriksen, JMT. Ruling out pulmonary embolism in primary care: Comparison of the diagnostic performance of "Gestalt" and the Wells rule. *Annals of Family Medicine,* 2016:14(3), 227–234.
8. Tinetti, ME, Fried, TR, Boyd, CM et al. Designing health care for the most common chronic condition—multimorbidity. *JAMA,* 2012:307(23), 2493–2494.
9. Hughes, LD, McMurdo, ME, Guthrie, B et al. Guidelines for people not for diseases: the challenges of applying UK clinical guidelines to people with multimorbidity. *Age and Ageing,* 2013:42, 62–69.
10. Donegan, L-A. Penn study: Electronic alerts significantly reduce catheter-associated urinary tract infections. *PenMedNews.* August 22, 2014.
11. Kelly, JW, Blackhurst, D, McAtee, W et al. Electronic hand hygiene monitoring as a tool for reducing health care-associated methicillin-resistant Staphylococcus aureus infection. *American Journal of Infection Control,* 2016:44, 956–957.
12. Robbins, GK, Lester, W, Johnson, KL et al. Efficacy of a clinical decision-support system in an HIV practice. *Annals of Internal Medicine,* 2012:157(11), 757–766.
13. Callen, J, Georgiou, A, Johanna, JL et al. The safety implications of missed test results for hospitalized patients: A systematic review. *BMJ,* 2011:20, 194–199.
14. Menon, S, Murphy, DR, Singh, H et al. Workarounds and test results follow-up in electronic health record-based primary care. *Applied Clinical Informatics,* 2016:7, 543–559.

15. Meyer, AND, Murphy, DR, Singh, H et al. Communicating findings of delayed diagnostic evaluation to primary care providers. *Journal of the American Board of Family Medicine*, 2016:29(4), 469–473.
16. Lilly, CM, Zubrow, MT, Kempner, KM et al. Critical care medicine: Evolution and state of the art. *Critical Care Medicine*, 2014:42(11): 2429–2436.
17. Desautels T, Calvert, J, Hoffman, J et al. Prediction of sepsis in the intensive care unit with minimal electronic health record data: A machine learning approach. *Journal of Medical Informatics*. 2016:4(3), e28.
18. Verma, A, Wang, AS, Feldman, MJ et al. Push-alert notification of troponin results to physician smartphones reduces the time to discharge emergency department patients: A randomized controlled trial. *Annals of Emergency Medicine*, 2017:70(3), 348–356.
19. Zafar HM, MIlls AM, Khorasani R, Langlotz CP. Clinical decision support for imaging in the era of the Patient Protection and Affordable Care Act. *Journal of the American College of Radiology*. 2012:9(12), 907–918.
20. Barnes, E. ACC-based software boosts appropriateness of heart scans. *Aunt Minnie*. July 23, 2012.
21. Agency for Healthcare Research and Quality. Physicians correctly identify fewer than half of drug pairs with potentially dangerous interactions. *AHRQ Newsletter*. 2009:245, 5–6.
22. Tjia, J, Field, TS, Garber, LD et al. Development and pilot testing guidelines to monitor high-risk medications in the ambulatory setting. *American Journal of Managed Care*, 2010:16(7), 489–497.
23. Persell, D, Dolan, NC, Friesema, EM et al. Frequency of inappropriate medical exceptions to quality measures. *Annals of Internal Medicine*, 2010:154(4), 225–231.
24. Genco, EK. Clinically inconsequential alerts: The characteristics of opioid drug alert and their utility in preventing adverse drug events in the emergency department. *Annals of Emergency Medicine*, 2015, 1–9(e-version).
25. Phansalkar, S, van der Sijs, H, Tucker, AD et al. Drug-drug interactions that should be non-interruptive in order to reduce alert fatigue in electronic health records. *Journal of the Medical Informatics Association,* 2012:20(3), 1–5.
26. Payne, TH, Hines, LE, Chan, RC et al. Recommendations to improve the usability of drug-drug interaction. *Journal of the American Medical Informatics Association*, 2015:22(6), 1243–1250.
27. Goel, VV, Poole, SF, Longhurst, CA et al. Safety analysis of proposed data-driven physiologic alarm parameters for hospitalized children. *Journal of Hospital Medicine*, 2016:11(12), 817–823.
28. Bonafide, CP, Localio, AR, Holmes, JH et al. Video analysis of factors associated with response time to physiologic monitor alarms in a children's hospital. *JAMA Pediatrics*, April 10, 2017:171, e1–e7. Online.
29. Schiff, GD, Amato, MG, Equale, T et al. Computerized physician order entry-related medication errors: Analysis of reported errors and vulnerability testing of current systems. *BMJ*, 2015:0, 1–8.
30. Hobson K. Study: Computerized order entry system has unintended consequences. *Wall Street Journal Health Blog*. September 27, 2010.
31. Nanji, KC, Rothschild, JM, Salzberg, C et al. Errors associated with outpatient computerized prescribing systems. *Journal of the American Medical Informatics Association*, 2011:18(6), 767–773.

32. Abramson, EL, Malhotra, S, Fischer, K et al. Transitioning between electronic health records: Effects on ambulatory prescribing safety. *Journal of General Internal Medicine*, 2011:26, 868–874.

33. Radley, DC, Wasserman, MR, Olsho, LE et al., Reduction in medication errors in hospitals due to adoption of computerized provider order entry systems. *Journal of the American Medical Informatics Association*, 2013:20, 1–7.

34. Page, N, Baysari, MT, Westbrook, JI. A systematic review of the effectiveness of interruptive medication prescribing alerts in hospital CPOE systems to change prescriber behavior and improve patient safety. *International Journal of Medical Informatics*, 2017:105, 22–30.

35. Brill, A. Overspending on multi-source drugs in Medicaid. *American Enterprise Institute for Public Policy Research*. March 28, 2011.

36. Scanning system tackles drug errors. *Federal Telemedicine News* [online]. December 3, 2014.

37. https://www.studentdoctor.net/2012/01/pharmacy-a-brief-history-of-the-profession/

38. http://jamanetwork.com/journals/jama/fullarticle/188076

39. Aisen, CF. Regenstrief institute puts clinicians in charge of computer-based decision support. *Indiana University*. Media Release. April 13, 2015.

40. https://www.forbes.com/sites/scottgottlieb/2015/05/14/how-many-people-has-obamacare-really-insured/#2563a1f1788a

41. Kaiser Permanente pilot reduces cardiac deaths by 73 Percent. *Kaiser Permanente News Center*. News release, March 17, 2009.

42. Blumenthal, D, Abrams, M, Nuzum, R. The affordable care act at 5 years. *New England Journal of Medicine*, 2015:372, 2451–2458.

43. Gupta, A. Association of the hospital readmissions reduction program implementation with readmission and mortality outcomes in heart failure. *JAMA Cardiology*, 2017. 2018:3(1), 44–53.

44. Evon Holladay, unpublished data.

45. Singer, SJ, Falwell A, Gaba DM et al. Identifying organizational cultures that promote patient safety. *Healthcare Management Review*, 2009:34(4), 300–311.

46. Cooper, J, Edwards, A, Williams, H et al. Nature of blame in patient safety incident reports: Mixed methods analysis of a national database. *Annals of Family Medicine*, 2017:15(5), 455–461.

47. Richardson, JE, Vest, JR, Green, CM et al. A needs assessment of health information technology for improving care coordination in three leading patient-centered medical homes. *Journal of the American Medical Informatics Association*, 2015:22, 1–8.

48. Bloch, C. Smartphones to improve eye care. *Federal Telemedicine News*. August 24, 2016.

49. http://jamanetwork.com/journals/jama/fullarticle/2588763

50. Quanta Magazine online. December 8, 2017.

51. Pekmezaaris, R, Schwartz, RM, Taylor, TN et al. A qualitative analysis to optimize a telemonitoring intervention for heart failure patients from disparity communities. *BMC Medical Informatics and Decision Making*, 2016:16(25), 1–9.

52. Kulshrestha, A, Kvedar, JC, Goyal, A et al. Use of remote monitoring to improve outcomes in patients with congestive heart failure: a pilot trial. *International Journal of Telemedicine Applications*, 2010:2010. Article no. 3.

53. Kitsiou, S, Paré, G, Jaana, M et al. Effects of home telemonitoring interventions on patients with chronic heart failure: An overview of systematic reviews. *Journal of Medical Internet Research*, 2015:17(3)e63, 1–30.

Chapter 10

1. Parks Associates 2017.
2. Rosen, S. Industry voices—The FCC's rural health care fund is a victim of its own success. *Fierce Healthcare.* November 27, 2017.
3. Center for Connected Medicine and The Health Management Academy. Top of mind for top U.S. health systems 2018. Online 2017, 1–31.
4. Wiklund, E. Kaiser CEO: Telehealth outpaced in-person visits last year. *mHealth Intelligence.* October 11, 2016.
5. Baker, LC, Johnson, SJ, Macaulay, D et al. Integrated telehealth and care management program for Medicare beneficiaries with chronic disease linked to savings. *Health Affairs*, 2011:9, 1689–1697.
6. Lowes, R. Telemedicine diagnoses okay within limits, AMA says. *Medscape.* Online June 17, 2016.
7. Saeb, S, Zhang, M, Karr, CJ et al. Mobile phone sensor correlates of depressive symptom severity in daily-life behavior: An exploratory study. *Journal of Medical Internet Research*, 2015:17(7)e|75, 1–11.
8. Jakicic, JM, Davis, KK, Rogers, RJ et al. Effect of wearable technology combined with a lifestyle intervention on long-term weight loss: The IDEA randomized clinical trial. *JAMA*, 2016:316(11), 1161–1171.
9. Finkelstein, EA, Haaland, BA, Bilger, M et al. Effectiveness of activity tracers with and without incentives to increase physical activity (TRIPPA): A randomized controlled trial. *The Lancet Diabetes and Endocrinology*, 2016:4(12), 983–995.
10. Bourne, S, DeVos, R, North, M et al. Online versus face-to-face pulmonary rehabilitation for patients with chronic obstructive pulmonary disease: Randomized controlled trial. *BMJ*, 2017:7, 1–11, e014580.
11. Bloch, C. VA's Telerehabilitation program. *Federal Telemedicine News.* July 12, 2015, ePub.
12. Aasch, D.A, Muller, RW, Volpp, KG Automated hovering in health care—watching over the 5000 hours. *New England Journal of Medicine*, 2012:367(1), 1–3.
13. Rice, S. Children's health Dallas testing 'digitized drugs' with sensors inside. *The Dallas Morning News.* August 19, 2016.
14. Zhang, Sarah. Why pharma wants to put sensors in this blockbuster drug. *Wired* [online]. September 21, 2015.
15. Trinity Health. Press release. July 18, 2017.
16. Kliff, S. A New Mexico experiment aims to fix doctor shortage—no new doctors required. *The Washington Post.* August 8, 2012.
17. Jaffe, S. Doctors' house calls saving money for medicare. *Kaiser Health News.* May 23, 2016.
18. Powers, BW, Rinefort, S, Jain, SH et al. Nonemergency medical transportation: Delivering care in the era of Lyft and Uber. *JAMA*, 2016:316(9), 921–922.
19. Blau, M. Six ways drones could change health care. *Scientific American STAT* [online]. June 13, 2017.
20. Bauer, JC, Ringel, MA. *Telemedicine and the Reinvention of Healthcare: The Seventh Revolution in Medicine.* New York, NY: McGraw-Hill. 1999, p. 8.
21. Bauer, JC, Ringel, MA. *Telemedicine and the Reinvention of Healthcare: The Seventh Revolution in Medicine.* New York, NY: McGraw-Hill. 1999, p. 8.

22. Ollove, M. State Prisons Turn to Telemedicine to Improve Health and Save Money. http://www.pewtrusts.org/en/research-and-analysis/blogs/stateline/2016/01/21/state-prisons-turn-to-telemedicine-to-improve

23. Moore, MA, Coffman, M, Jetty, A et al. Family medicine physicians report considerable interest in, but limited use of, telehealth services. *Journal of the American Board of Family Medicine*, 2017:30(1), 320–330.

24. Update on Military Telehealth. *Federal Telemedicine News*. August 13, 2014.

25. McConnochie, KM, Wood, NE, Herendeen, NE et al. Acute illness care patterns with use of telemedicine. *Pediatrics*, 2009:123(6), e989–e995.

26. Boyle, A. Maryland pediatric practices feel the ripple effect of school telemedicine programs. *FierceHealthcare*. July 5, 2017.

27. North, F, Odunukan, O, Varkey, P et al. The value of telephone triage for patients with appendicitis. *Journal of Telemedicine and Telecare*, 2011:17, 417–420.

28. Davis, MS, Harrison, KL, Rice JF et al. A model for effective and efficient hospice care: Proactive telephone-based enhancement of life through exellent caring, "teleCaring" in advanced illness. *Journal of Pain and Symptom Management*, 2015:30(3), 414–418.

29. Pande, RL. Leveraging remote behavioral health interventions to improve medical outcomes and reduce costs. *The American Journal of Managed Care*, 2015:21(2), e141–e151.

30. Richter, KP. Comparative and cost effectiveness of telemedicine versus telephone counseling for smoking cessation. *Journal of Medical Internet Research*, 2015:17(5), 1–15. e113.

31. Mohr, DC, Ho, J, Reifler, D et al. Effect of telephone-administered vs face-to-face cognitive behavioral therapy on adherence to therapy and depression outcomes among primary care patients. *JAMA*, 2012:307(21), 2278–2285.

32. Ernsäter, A, Winblad, U, Engström, M et al. Malpractice claims regarding calls to Swedish telephone advice nursing: What went wrong and why? *Telemedicine and Telecare*, 2012:18, 379–383.

33. Bidargaddi, N. Efficacy of a web-based guided recommendation service for a curated list of readily available mental health and well-being mobile apps for young people: Randomized controlled trial. *Journal of Medical Internet Research*, 2017:19(5), e141.

34. Goldsmith, DM, Safran, C. Using the web to reduce postoperative pain following ambulatory surgery. *Journal of the American Medical Informatics Association*, 1999, 780–784.

35. Hanlon, P, Daines, L, Campbell, C et al. Telehealth interventions to support self-management of long-term conditions: A systematic metareview of diabetes, heart failure, asthma, chronic obstructive pulmonary disease, and cancer. *Journal of Medical Internet Research*, 2017:19(5), 1–16. e172.

36. Wasson, J, Gaudette, C, Whaley, F et al. Telephone care as a substitute for routine clinic follow-up. *JAMA*, 1992:267(13), 1788–1793.

37. Darkins, A, ed. Scaling-up telehealth programs. *ATA Federal Telemedicine Policy Summit*. June 27–28, 2013.

38. American Telemedicine Association Member Update. 2002–21.

39. Shah, M, Gillespie, SM, Wood, N et al. High-intensity telemedicine-enhanced acute care for older adults: An innovative healthcare delivery model. *Journal of the American Geriatric Society*, 2013:61(11), 200–2004.

40. Mehrotra, A, Paone, S, Martich, GD et al. A comparison of care at E-visits and physician office visits for sinusitis and urinary tract infection. *JAMA Internal Medicine*, 2013:173(1), 72–74.

41. Egede, LE. Psychotherapy for depression in older veterans via telemedicine: A randomized, open-label, non-inferiority trial. *The Lancet Psychiatry*, 2015:2(8), 693–701.

42. Stubbings, DR, Rees, CS, Roberts, LD et al. Comparing in-person to videoconference-based cognitive behavioral therapy for mood and anxiety disorders: Randomized controlled trial. *Journal of Medical Internet Research*, 2013:15(11), 1–14.

43. Sucala, M, Schnur, JB, Constantino, MJ et al. The therapeutic relationship in e-Therapy for mental health: A systematic review. *JMIR*, 2012:14(4), 1–11.

44. Fortney, JC, Pyne, JM, Mouden, SB et al. Practice-based versus telemedicine-based collaborative care for depression in rural federally qualified health centers: A pragmatic randomized comparative effectiveness trial. *American Journal of Psychiatry*, 2013:170(4), 414–418.

45. https://hms.harvard.edu/news/mental health line

46. Tam, T, Cafazzo, JA, Seto, E et al. Perception of eye contact in video teleconsultation. *Journal of Telemedicine and Telecare*, 2007:13, 35–39.

47. Livingston, SA. So, be honest. Have you lied to your doctor? *The Washington Post*. July 23, 2015.

48. Canidate, S. The use of avatar counseling for HIV/AIDS health education: The examination of self-identity in avatar preferences. *Journal of Medical Internet Research*, 2017:19(12), 1–7.

49. Brown, N. State Medicaid and private payer reimbursement for telemedicine: An overview. *Journal Of Telemedicine And Telecare* [serial online], 2006:12(Suppl. 2), S32–S39. Available from: MEDLINE Complete, Ipswich, MA. Accessed September 12, 2017.

50. http://www.cchpca.org/store-and-forward

51. Abrams, L. Where ER doctors work entirely via webcam. *The Atlantic Daily*. Online December 11, 2012.

52. Hawkins, HA, Lilly, CM, Kaster, DA et al. ICU telemedicine Co-management methods and length of stay. *Chest*, 2016:150(2), 314–319.

53. Olayiwola, JN, Anderson, D, Jepeal, N et al. Electronic consultations to improve the primary care-specialty interface for cardiology in the medically underserved: A cluster-randomized controlled trial. *Annals of Family Medicine*, 2016:14(2), 133–140.

54. Scalvini, S, Zanelli, E, Volterrani, M et al. A pilot study of nurse-led, home-based telecardiology for patients with chronic heart failure. *Journal of Telemedicine and Telecare*, 2014:10(2), 113–117.

55. Chetney, R. The cardiac connection program: Home care that doesn't miss a beat. *Home Healthcare Nurse*, 2003:21(10), 680–686.

56. Stewart, S, Vandenbroek, AJ, Pearson, S et al. Prolonged beneficial effects of a home-based intervention on unplanned readmissions and mortality among patients with congestive heart failure. *Archives of Internal Medicine*, 1999:139, 257–261.

57. Krypel, K, Hutchison, M. How lay health care workers can add high touch to high tech. *Health Affairs Blog*, June 11, 2015, 1–4. healthaffairs.org/blog/2015/06/11

58. Tam, A, Leung, A, O'Callaghan, C et al. The role of telehealth in perioperative medicine for regional and rural patients in Queensland. *Internal Medicine Journal of the Australasian College of Physicians*, 2017:47(8), 933–937.

59. Teleaudiology makes a Difference. *Federal Telemedicine News*. Online August 20, 2014.

60. Walgreens press release. December 11, 2017.

61. Galewitz, P. Your doctor will see you in this telemedicine kiosk. *Kaiser Health News.* June 21, 2016.

62. Murphy, DR. The burden of inbox notifications in commercial electronic health records. *JAMA Internal Medicine* [online], 2016:176(4), 159–160.

63. O'Toole, A, Joo, J, DesGroeilliers, JP et al. The association between question type and the outcomes of a dermatology eConsult service. *International Journal of Dermatology*, 2017:epub, 1–6.

64. Resneck, JS, Abrouk M, Steuer M et al. Choice, transparency, coordination and quality among direct-to-consumer telemedicine websites and apps treating skin disease. *JAMA Dermatology*, May 15, 2016, e1–e8, jamadermatology.com

65. Catarino, R, Vassilakos, P, Scaringella, S et al. Smartphone use for cervical cancer screening in low-resource countries: A pilot study conducted in Madagascar. *PLOS ONE*, 2015:10(7), e0134309.

66. Beck, M. How telemedicine is transforming health care. *The Wall Street Journal.* June 26, 2016.

67. Belluck, P. Birth control via app finds footing under political radar. *The New York Times.* June 19, 2016.

68. Gomperts, R, van der Vleuten, K, Jelinska, K et al. Provision of medical abortion using telemedicine in Brazil. *Contraception.* November 14, 2013.

69. Grossman, DA, Grindlay, K, Buchacker, T et al. Changes in service delivery patterns after introduction of telemedicine provision of medical abortion in Iowa. *American Journal of Public Health*, 2013:103(1), 73–78.

70. Gold, A. Telemedicine-enabled abortion restrictions spreading. *FierceHealthIT.* August 12, 2013.

71. Hagland, M. Telementoring at UPMC: The newest frontier in surgical training. *Healthcare Informatics.* July 25, 2012.

72. WoundMatrix's Next GenSystem. *Federal Telemedicine News.* May 5, 2015.

73. Sweeney, E. Survey: More than half of patients prefer telehealth visits to in-person care. *FierceHealthcare.* July 17, 2017.

74. Brohan, M. Choosy moms choose more digital healthcare. *Internet Health Management.* November 7, 2016.

Chapter 11

1. Himmelstein, DU, Woolhandler, S. The current and projected taxpayer shares of US health costs. *American Journal of Public Health*, March 2016:106(3), 449–452. doi:10.2105/AJPH.2015.302997. Epub January 21, 2016.

2. http://www.usgovernmentspending.com/spending_chart_2006_2021USb_18s2li111mcn_14t

3. Guy, RJ, Micallef, JM, Mooney-Somers, J et al. Evaluation of chlamydia partner notification practices and use of the "Let them know" website by family planning clinicians in Australia: Cross-sectional study. *Journal of Medical Internet Research*, 2016:18(6), 1–11. e173.

4. Paul, MJ, Dredze, M, Broniatowski, D. Twitter improves influenza forecasting. *PLOS Currents Outbreaks*, October 28, 2014. Edition 1. doi:10.1371/currents. outbreaks.90b9ed0f59bae4ccaa683a39865d9117

5. Sugawara, T, Ohkusa, Y, Ibuka, Y et al. Real-time prescription surveillance and its application to monitoring seasonal influenza activity in Japan. *Journal of Medical Internet Research*, 2012:14(1), 1–9.

6. Dzierzak, L. AI scans Twitter for signs of opioid abuse. *Scientific American Online*. October 30, 2017.

7. Online tool predicted Ebola outbreak before WHO announcement. *iHealthBeat*. August 11, 2014.

8. Liu, K, Huang, S, Miao, ZP et al. Identifying potential norovirus epidemics in China via internet surveillance. *Journal of Medical Internet Research*, 2017:19(8), 1–11. e282.

9. https://www.cdc.gov/mmwr/preview/mmwrhtml/mm6332a1.htm?s_cid=mm6332a1_w

10. Ayers JW, Althouse BM, Allem JP et al. Seasonality in seeking mental health information on Google. *American Journal of Preventive Medicine*. 2012:42, 539–549.

11. Teng, J, Thomson, DR, Lascher, JS et al. Using mobile health (mHealth) and geospatial mapping technology in a mass campaign for reactive oral Cholera Vaccination in rural Haiti. *PLOS Neglected Tropical Diseases,* July 31, 2014:8(7), e3050.

12. Penn Medicine contest maps 1,400 lifesaving AEDs via crowdsourcing contest fueled by smart phones. *Penn Medicine News* (news release). November 4, 2012.

13. Wang, S, Paul, MJ, Dredze, M et al. Social media as a sensor of air quality and public response in China. *Journal of Medical Internet Research*, 2015:17(3), 1–10. e22.

14. Yom-Tov, E, Borsa, D, Hayward, AC et al. Automatic identification of web-based risk markers for health events. *Journal of Medical Internet Research*, 2015:17(1), 1–13, e29.

15. Wong, CA, Sap, M, Schwartz, A et al. Twitter sentiment predicts affordable care act marketplace enrollment. *Journal of Medical Internet Research*, 2015:17(2), 1–8, e51.

16. Wikipedia—"Louis B. Rosenberg." Accessed 7-28-17.

17. Study: Negative Tweets associated with higher heart disease deaths. *iHealthBeat*. January 22, 2015.

18. https://www.cdc.gov/mmwr/preview/mmwrhtml/mm4818a1.htm

Chapter 12

1. Meza, JP, Passerman, DS. *Integrating Narrative Medicine and Evidence-Based Medicine: The Everyday Social Practice of Healing.* Boca Raton, FL: CRC Press. 2011.

2. Helbing, D, Frey, BS, Gigerenzer, G et al. Will democracy survive big data and artificial intelligence? *Scientific American*. 2017.

3. https://www.ted.com/talks/deb_roy_the_birth_of_a_word

4. Loyd, L. Listening to doctors and patients talk. *Philly.com*. January 14, 2008.

5. Gemming, L, Doherty, A, Utter, J et al. The use of a wearable camera to capture and categorize the environmental and social context of self-identified eating episodes. *Appetite*, 2015:92, 118–125.

6. Reardon, S. Project ranks billions of drug interactions. *Nature*, 2013:503, 449–450.

7. Greenmeier, L. Crowd-sourced medical research gets Apple assist. *Scientific American* [online]. March 16, 2015.

8. Kansagra, AP, Yu, JP, Chatterjee, AR et al. Big data and the future of radiology informatics. *Academic Radiology*, 2016:23, 30–32.

9. IBM, four drugmakers donate chemical database to NIH. *iHealthBeat*. December 9, 2011e.

10. Parkikh, RB. Integrating predicative analytics into high-value care: The dawn of precision delivery. *JAMA*, 2016:315(7), 651–652.

11. Zeltner, B. MetroHealth, Explorys use huge patient database to revolutionize medical research. *The Plain Dealer*. August 19, 2012.

12. Tannen, RL, Weiner, MG, Xie, D et al. A simulation using data from a primary care database closely replicated the women's health initiative trial. *Journal of Clinical Epidemiology*, 2007:60, 686–695.

13. Olfson, M, Marcus, SC. Decline in placebo-controlled trial results suggests new directions for comparative effectiveness research. *Health Affairs*, 2013:32(6), 1116–1125.

14. Schmidt, C. Many pediatric studies are a waste of time. *Scientific American.* September 1, 2017.

15. Holland, CM. iTunes song-gifting is a low-cost, efficient recruitment tool to engage high-risk MSM in internet research. *AIDS and Behavior*, 2015:19, 1914–1918.

16. Whitaker, C, Stevelink, S, Fear, N et al. The use of Facebook in recruiting participants for health research purposes: A systematic review. *Journal of Medical Internet Research*, 2017:19(8), 1–11. e290.

17. Researchers: Increased online chatter could jeopardize clinical trials. *iHealthBeat* [online]. July 30, 2014.

18. Jacobs, BP, Bent, S, Tice, JA et al. An internet-based randomized, placebo-controlled trial of kava and valerian for anxiety and insomnia. *Medicine*, 2005:84(4), 197–207.

19. Molteni, M. Biology's roiling debate over publishing research early. *Wired Science* [online]. July 8, 2017.

20. Molteni, M. *Wired Science* [online]. July 8, 2017.

21. Desprez, EE, Chen C. Medical journals have a fake news problem. *Bloomberg Businessweek*. September 4, 2017, pp. 52–56.

22. Schlermeir, Q. Hundreds of German universities set to lose access to Elsevier journals. *Nature* [online]. December 5, 2017.

23. Moseley, ET, Hsu, DJ, Stone, DJ et al. Beyond open big data: Addressing unreliable research. *Journal of Medical Internet Research*, 2014:16(11), 1–17. e259.

24. Greenberg, SA. How citation distortions create unfounded authority: analysis of a citation network. *BMJ*, 2009:339, 210–213.

Chapter 13

1. Meyer, AND, Payne, VL, Meeks, DW et al. Physicians' diagnostic accuracy, confidence and resource requests: A Vignette study. *JAMA Internal Medicine*, 2013:173(21), 1952–1959.

2. McKendrick, D, Cumming, GP, Lee, AJ. Increased use of Twitter at a medical conference: A report and a review of the educational opportunities. *Journal of Medical Internet Research*, 2012:14(6), e176.

3. Wenger, N, Méan, M, Castioni, J et al. Allocation of internal medicine resident time in a Swiss hospital: A time and motion study of day and evening shifts. *Annals of Internal Medicine*, 2017:166, 579–586.

4. http://medicalfuturist.com/top-10-virtual-medical-sites-in-second-life/

5. Jauhar, S. Empathy gadgets. *New York Times*. July 29, 2017.

6. Ryoo, EN, Ha, EH. The importance of debriefing in simulation-based learning: Comparison between debriefing and no debriefing. *Computers, Informatics, Nursing,* 2015:33(12), 538–545.

7. Brisson, GE, Tyler, PD. Medical student use of electronic health records to track former patients. *JAMA Internal Medicine,* June 15, 2016:176(9), 1395–1397.

8. Dillon, CL. Distance education research and continuing professional education: Reframing questions for the emerging information infrastructure. *Journal of Continuing Education in Health Professions,* 1996:16, 5–13.

9. Liyanagunawardena, TR, Williams, SA. Massive open online courses on health and medicine: Review. *JMIR,* 2014:16(8), e191.

10. Rural Chinese doctors use video, internet for medical training. *iHealthBeat* [online]. July 10, 2007.

11. Sedrak, MS, Myers, JS, Small, DS et al. Effect of a price transparency intervention in the electronic health record on clinician ordering of inpatient laboratory tests. *JAMA Internal Medicine,* April 21, 2017:177(7), 939-945

Chapter 14

1. https://www.solutionreach.com/blog/are-senior-citizens-engaging-in-healthcare-technology

2. Lungu, A, Sun, M. Time for a change: College students' preference for technology-mediated versus face-to-face help for emotional distress. *Telemedicine and e-Health,* 2016:20(12), 1–10.

3. Paj, A. Survey: Patients prefer doctors who offer email communication. *Mobilehealthnews,* [online] June 3, 2014.

4. Pennic, F. Should physicians tailor patient engagement based on age? *HIT Consultant* [online]. January 16, 2015.

5. Kraschnewski, JL, Chuang, CH, Poole, ES et al. Paging "Dr. Google": Does technology fill the gap created by the prenatal care visit structure? Qualitative focus group study with pregnant women. *Journal of Medical Internet Research,* 2014:16(6), 1–11.

6. Reed, M, Graetz, I, Gorden, N et al. Patient-initiated e-mails to providers: Associations with out-of-pocket visit costs and impact on care-seeking and health. *American Journal of Managed Care,* 2015:21(12), e632–e639.

7. Shenkin, BN, Warner, DC. Giving the patient his medical record: a proposal to improve the system. *New England Journal of Medicine,* 1973:289, 688–692.

8. Landi, H. Survey: 1 in 3 healthcare consumers lack easy access to medical records. *Healthcare Informatics* [online]. 2017.

9. Haun, K, Topol, EJ. The health data conundrum. *The New York Times.* January 2, 2017.

10. Jacob, JA. Patient access to physician notes is gaining momentum FREE. *JAMA,* 2016:315(23), 2510–2511.

11. Walker, J, Darer, JD, Elmore, JG et al. The road toward fully transparent medical records. *New England Journal of Medicine,* 2014:370(1), 6–8.

12. Delbanco, T, Walker, J, Bell, SK et al. Inviting patients to read their doctors' notes: A quasi-experimental study and a look ahead. *Annals of Internal Medicine,* 2012:157, 461–470.

13. Palen, TE, Ross, C, Powers, JD et al. Association of online patient access to clinicians and medical records with use of clinical services. *JAMA*, 2012:308(19), 2012–2019.

14. Ford, EW, Hesse, BW, Huerta, TR et al. Personal health record use in the United States: forecasting future adoption levels. *Journal of Medical Internet Research*, 2016:18(3), 1–7.

15. Hirsch, MD. Patient review of medication lists can improve accuracy of their EHRs. *FierceEMR*. October 6, 2014.

16. Wright, E, Darer, J, Tang, X et al. Sharing physician notes through an electronic portal is associated with improved medication adherence: Quasi-experimental study. *Journal of Medical Internet Research*, 2015:17(10), 1–9. e226.

17. Bell, SK. When doctors share visit notes with patients: A study of patient and doctor perceptions of documentation errors, safety opportunities and the doctor-patient relationship. *British Medical Journal*, 2017:26, 262–270.

18. Krakta, A, Wong, CA, Herrmann, R. Finding health care prices online—how difficult is it to be an informed healthcare consumer? *JAMA Internal Medicine* [online]. December 4, 2017, E1–E2.

19. Patients doubt doctors' advice when it conflicts with online Info. *iHealthBeat* [online]. July 30, 2008.

20. Rumball-Smith, J, Shekelle, PG, Bates, DW. Using the electronic health record to understand and minimize overuse. *JAMA*, 2017:317(3), 257–258.

21. *iHealthBeat* [online]. April 18, 2012.

22. http:www.pewinternet.org/files/~/media/FilesReports/PIP_HealthOnline.pdf

23. [Kanthawala, S, Vermeesch, A, Given, B Search engine ranking, quality and et al. Answers to health questions: Internet search results versus online health community responses. *Journal of Medical Internet Research*, 2016:18(4), e95.

24. Heilman, JM, West, AG. Wikipedia and medicine: Quantifying readership, editors, and the significance of natural language. *Journal of Medical Internet Research*, 2015:17(3), 1–15. E62.

25. Fu, LY, Zook, K, Spoehr-Labutta, Z et al. Search engine ranking, quality and content of web pages that are critical versus noncritical of human papillomavirus vaccine. *Journal of Adolescent Health*, 2016:58(1), 33–39.

26. Wilson, K, Keelan, J. Social media and the empowering of opponents of medical technologies: The case of anti-vaccinationism. *Journal of Medical Internet Research*, 2013:15(5), 1–9.

27. Hasty, RT, Garbalosa, RC, Barbato, VA et al. Wikipedia vs peer-reviewed medical literature for information about the 10 most costly medical conditions. *Journal of the American Osteopathic Association*, 2014:114(5), 368–373.

28. Health Information and Management Systems Society. *HIMSS Newsbreak* [online]. November 25, 2002.

29. Wikipedia. Health on the net foundation. https://en.wikipedia.org/wiki/Health_On_the_Net_Foundation

30. Verel, D. Google to reshape how it provides health information, Mayo clinic joins as a partner. *Medcitynews*. February 10, 2015. https://medcitynews.com/2015/02/google-seeks-bring-accuracy-online-health-information/

31. Doctors using YouTube for patient education, professional networking. *iHealthBeat* [online]. June 19, 2012.

32. Fox, S, Duggan, M. Mobile health 2012. *Pew Research Center*. 2012.

33. Richtel, M. Poorer kids waste more time on gadgets. *The Denver Post*. May 30, 2012, 18A.

34. https://www.cbsnews.com/news/study-allowing-organ-donation-status-on-facebook-increased-number-of-donors/
35. Kardaras, N. *Glow Kids: How Screen Addiction Is Hijacking Our Kids.* New York, NY: St. Martin's Press. 2016.
36. Shakya, HB, Christakis, NA. Association of facebook use with compromised well-being: A longitudinal study. *American Journal of Epidemiology*, 2017:185(3), 203–211.
37. Cotton, SR, Anderson, WA, McCullough, BM. Impact of internet use on loneliness and contact with others among older adults: Cross-sectional analysis. *Journal of Medical Internet Research*, 2013:15(2), 1–13. e39.
38. Schulman, C, Kuchkarian, FM, Withum, KF et al. Influence of social networking websites on medical school and residency selection process. *Postgraduate Medical Journal*, 2012:0, 1–5.
39. Doctors taking proactive approach to online rating, review sites. *iHealthBeat* [online]. May 20, 2014.
40. Poor bedside manner is most common critique in online doctor ratings. *iHealthBeat* [online]. May 2, 2013.
41. Gao, GG, McCullough, JS, Agarwal, R et al. A changing landscape of physician quality reporting: Analysis of patients' online ratings of their physicians over a 5-year period. *Journal of Medical Internet Research*, 2012:14(1), 1–10.
42. Murphy, GP, Awad, MA, Osterberg, EC et al. Web-based physician ratings of California physicians on probation. *Journal of Medical Internet Research*, 2017:19(8), 1–7. e254.
43. Okike, K, Peter-Bibb, TK, Xie, KC et al. Association between online rating and quality of care. *Journal of Medical Internet Research*, 2016:18(12), 1–6. e324.
44. Study: Hospitals' readmission rates correlate with Facebook ratings. *iHealthBeat* [online]. March 16, 2015.
45. Timian, A, Rupcic, S, Kachnowski, S et al. Do patients "Like" good care? Measuring hospital quality via Facebook. *American Journal of Medical Quality*, 2013:20(10), 1–9.
46. Peter, D. Hospital rating websites vary widely in rankings, study finds. *iHealthBeat*. March 3, 2015.
47. Ryan, AM, Nallamothu, BK, Dimick, JB. Medicare's public reporting initiative on hospital quality had modest or no impact on mortality from three key conditions. *Health Affairs*, 2012:31(3), 585–592.
48. Fung, C, Lim, YW, Mattke, S et al. Systematic review: The evidence that publishing patient care performance data improves quality of care. *Annals of Internal Medicine*, 2008:148(2), 111–123.
49. American Medical Association. How to manage your online reputation: Top 4 tips. *AMA Wire*. December 3, 2014, online. (and other sources)
50. Liang, Y, Zheng, X, Zeng, DD et al. Exploring how the tobacco industry presents and promotes itself in social media. *Journal of Medical Internet Research*, 2015:17(1), 1–11. e25.
51. NIH establishes Down syndrome patient registry. *NIH news release*. October 26, 2012.
52. Merrill, M. Social media could 'accelerate clinical discovery'. *Healthcare IT News*. March 25, 2011.
53. Koppe, H, van de Mortel, TF, Ahem, CM et al. How effective and acceptable is Web 2.0 Balint group participation for general practitioners and general practitioner registrars in regional Australia? A pilot study. *Australian Journal of Rural Health*, 2015:24(1), 16–22.

54. Peebles, R, Wilson, JL, Litt, IF et al. Disordered eating in a digital age: Eating behaviors, health, and quality of life in users of websites with pro-eating disorder content. *Journal of Medical Internet Research*, 2012:14(5), 1–10.

55. Mackey, TK, Liang, BA. Global reach of direct-to-consumer advertising using social media for illicit online drug sales. *Journal of Medical Internet Research*, 2013:15(5), e105.

56. Advocates concerned about drug companies' use of social media. *iHealthBeat* [online]. July 26, 2011.

57. http://www.rankedhealth.com/

58. Wearable tattoo sends alcohol levels to your cell phone. National Institute of Biomedical Imaging and Bioengineering. *Science Highlight*. October 17, 2016.

59. Rock Health Consumer survey data.

60. www.ihealthbeatorg/articles/2015/11/5/survey-nearly-half-of…

61. Accenture: Hospitals missing out on millions. *Health Management Technology*. April–May 6, 2016.

62. Lee, JM, Hirschfeld, E, Wedding, J. A patient-designed do-it-yourself mobile technology system for diabetes. *Journal of the American Medical Association,* 2016:315(14), 1447–1448.

63. Long, JA, Jahnle, EC, Richardson, DM et al. Peer mentoring and financial incentives to improve glucose control in African American veterans, a randomized trial. *Annals of Internal Medicine*, 2012:156, 16–424.

64. Murphy, J. Memory loss? There's an app for that. *MDLinx*. August 5, 2016.

65. Sharpe, R. Many health apps are based on flimsy science at best, and they often don't work. *The Washington Post*. November 12, 2012.

66. Apps for detecting skin cancer can misdiagnose lesion, study finds. *iHealthBeat*. January 17, 2013.

67. Brinker, TJ. Photoaging mobile apps in school-based melanoma prevention: Pilot study. *Journal of Medical Internet Research*, 2017:19(9), 1–10. e319.

68. McDermott, MT. Hacks can ease the trials of aging. *The New York Times*. August 15, 2016.

69. Edmiston, CJ, Krepel, CJ, Edmiston, SE. et al. Empowering the surgical patient: A randomized, prospective analysis of an innovative strategy for improving patient compliance with preadmission showering protocol. *Journal of the American College of Surgeons*, 2014:219(2), 256–264.

70. Välimäki, M, Kannisto, KA, Vahlberg, T. et al. Short text messages to encourage adherence to medication and follow-up for people with psychosis (mobile. net): Randomized controlled trial in Finland. *Journal of Medical Internet Research*, 2017:19(7), e245.

71. Uy, C, Lopez, J, Trinh-Shevrin, C. et al. Text messaging interventions on cancer screening rates: A systematic review. *Journal of Medical Internet Research*, 2017:19(8), 1–12. e296.

72. Regan, AK, Bloomfield, L, Peters, I. et al. Randomized controlled trial of text message reminders for increasing influenza vaccination. *Annals of Family Medicine*, 2017:15(9), 507–515.

73. Hall, AK, Cole-Lewis, H, Bernhardt, JM. et al. Mobile text messaging for health: A systematic review of reviews. *Annual Review of Public Health*, 2015:36, 393–415.

74. Luengo-Oroz, MA, Arranz, A, Frean, J et al. Crowdsourcing malaria parasite quantification: An online game for analyzing images of infected thick blood smears. *Journal of Medical Internet Research*, 2012:20(6), 1–11.
75. Herz, NS, Mehta, SH, Sethi, KD et al. Nintendo Wii rehabilitation ("Wii-hab") provides benefits in Parkinson's disease. *Parkinsonism and Related Disorders*, 2013:19(11), 1039–1044.

Glossary

1. Graham, R, Mancher, M, Wolman, DM et al., eds. *Clinical Practice Guidelines We Can Trust*. Washington DC, National Academies Press. 2011, p. 29.
2. Sackett DL. Evidence -based medicine. Seminars in Perinatology, 1997:21(1), 3–5.
3. Hafferty FW, Franks R. The hidden curriculum, ethics teaching, and the structure of medical education. *Academic Medicine*, 1994:69(11), 861–871.

Suggested Reading

Alkureishi, ML, Lee, WW, Frankel, RM. Patient-centered technology use: Best practices and curricular strategies. In *Health Professionals' Education in the Age of Clinical Information Systems, Mobile Computing and Social Networks.* Shachak, A, Borycki, EM, Reis, SP, eds. London, Academic Press, 2017, pp. 201–232. The best how-to about teaching and employing best practices when engaging the patient-provider-computer triad.

Antonovsky, A. Islands rather than bridgeheads: The problematic status of the Biopsychosocial model. *Family Systems Medicine,* 1989:7(3), 243–253.—An analysis, 12 years after the biopsychosocial model was first proposed, of how and why it had failed to make much headway in broadening the focus of the biomedical model that has held sway since the early 20th Century. (See Engel GL.)

Aronson, Sidney H. The Lancet on the telephone 1876–1975. Medical history. *Lancet,* 1977:21, 69–87.—A fun, fascinating account of the introduction of telephones into medical practice. This fresh look at how a technology that we have long taken for granted came to permeate the everyday lives of patients and professionals lends some insight into where other technologies that we are on the way to taking for granted will lead us.

Bauer, JC. *Paradox and Imperatives in Health Care: Redirecting Reform for Efficiency and Effectiveness, revised ed.* Boca Raton, FL: CRC Press. 2014.—A cogent argument for placing the primary focus on quality in healthcare, with favorable economics to follow.

Bauer, JC, Ringel, M. *Telemedicine and the Reinvention of Healthcare.* New York, NY: McGraw Hill. 1999.—Though the technology discussed is dated, the basic principles still hold up.

Chen, JH, Asch, SM. Machine learning and prediction in medicine—beyond the peak of inflated expectations. *New England Journal of Medicine,* 2017:376(26), 2507–2509.—A brief, clear-eyed view of where we are at with machine learning based artificial intelligence and where we are likely to go in the next few years.

Daimler, AG. Mercedes-Benz 2014 S-Class production Sindelfingen plant. June 30, 2013 https://www.youtube.com/watch?v=TvKAN_UPVY4—An astounding view of an automobile assembly line that has been automated with robots to the extent that just about the only humans one sees in the video of the plant are pushing brooms.

Donde, J. Self-driving cars will kill people. Who decides who dies? *Wired* [online], September 21, 2017. https://www.wired.com/2014/05/self-driving-cars-will-turn-surveillance-woes-into-a-mainstream-issue/—How to inject human values into

AI-driven systems is the main theme of this article, presented in the form of the "trolley problem," an ethical thought experiment that has challenged humans to examine the values upon which we base (or ought to base) ethical decisions.

Engel, GL. The need for a new medical model: A challenge for biomedicine. *Science,* 1977:196(4286), 129–136.—The foundational document for the biopsychosocial model of clinical science, a model that has been taken seriously but has gained little traction in supervening the standard biomedical model, which holds the territory of healthcare in much narrower focus.

Gawande, A. The cost conundrum. *New Yorker Magazine.* June 1, 2009.—An exceptionally clear article that elucidates the misalignment of health and financial incentives in American healthcare.

Graham, R, Mancher, M, Miller, D et al. eds. *Clinical Practice Guidelines We Can Trust.* Washington, DC: National Academies Press. 2011. https://www.ncbi.nlm.nih.gov/ books/NBK209539/—Report of a high-powered group convened by the Institute of Medicine. A detailed look at clinical practice guidelines, how to choose them, produce them and put them to use. Published as a 232-page book and available for free download.

HealthIT.gov. What is workflow redesign? Why is it important? June 10, 2013. http:www .healthit.gov/providers-professionals/faqs/ehr-workflow-redesign—If you are a do-it-yourselfer, this is a good place to start learning about practice workflow redesign.

Helbring, D, Frey, BS, Gigerenzer, G et al. Will democracy survive big data and artificial intelligence? *Scientific American* [online]. January 25, 2017. https://www.scientificamerican.com/article/will-democracy-survive-big-data-and-artificial-intelligence/?WT .mc_id=SA_BS_20170303—Just what it says, a hard look at the brave new world of AI and big data.

Institute of Electrical and Electronics Engineeers. Ethically aligned design: A vision for prioritizing human wellbeing with artificial intelligence and autonomous systems, version 1. 2016. http://standards.ieee.org/develop/indconn/ec/ead_v1.pdf—A good starting point for thinking about the role of technology in our culture, written by geeks-in-the-know.

Jordan, B. *Technology and Social Interaction: Notes on the Achievement of Authoritative Knowledge in Complex Settings.* Palo Alto, CA: Institute for Research and Learning. 1992. Report #IRL92-0072—A fascinating sociological/anthropological study that compares the cultures of the airline situation room, where teams of workers coordinate the complex, rapidly changing, high stakes process of flight arrivals and departures to the delivery room, where nurses and doctors work together in managing the complex, rapidly changing, high stakes birth process.

Lanier, J. You are not a gadget. New York, NY: Vintage. 2011.—The author, who has a foot in the world of advanced computing and another in the world of ancient and rare musical instruments, composing and performing. His analysis of the complex border between cyberspace and meatspace, and what parts of our lives ought to be relegated to each, is quite provocative.

Lewis-Kraus, G. Going neural. *New York Times Magazine.* December 18, 2016. pp. 40–49, ff.—An intelligent, digestible article about how neural nets work to produce artificial intelligence. Though the field of AI is changing at blazing speed, this is a good place to get an idea of the basic principles on which they function.

Markoff, J. *Machines of Loving Grace: The Quest for Common Ground between Humans and Robots.* New York, NY: HarperCollins. 2015.—A cogent discussion of the past, current and future role of technology in human life.

Minkler, M, Wallerstein, N, eds. *Community-Based Participatory Research for Health: From Process to Outcome,* 2nd ed. San Francisco, CA: Jossey-Bass/Wiley. 2008.—A good place to start learning about community-engaged research, a topic I hope it will become ever more important to understand as time goes on. Contains both theoretical discussion and case studies.

O'Neil, C. *Weapons of Math Destruction: How Big Data Increases Inequality and Threatens Democracy.* New York, NY: Crown Publishing Group/Penguin Random House. 2016.—A maddening and scary account of how big data, even when collected, analyzed and wielded with the best of intentions, all too often makes things worse by reinforcing prejudices, creating self-fulfilling prophecies and manipulating us. An extremely well made argument for putting people, values and culture at the center of any project, ahead of big data.

Pho, K, Gay, S. *Establishing, Managing and Protecting Your Online Reputation: A Social Media Guide for Physicians and Medical Practices.* Phoenix, MD: Greenbranch Publishing. 2013.—A plea for the importance of getting online because that's where the patients are and a how-to for doing it. The authors conclude, "The biggest risk of social media in health care is not using it at all."

Ranked. Ranked: Curated health apps and devices. http://www.rankedhealth.com/—A curated website, founded by MIT spinoff Hacking Medicine Institute, that reviews digital health devices and apps.

Richards, NH. The dangers of surveillance. *Harvard Law Review*, 2013:126, 1934–1958.—A lawyer's view of the dilemmas that widespread surveillance and use of the big data it generates pose to individuals, society and culture.

Sax, D. *The Revenge of Analog: Real Things and Why They Matter.* PublicAffairs, New York, NY. 2017.—An intelligent appreciation of the non-digital world we actually live in, in all its subtlety, clumsiness and beauty.

Solomon, MZ, Bonham, AC. eds. Ethical oversight of learning health care systems. *Hastings Center Report*, 2013:43(1), s1–s46.—A deep and thoughtful look at the blurring of the boundary that is occurring between clinical care and medical research, impelled in large part by the spread of information technology.

Standage, T. *The Victorian Internet.* New York, NY: Walker and Company. 1998.—This story of a previous revolution in electronic communications sheds light on the current one.

Wyatt, JC, Thimbleby, H, Rastall, P et al. What makes a good clinical app? Introducing the RCP health informatics unit checklist. *Clinical Medicine*, 2015:15(6), 519–521.—A nice checklist of what factors to consider when choosing a health app.

Index

3 20